CITY ON LEAVE
A HISTORY OF BERLIN
1945–1962

CITY ON LEAVE

A History of Berlin

1945–1962

BY

PHILIP WINDSOR

FREDERICK A. PRAEGER

Publisher

NEW YORK

BOOKS THAT MATTER

Published in the United States of America in 1963
by
Frederick A. Praeger, Inc., Publisher
64, University Place, New York 3, N.Y.

Library of Congress Catalog Card Number: 63-11480

Printed in Great Britain
by R. & R. Clark, Ltd.,
Edinburgh

To
MY PARENTS

Contents

Introduction

SINCE 1945 Berlin has played a dominant part in international relations. It has become one of the two or three problems which are capable of starting a world war. If the world's two leading powers have shown again and again that they are determined to avoid a conflict there, each has also shown some desire to exploit these fears to maintain or improve its position. They have always drawn back at the last minute, and sometimes the German authorities have themselves acted to save the world from the imminent risk of war. But the danger is still present.

This history, and the fact that the Berlin problem arises inevitably out of the city's political status and geographical position, have given the 'Berlin crises' of the past seventeen years an appearance of continuity which they do not in fact possess. The motives which inspired the Blockade were quite different from those which lay behind Khrushchev's ultimatum in 1958; and the crisis which this touched off had radically changed in nature by 1961.

This book is an attempt to show how these different crises arose out of the setting of international relations, and the changing problem of Germany since the end of the Second World War. I have tried to show the motives of each side, and to relate the part played by the Germans themselves in these years—the East Germans as well as their overlords, the West Berliners as well as their protectors, who in fact often followed German initiatives. But Berlin has not always been a significant problem: when the evolution of Germany, or the requirements of Russian policy allowed it, it has been forgotten—sometimes for a long period. There are signs in 1962 that this may again be happening. Yet West Berlin still has peculiar problems to face, and its existence will be precarious as long as the Cold War goes on. So I have also given an account of the growth of the city of West Berlin, of the political leadership it has been given, and of its relationship with the Federal Republic.

I have enjoyed much generous help and hospitality while writing. I should particularly like to express my gratitude to the

INTRODUCTION

Warden and Fellows of St. Antony's College, Oxford, who made it possible for me to go to Berlin, and to come back and write; to Professor Hans Herzfeld and the Friedrich-Meinecke Institut of the Free University of Berlin, and to Dr. Albrecht Lampe of the Landesarchiv Berlin for their encouragement and help in finding material; to Professor Ferdinand Friedensburg; to Professor Richard Lowenthal and Mr. Harold Hurwitz for their penetrating answers to a number of confused questions; to the late Senator Paul Hertz for providing me with material and enlightening my mind on economic issues; to Herr Eberhard Hesse, General Secretary of the SPD in Berlin, and a Member of the House of Representatives; to Dr. Hans Hirschfeld, formerly Press Chief of the City Government; to Dr. Georg Kotowski of the Friedrich-Meinecke Institut, and a Member of the CDU Fraktion of the House of Representatives; Dr. Friedrich Zipfel of the Free University; and Colonel Guyon, formerly Chief of Police in the British Military Government in Berlin, for much valuable information and advice; to Herr Wolfgang Leonhard for his frank and generous explanations of the situation after 1945; and to Herr Wilhelm Cornides of the Deutsche Gesellschaft für Auswärtige Politik. I am greatly indebted to Dr. Gerhard Ritter of the Free University for his ready assistance and advice. I am deeply grateful to Mr. James Joll of St. Antony's College for his constant kindness and encouragement, and to Mr. Peter Calvocoressi for the unfailing patience with which he guided this book towards publication. Finally, I owe a great deal to Mrs. Shirley Bowler, Mrs. Rose Kloegman, and Miss Penelope Mason for bringing order to a chaotic manuscript.

PHILIP WINDSOR

Chapter One

THE DIVISION OF GERMANY

W HEN the three leaders of the Grand Alliance met at Yalta
in February 1945, they were all anxious to avoid a European settlement. Their conference was directed primarily to
the final organisation of victory and the smooth achievement of
a German surrender. They preferred to postpone decision on
other matters because they were convinced that the Alliance
should be preserved in the post-war world. Premature commitments could have provoked a disastrous conflict, but each
hoped that with time his own intentions could be fulfilled (and
those of his partners frustrated) by means of the Alliance itself.
In their awareness of conflicting aims, and in their efforts to dis-
sipate suspicion, they counted on Germany to keep them
united; and while the future influence of France, the future
shape of Poland, the régimes of all the Eastern European states
were left to later determination, they hoped to square the circle
of their ambitions by collaborating in Germany. And each
believed that their designs for Germany would secure him the
greatest possible room for manœuvre in attaining his subsequent
objectives.

From previous meetings and the work of their Foreign
Ministers in the European Advisory Commission, they had
brought with them certain common assumptions which were to
provide the basis of their policies and ensure that even the
vaguest agreements would maintain collaboration. These were
still taken for granted at Yalta, but because they could not resolve their equivocations on the rest of Europe, they later dis-
carded these intentions and entered the defeated Reich without
forming any new principles to govern their conduct.

Chief of these rejected undertakings was their plan for dismemberment. They had understood that the German state
would cease to exist, that it would never again be restored, and
that until the succession had been determined, each of the
Allies would administer part of its territory. During the period
of occupation, the necessity of agreeing on the form of

dismemberment would oblige them to pursue common policies; and after the establishment of the substitute states, the threat of an eventual reunification would still force the Three Powers to join forces in upholding 'the peace of the world'. This was their only guarantee for the future of the alliance.

Yet within a few weeks of signing the communiqué which envisaged 'the complete . . . dismemberment of Germany', they had all abandoned this decision. The occupation of their respective zones was to lead, not to the dismembering of the country by agreement among the victors, but to her partition between them. The Cold War did not represent the initial intentions of either side, but the collapse of the hopes which they had attached to the Alliance, and the partition of their original enemy, was their minimum compensation for this loss. The outlines of this development were already visible at the end of the war; and the brusque changes which converted the leading allies into competitors for the mastery of Europe were brought about between the meetings at Yalta and Potsdam. During these months it became clear that it was no longer possible to defer decision on the vital issues of Europe's future; and that the attempt to do so, far from ensuring collaboration over Germany, was leading instead to a struggle for pre-emptive victory and the rapid establishment of control. This applied most fully to the Soviet Union, least to the United States; yet all three powers had certain definable motives which made this evolution almost predictable.

Of the three, one can be least certain about Stalin. It is possible that his motives were more contradictory than they appear here. But he seems to have come to the conference with two predominant considerations. The first was that if Anglo-American presence in Europe were inevitable for the next few years, Soviet influence could only be established by consolidating its base in the East. To this end, he had shown himself prepared to define spheres of influence with Churchill* which would have given him a determining influence in Roumania and Bulgaria, while leaving the British supreme in Greece, and retaining Jugoslavia and Hungary as buffer states between them. Until his control over these areas was secured, he did not desire any similar arrangements in Germany, though he may well have

* At Moscow, October 1944.

hoped for the same success from a later dismemberment that the division of Eastern Europe was to assure him there. But he had no intention of seeing Germany divided for the time being.

There appear to have been two reasons for this hesitation: Russia urgently needed reparations to restore production in her western provinces, and to permit a planned industrial expansion. Such payments, particularly the transfer of installations from all parts of Germany to Russia, could only be secured by arrangement with the Western Powers. This gave the question of reparations a weight in Soviet diplomacy, during and after the war, which did much to counteract the overwhelming strength of the Red Army. Secondly, by maintaining a flexible attitude to Germany, by co-operating with his Allies and extorting concessions from them (as he succeeded in doing in the case of Poland), he might hope to prepare the ground for a political victory which would embrace the whole of Germany. If this is true, there were strong reasons for preserving an alliance 'securing lasting peace and the fruits of victory', as Stalin himself expressed it at Yalta.[1]

In any case the war was not over. Stalin's other main consideration lay in his old fears of a separate Western peace with Germany which would direct a stronger resistance against the Soviet Union. The next months were to show that these were still alive. Russian victories, on the other hand, could turn the situation further in his favour before the next meeting of the Allied leaders. The continuation of the Alliance into peace time would then further his aims.

That he had no ulterior intention of disrupting Allied plans after victory would seem to be confirmed by the instructions that were given in Moscow to the group of German Communists which was to take over the political organisation of the Soviet Zone at the end of the war. Shortly after the Yalta Conference, they were told that on returning to Germany they were to form a coalition of anti-fascist forces, which would concentrate on the fulfilment of the 'bourgeois-democratic revolution' of 1848. They were expressly forbidden to found any Communist Party and were told how to reply to 'leftist' criticisms of this decision. The significance of the term 'bourgeois-democratic' will be discussed later. But it is clear that at the time the 'Ulbricht Group' and the political staff of Marshal Zhukov's army intended to prepare for an extension of the anti-fascist coalition to the whole of Germany within the framework provided by the Alliance.*

Stalin therefore had weighty reasons for persevering in his association with the United States and Great Britain. In avoiding too distinct a settlement in Germany (or Poland, or Jugoslavia), he could hope to ensure the greatest gains, while profiting from the alliance for immediate purposes. The chief of these was reparations; and his two partners might have been justified in calculating that until his minimal demands had been met in this sphere, he would have been willing to co-operate with them in other ways. (He may also have been tempted to rely at this stage on the chances of an American loan, which would have enabled him to begin reconstruction as soon as peace was restored.)[2] If they had had definite views of the political future of Germany, they might have ensured a measure of acquiescence by this means; but neither Churchill nor Roosevelt was willing to risk an early commitment—not because they failed to recognise the dangers of Russian ambition in Central Europe, but because each feared that the other's remedy might entail the perils of a third world war.

Churchill, in ignorance of conditions in Germany, without any means of judging how long resistance would last, and in mounting despair at the unchecked advance of Soviet power, was convinced that the only insurance against this menace would be a temporary division of spheres of influence in which the presence of American armies would preserve the interests of Western Europe. But there was no prospect for the moment of securing American consent to such proposals, and he judged that the best hope of an acceptable agreement in future lay in the avoidance of immediate decision: 'Treatment of Germany after the war', he had written to Eden a month earlier. 'It is much too soon for us to decide these enormous questions. Obviously when German organised resistance has ceased, the first stage will be one of severe military control. . . . We have

* Wolfgang Leonhard, one of the members of the Ulbricht Group, has described these instructions and the abrupt change of line a few months later in his book *Child of the Revolution*. Mr. Leonhard has also told me that it was understood by all members of the group that the anti-fascist coalition, and the measures (such as land reform) which were to accompany its formation, were to provide the basis for a political organisation of the whole of Germany.

yet to settle the practical questions of the partition of Germany, the treatment of the Ruhr and Saar industries etc. . . . but I doubt if any final decision will be reached (at the conference). No one can foresee at the present moment what the state of Europe will be, or what the relations of the Great Powers will be. . . .'[3] Perhaps he hoped that the first stage of military control would restore him some flexibility in the handling of particular problems. Certainly his position had not changed at the conference. The treatment of Germany, he told his partners, raised questions which needed profound study, and no final decision could be reached until an examining commission had reported on the problems involved, nor until the British government had carefully considered the attitude of its allies.[4] Similarly, he insisted that the Russian reparations claim could not be discussed until the condition of German industry had been examined. It seems clear that he regarded Roosevelt's ideas on the organisation of world peace with much reserve, except in so far as they represented an extension of the alliance itself. His account of the discussions of the 'World Instrument for Peace' and the 'World Organisation' which had been agreed on at Dumbarton Oaks, shows that he was concerned above all that this should not become an instrument for the dismantling of the British Empire, and that the Great Powers should maintain their concert. He was at all events convinced that in itself no organisation could hope to prevent a German resurgence, or check Soviet ambitions in Europe, and that the illusion that it could do so might well prove dangerous. He was for this reason deeply concerned to retain the American armies in Europe, and when he learned that Roosevelt had decided to limit the occupation period to two years, he pressed immediately for French participation in the control of Germany and the re-creation of a 'strong France'.

On the basis of a three-power contribution to the garrisons of West Germany, he also hoped that the World Organisation might provide an instrument of genuine accord with the Soviet Union and help to prevent Poland and the whole of Eastern Europe from falling to total Russian domination. In discussions on Poland at Yalta he said without any equivocation: 'Poland must be mistress in her own house and captain of her own soul. Such freedom must not cover any design by Poland, or by any Polish group, possibly in intrigue with Germany, against Russia;* but the World Organisation that was being set up would surely never tolerate such action *or leave Russia to deal with it alone*.'⁵

Churchill was cautiously optimistic over the results of Yalta. Like Stalin, he hoped that the skeleton agreement of the conference would still enable him to influence the course of events after the war. For both this meeting was intended to establish a diplomatic basis for their further purposes. Both hoped to carry these out within the Alliance, and particularly by winning American consent—though Churchill was under no illusions about the extent of his power should he fail to do so. Although their mistrust mellowed for a while during their meeting, both were fully justified in their intense suspicion of the other's purpose. And both realised that between these, and Roosevelt's approach to the organisation of peace, there lay a no-man's-land, which with military luck and diplomatic skill could be turned to great advantage.

There is no doubt that Roosevelt understood his position in the plans of his allies, and regarded himself as a mediator between the two contenders. Nor did he underestimate the menace of Russian ambition. But for him the conference had two overriding purposes. It was only by their simultaneous attainment that he believed that the Alliance could be preserved in the post-war period.⁶ The first was 'to sustain the concert of military action against Germany' (which had been gravely threatened by the dissensions of the last months) 'until the war was won, and to manage the German surrender smoothly'.⁷ He was not willing to see a discussion of the modalities of surrender develop into an apportionment of claims. He had been deeply disturbed by the overwhelming evidence of Russian intentions towards the separate Eastern European states† and believed that the best way of restraining them was to work closely together with the Soviet Union in the administration of Germany. This was to be a local form of practical co-operation between the Great Powers—which he was at the same time attempting to

---

* In the correspondence over Poland which the three had conducted between the Warsaw Rising and the Yalta Conference, Stalin had insisted that the Polish problem and that of Soviet security were inseparable.

† More so, it seems, than his immediate advisers. See Feis, *Between War and Peace*, p. 78.

develop into a global system through the World Organisation for peace. It was above all essential that the two gigantic countries should work together in establishing the pattern of the new world; and his second main purpose was therefore to obtain Russian assent to this new body of states and reach agreement on a method of voting which would preserve scope for collaboration among the Great Powers while ensuring that the lesser would not be ignored. He was deeply distrustful of a settlement of outstanding problems through private arrangements between the Great Powers, which he regarded as the origin of power-conflicts and wars.* Stalin's concessions in the question of organising the Security Council, and in reducing to three the number of votes demanded by the Soviet Union, were taken by him as substantial signs of good faith. The impression that the United States had gained a diplomatic triumph—that the Soviet Union had made far greater concessions than they on all points which concerned the World Organisation†—does not seem to have induced the American delegation to question the Russian scale of priorities, or seek any firmer engagements in matters of more immediate moment to the fate of Europe. This optimism may have been encouraged by Stalin's apparent readiness to agree that the Polish government, which had been set up at the Russian occupation, should be 'reorganised' at the end of the war, and not merely 'enlarged' as had been feared. If, as both Roosevelt and Churchill still hoped, it were possible to secure an independent, democratic government in Poland, the greatest obstacle to full co-operation would be removed. But the essential proof of Roosevelt's policy and Russia's purposes would be found in Germany.

Perhaps Roosevelt believed that here the Three Powers would be obliged to work together in elaborating their policies. The definition of boundaries, the securing of reparations, the restoration of peaceful economic production, the punishment of war criminals and the elimination of militarism, would all demand the closest consultation. In fact the vaguer the agreements on Germany, the greater the necessity of reaching preliminary consent to new decisions after the war.

* This view is expounded by Roosevelt's Secretary of State at the time of the Conference, Edward R. Stettinius, jr., in his book, *Roosevelt and the Russians.*

† Stettinius and Hopkins both emphasised this judgement.

But the compromises of Yalta could not be developed any further. Certain principles on the treatment of Germany after the war had been evolved over the previous years, but they could not be realised in the context of the different interpretations which each member attached to the Alliance as victory drew near. It was to the Foreign Ministers that the three looked for the provisions of unified treatment. They had now, essentially, to consider two matters, both of which presupposed that the period of occupation would be governed by common decisions, but neither of which could be settled without working out the details of the application of earlier principles. These were: reparations, and the future dismemberment of Germany. The first embraced a great range of economic and administrative policies which would have to be carried out by all the occupation powers.* The second implied that after the rapid attainment of certain objectives, the Allies would work together in establishing the successor states.

The point of departure for all subsequent debate on the 'treatment of Germany' had been the Anglo-American declaration of January 1943. As it became clear that they were going to win the war, the two leaders had decided on the enforcement of unconditional surrender. In view of the enemy that they were fighting, this may have been a just and wise decision; but it carried certain ineluctable implications, that, in view of their ally in the struggle, should have been well considered. The first was the annihilation of the German state, and the consequent transfer of all authority to the occupying Powers. The second was that if Germany were ever to exist as a separate state again, it could only be by agreement among the victors. The third, that if conflict between them were to be avoided they would have to reach an early understanding on the nature of their administration, and the form of the future state. This had been attempted in earlier meetings between the leaders.

It had been decided that partition was preferable to one central tripartite administration. This had been discussed at the first Quebec Conference of 1943, and agreed at the meeting in Teheran later in the same year. Here, too, the Allies agreed that partition should be the preliminary to dismemberment.

---

* For this reason Stalin suggested, and Churchill opposed, the settlement of a fixed total of reparations as a preliminary to the discussion of means.

Although the three leaders were uncertain how this would be carried out (Roosevelt spoke of the creation of five new states, Churchill of an Austro-Bavarian state), they were all persuaded that an essential post-war task of the alliance would be to prevent reunification. Stalin remarked that such attempts would have to be restrained by economic measures or, if necessary, by force. They also believed that in the interim they would be concerned together in the denazification, demilitarisation and economic administration of the country.*

At Teheran the European Advisory Commission was projected. Its chief task was the demarcation of the zonal boundaries, and this was completed only three months before the conference at Yalta. To symbolise the intention of maintaining a unified control of Germany, and of preventing the zonal divisions from developing into permanent partition, it was also decided, after much dispute, that Berlin should be administered by all the occupying powers as an enclave in the Soviet Zone. The old capital was to become the new seat of the Control Council, which would provide the machinery for the co-ordination of national policies. The general basis for common action in Germany had thus been laid when the Yalta Conference began; the Foreign Ministers, who headed the Advisory Commission, were henceforth to be charged with the elucidation of further problems. But the preservation of the Alliance now depended on the postponement of decision, while the policies already formulated demanded that the three should reach rapid concurrence before the diversity of administration in the respective zones should prejudice the future. This was the heart of the matter, and only a remarkable unity of purpose in the concluding months of the war could have given the Foreign Ministers any hope of success. Instead, their assumptions were foundering already, and the new policies after Yalta did not extend their agreements, but prepared for greater divergencies.

This central difficulty first took overt form in the question of reparations. For understandable reasons it was accorded primacy of treatment. It represented a vital interest for the Soviet Union and a secondary consideration for the United States, on

* It was *after* this that Churchill and Roosevelt gave their short-lived approval to the Morgenthau Plan of September 1944 for the internationalisation of Germany's main industrial resources, and the general pastoralisation of the country.

which Roosevelt was disposed to make concessions to Stalin. Since it had first been raised at the time of Beaverbrook's and Harriman's visit to Moscow in 1941, this had been the recurring theme of all subsequent negotiations with Russia. By 1945, it had come to symbolise for Stalin Russia's emergence as a decisive world power: he described the later proposal of French participation in the Reparations Commission as an insult and an attempt to humiliate the Soviet Union. For more practical purposes it also represented the quickest and most effective way of restoring Soviet industry in the west of Russia. During the war, the Russians had acquired a vast experience of the transfer and re-erection of whole industries; and the denuded areas could now be equipped by the same means. Lastly, a flexible adjustment of his claims to the political needs of the moment offered Stalin great opportunities for influencing the future development of Germany.

Concerned, therefore, to provide a diplomatic foundation for his later contentions, he proposed as a basis for discussion that Germany should be required to pay a total of 20 milliard dollars, of which half was to go to the Soviet Union. The claim could be substantiated by a double standard of calculation: the extent of Russian losses on the one hand, and the importance of her contribution to victory on the other. This was unexceptionable. Churchill did not dispute it, but opposed the attempt to name any total, even as a basis for discussion, until conditions inside Germany were better known. Both he and Roosevelt were concerned essentially with Germany's capacity to pay: by removing the argument from this sphere, Stalin avoided the implications of a central administration which were contained in any realistic assessment.*

The agreed total was to be raised from three sources: industrial levies in the first two years after the war; annual deliveries from current production for a period to be determined; and the employment of German labour in reconstruction. This was the basis on which the Reparations Commission was to do its work.

But a whole complex of other problems was connected with that of reparations, each of which should have been settled be-

* The United States agreed to this figure as a basis for discussion. The British disagreement appeared in the communiqué; but subsequent Russian statements insisted that the claim to 10 milliard dollars had been recognised at Yalta.

fore any concrete discussion was possible: the future Eastern frontiers of Germany; the co-ordination of administrative policies in the period of occupation; the nature of Germany's economic development, and her standard of living. All these questions were left in abeyance at Yalta, and though some of them were to be studied separately, the general approach to their solution was to be through agreement on reparations instead of the reverse. It was clearly impossible for the Ministers of the Commission to fix a level of payments without certain knowledge of the future Eastern frontier: if the lands between the Eastern and Western Neisse were to be granted to Poland, an important economic asset would be lost, and the standard of living of the rest of the country reduced by the need to support some millions of displaced Germans. Until economic administration had been co-ordinated, the main lines of development ascertained, and the standard of living determined, no one could say how reparations were to be effected, nor what form interzonal exchanges were to take.

If reparations were to be determined before these problems were resolved, agreement was needed at least on the extent of tripartite control, and on the direction in which the occupying powers would develop their zones. Two decisions had already been made. Supreme authority was to be exercised by the Allied Control Council, sitting in the Three Power city of Berlin and working on the principle of unanimity. And further aims were defined on the assumption of dismemberment; another special commission was to study this question. It was expected that its report would indicate the course of future action. These conclusions were inseparably connected. The multilateral administration of Berlin had been recommended in September 1944 as an earnest of continuing collaboration, but the only guidance for the Control Council in its pursuit of common decisions would be provided by the report of the Dismemberment Commission. If the idea of dismemberment were abandoned, the governors of Germany would begin their administration without any notion of their final objectives.

The conference adopted one other recommendation of the European Advisory Commission. This was the association of France in the occupation of Germany. If the Three Powers had agreed on their purposes this would have been of little import.

But the allocation of a zone to France and later of a sector in Berlin, with a voice in the unanimous decisions of the Control Council, meant in the actual circumstances a further obstacle to the determination of definite policies. The exclusion of French representatives from Yalta and Potsdam aggravated the difficulty, for the French thereafter maintained a calculated truculence in allied discussion of Germany to demonstrate their independence.

All these circumstances were far less clear at the time than they have since become. The three leaders may well have left Yalta convinced that it would be possible for them to collaborate peacefully until the occupation was over, and that the deferment of essential decisions would in the meantime reinsure them against disruptive ambition or hostile enclosure. It was almost imperceptibly that it led instead to the partition of Germany.

When Churchill and Truman met Stalin at Potsdam, conditions had vastly altered. These changes had been brought about in the final months of war, and though all still hoped to continue the policy of collaboration, at least in certain essentials, their expectations were tempered by great reserve.

Stalin's suspicions were perhaps the first to be revived. He seems to have been disturbed by the unexpectedly quick advance of the armies in the West. He was tempted to infer collusion with the German forces, and this was intensified when Churchill and Roosevelt told him at the beginning of March that their representatives had begun exploratory conversations with General Karl Wolff, the commander of the SS in Italy, to see if a surrender of Kesselring's armies could be negotiated. This surrender would be unconditional. The Russians were invited to send a representative. Exchanges between the three continued for weeks, Stalin persisting in his charges of bad faith, the others in their invitation. Stalin may have wished to obstruct negotiations and so prolong the war in the West by consistently ignoring the invitation; or the knowledge that Himmler was still hopeful of a separate peace with the Anglo-American forces, which would enable the remaining German armies to concentrate in the East, may have made him suspicious of any contacts with an SS General.

Churchill was at the same time increasingly disquieted by Stalin's mounting ambitions in Eastern Europe. His evident intention of securing the mastery of Poland through the Lublin (now Warsaw) government, Tito's expansion in the Balkans, and the fear that the Russian armies might strike across North Germany into Scandinavia, awoke his worst suspicions. Russia might now be able to dominate the greater part of Germany's perimeter and obtain the effortless mastery of Europe. The dismemberment of the Reich would only help him to achieve this.

The last month of Roosevelt's life was dominated by the dissensions between his allies. It was also clear to him that Stalin had no intention of allowing any arrangements made at Yalta to moderate his ambitions in Poland. The accord, he told the President on April 7th, had provided that the existing Polish government should be the 'kernel' of the new one.

In this atmosphere of growing suspicion the idea of dismemberment was dropped. 'I hardly like to consider dismembering Germany until my doubts about Russia's intentions have been cleared away', said Churchill in March. Roosevelt, though he does not appear to have decided at any point that it should be finally abandoned, was reluctant to embark upon it; and his State and War Departments, and the Joint Chiefs of Staff, were by now all advising him against it.* Stalin had similarly changed his mind. On March 26th his representatives on the Dismemberment Commission had said that dismemberment should not be regarded as a settled policy, but as a threat to hold over the Germans, should they prove recalcitrant. This was also the opinion of the British member, and the topic never afterwards received serious discussion.†

The Allies, therefore, ended the war without having even the most general conception of the future of Germany, nor the most tenuous basis of united policy in their zones. And while relations between them continued to deteriorate, no one of the Western Powers seemed able to produce a settled plan for its own zone, or any firm prospects of agreement with the Soviet

* Though Roosevelt seems to have been as much influenced by his anxiety over Germany as by his suspicions of Russia. Another factor in American calculations was the impression that Russia was in any case reconsidering the whole question. See Feis, *Between War and Peace*, p. 236.

† In his victory message of May 9th, Stalin announced that Russia had no intention of dismembering Germany.

Union. One may assume that the Russian governors of East Germany did have certain immediate objectives, which will be examined in a later chapter. But victory would reveal that the other Three Powers had no specific intentions even towards their own zones, and that in all-German affairs their own lack of initiative was too easily translated into compliance with Soviet moves.

This tendency was strengthened by the developments of the last month of war. At the beginning of April, Churchill voiced his darkest forebodings in a message to Roosevelt, which ended: 'If they [the Russians] are ever convinced that we are afraid of them and can be bullied into submission, then indeed I shall despair of our future relations with them and much else'.[8] But a week later Roosevelt died. He was the only man on whom both Russia and Britain could by now rely as an intermediary, or who still had sufficient weight with both sides to induce an acceptable compromise, however temporary, in the approaching struggle for the control of Germany. His successor had not been kept informed of all the developments of the past months, and had, moreover, to rely on the advice of a group of men who, though they had been close to the President, did not fully share his anxiety and were inclined to discount Churchill's pessimism. As the Four Powers moved into their zones of occupation, Truman was therefore anxious to put Russian intentions yet again to the test, and the arguments that Churchill used may in part have strengthened him in this resolve.

The war ended along lines unsatisfactory to both sides. At the time of capitulation Anglo-American forces were in possession of large tracts of territory that had been assigned to Russian occupation. The Soviet armies were in exclusive control of Berlin and Vienna, as well as parts of Austria within the Western Zones. Neither side was prepared to move without some preliminary guarantees from the other; but Churchill, above all, was disposed to force a showdown over the matter, using it to bring Stalin to the early conference which he was simultaneously urging on Truman. He was now convinced that the decisions which had been postponed at Yalta could be delayed no longer. To Eden in San Francisco he wrote that the Allies should not retreat from their positions 'until we are satisfied about Poland and also about the temporary nature of the Russian occupation of Germany'.[9] But Truman regarded this as a purely military matter,* and he continued in this attitude until the beginning of June. Stalin and Zhukov also insisted that the reasons for delay in admitting the Anglo-American forces to Berlin were purely military. All routes of access to Berlin would be blocked for weeks by the re-deployment of Soviet troops. But at the same time the Soviet authorities made the proper occupation of the respective zones a condition for beginning the regular work of the Allied Control Council. To this Truman replied that the withdrawal of forces was one of the matters to be settled in the Control Council itself. Thus, though no one of the three had any intention of going back on the arrangements made by the Advisory Commission, the case became a symbol of the difficulties which the Alliance encountered at the very beginning of its period of government—and also of the trust which the President and his advisers placed in the machinery of collaboration. So it came about that the final agreement that the Western forces should withdraw from their own zones, and simultaneously occupy Berlin at the beginning of July, was reached at the same time that Zhukov ordered the creation of a Communist Party in Berlin and the Eastern Zone. The Russian attempt to organise Berlin in Soviet interests will be discussed in the next chapter; but it was in any case becoming clear that the campaign for the political conquest of Germany was no longer to be delayed.

This was confirmed by a number of unilateral decisions which were taken by the Russians immediately after the end of the war. All these attempted to anticipate the agreements, which, it was understood at Yalta, would be worked out together by the Three Powers, once they had secured possession of Germany. As Stalin had requested without success in February, Poland had now been entrusted with the administration of the territory between the Eastern and the Western Neisse. Secondly, troops and industrial experts had begun wholesale dismantling in the Eastern Zone, without any reference to the Western Allies or any report to the Reparations Commission. Thirdly, Zhukov ordered, on June 10th, that 'anti-fascist' parties and trade

* 'As to the actual movement of US forces, you should state that ... this is primarily a military matter. . . .' Truman to Eisenhower: H. S. Truman, *Year of Decision*, p. 224. See also Feis, *Between War and Peace*, p. 111.

unions were to be established immediately in the Soviet Zone, although it was originally provided that such steps were to be taken only after joint consultation.

Germany was thus already being divided before the powers that had assumed responsibility for her destiny met again. The attempts they had made to provide a basis for collaboration had failed before they were even tested. If these divergencies were not to develop into a permanent partition, new action was urgently necessary. For this, only one means remained: the creation at Potsdam of a central German authority, to carry out the instructions of the Control Council in all four zones. The only alternative to partition was centralisation.

But in the circumstances of the time this was impossible. None of the Western Powers had any settled ideas on its future policy in Germany. Their first preoccupation was to ensure co-operation with the Russians in the face of the German population. All were concerned to secure certain guarantees against German resurgence; and France in particular looked to Russian support in attaining her own ends. The British and American administrations had, moreover, urgent practical reasons for obtaining early agreement with the Soviet authorities. They were incapable of feeding their own zones, and would depend on the delivery of food from the East. Otherwise, they had few opportunities of judging Russia's further intentions, since the Allied Control Council was not officially opened until July 30th, when the Potsdam Conference was nearly over.

Potsdam therefore represented another deferment of decision. The chief concern of the meeting was indeed not with Germany, but the general organisation of peace—the treaties with the satellite states, and the admission of Italy to the United Nations. As far as the particular question of Germany was broached, the conference could do little more than reaffirm old principles and ratify accomplished Russian actions. When Stalin assured his allies that the question of Poland's western frontier was not yet finally settled, they agreed that the territory beyond the Eastern Neisse should remain under Polish administration until a German peace-treaty was signed. In response to the widespread dismantling that had already been carried out, they attempted to reach a compromise which finally provided that each power was to settle its reparations requirements primarily from its own zone; but Russia was also promised 25 per cent of the industrial plants that were to be dismantled in Western Germany, in return for which she was to make certain deliveries of raw materials and manufactured goods to the West.* This arrangement was of crucial importance. It admitted the principle of administrative decentralisation, and specified that reparations were henceforth to be directed separately in each of the four zones. Just as the admission of France and Poland to the control of German territory had disorganised the conception of exclusive three-power control, so now the principles of unified direction were forgotten.

Partly, perhaps, as a result of the *faits accomplis* with which he had been confronted, Truman proposed at the first meeting of the conference that the Control Council should begin its meetings forthwith, and presented a formula to define its powers. This was more emphatic than the previous drafts in its insistence on the supreme authority of the Council in all but exclusively zonal affairs.[10] But there were no new reasons for this change; they had applied with equal force at the end of the war. It could have been prompted only by distrust— and Molotov objected vigorously. The new wording was withdrawn, and replaced by a virtually unaltered renewal of the earlier draft. But though it was becoming increasingly clear that the victorious powers had retained no common principles but those of demilitarisation and denazification, the American delegation was by now convinced that concessions would have to be made to the Soviet Union to ensure her amenability in the final organisation of the United Nations. This policy was partly a reversal of Roosevelt's. He seems to have intended rather to make the administration of Germany a test case of Russia's intentions. This was still, on the surface, true, but agreement on matters of principle was regarded as more important than collaboration on substantive issues. Thus, though large concessions were made at Potsdam, the 'package deal' by which Russian assent was given to the principles of the Agreement seemed still to provide the basis for common policies in the immediate future.

* An account of the discussions in the Reparations Commission, and the reluctant agreement to refer the matter to the Potsdam Conference, is given in Feis, *Between War and Peace*, pp. 254-258.

In exchange for provisional recognition of the Oder-Neisse Line, and the compromise on the modalities of reparations, the Russian delegation agreed to support the admission of Italy to the United Nations and join in issuing the Potsdam Declaration of Principles on the treatment of Germany.

These principles now represented all that the Three Powers* had to go on in co-ordinating their future policies in Germany. They were divided into political and economic sections. Both implied in some degree a confession of failure. Though the Control Council was still recognised as the supreme authority, and the inter-allied status of Berlin was reaffirmed, the decision was taken to decentralise the political structure—with a view to preparing 'the eventual reconstruction of German political life on a democratic basis', and enabling the Germans 'in due course to take their place among the free and peaceful peoples of the world'. How this was to be achieved without any centralised political structure was left for later consideration; the only approach to the problem at present was the decision that free local elections could be held in the various zones when their respective governors deemed that the time had come. There were no provisions for co-ordinating these, nor for securing the 'uniformity of treatment of the German population throughout Germany', which the principles also demanded. It was emphasised in the original American draft, and still repeated in the final declaration, that the creation of a central German government was to be indefinitely postponed, though central German administrative machinery might be used for 'economic activities of national scope'. In fact, the only hope of maintaining even a skeletal framework for inter-allied administration lay in the rapid creation of such German machinery. No German authority, even if fully approved by all the Allies, could at that stage have exerted any pressure whatsoever on any of them; but a single authority would have meant that the Four Powers were obliged, at least in principle, to work out common policies in all questions of national importance. The mere existence of the Control Council did nothing to ensure this, offering rather a forum for their disagreements. The declaration had foreseen certain essential German administrative departments headed by state secretaries, but even these were never established; and a

* France did not consider herself bound by the Potsdam Agreement.

struggle for the control of any future central authority would become inevitable from the moment that the economic and political policies of Russia and the Western Powers began to diverge.

That they should diverge was scarcely prevented by the economic principles, which offered no basis of common interpretation. They laid it down that common policies should be established in all the vital sectors of the national economy—among them mining and industry; agriculture; wages, prices and rationing; import and export programmes; currency, banking, and taxation; and reparations. In all these matters it was essential to establish a firm distinction between denazification and economic development, yet this was never done. In some, it would be natural for the Russians to argue that later economic and social programmes were logical extensions of denazification—notably in agriculture. In others, it would be easy to accuse authorities actuated purely by economic motives of fostering Nazism. The founding of the Communist Party in East (and subsequently West) Germany should have warned the governments of the other zones that immediate distinction between central economic policies and local political organisations was vital to the preservation of the Alliance even in its most attenuated form; but they do not appear to have observed this. The American and British governments were still concerned, above all, with the task of ending the 'German Problem', and were no doubt persuaded that the Control Council and the now permanent Council of Foreign Ministers would in their periodic meetings ensure agreement on essentials.

This rudimentary machinery could have been used to achieve some compromise, and the observance of policies already agreed on, as it was at the end of the Berlin Blockade. But it served more often as a vehicle for legalistic conflicts; and this was largely because the Western Powers had no definite idea of what they wanted to do in Germany. Neither side seems yet to have contemplated a permanent division of the country; but the 'ambiguities' of the Soviet threat were first being formulated in practice; and it was bound to lead to division unless the others rapidly devised energetic measures of preventing this. The general policies of the Occupation Powers will be discussed in a later chapter, but for the moment the others desired above all a comfortable *modus vivendi* with the Soviet Union. The new British government was at first far more convinced than Churchill had been that some form of understanding was possible, and still concentrated on preventing a German resurgence. In this they took Soviet participation for granted. But they were not prepared to bargain with the resources that they controlled* for an international direction of Germany's development, and without this, no alternative to division could be contrived. In any case it had become increasingly clear during Churchill's last months of office that, with the end of the war, Britain's influence in world affairs was greatly reduced. His departure confirmed the fact, that the 'Big Three' no longer existed, and the United States would henceforth bear the prime responsibility for meeting the challenge from Russia.

Although Roosevelt had spoken for the whole country in international conferences, his death revealed considerable divisions of opinion inside his government. The War and State Departments and the Joint Chiefs of Staff had different counsels to offer his successor. The only document that they had given Generals Eisenhower and Clay to guide them in the government of Germany, JCS/1067, reflected their contest for influence in its entirely negative instruction. It was an echo of the Morgenthau Plan that bore no relation to the conditions inside the country nor to the problems which the Soviet administration now presented. The Military Governor and his Deputy had already had to make many primary decisions in their relations with the Soviet authorities; without any other directives, they were anxious to collaborate as closely as possible both with the Russians and with their other Allies.†

The French government was at this stage determined on certain specific objectives, notably the detachment of the Saar and the Ruhr from German control, and anxious to restore some flexibility to its relations with the Anglo-Saxons through a *rapprochement* with the Soviet Union. These purposes seemed to combine well for a time, particularly as long as the French Communist Party was represented in the government. Until the

* Bevin's personal objections to Stalin's proposal for the internationalisation of the Ruhr secured its withdrawal.

† Eisenhower had wished to continue SHAEF as an instrument of integrated Western occupation, but apparently without prejudice to relations with Russia.

middle of 1946, Bidault hoped that Russian support could be won in return for French backing over the creation of the central German authorities which had been envisaged at Potsdam. Meanwhile, France refused to be bound by the Potsdam Agreement, and showed unrelenting hostility to any measures of centralisation.

All the Western Powers were thus, for different reasons, convinced that collaboration with the Soviet Union in Germany was their essential task. The struggle for the country came upon them almost unawares, and at the outset none was capable of answering the scarcely defined Russian threat. This threat would not become manifest until they were all forced to face the need of defining common economic policies and erecting a central German authority. But there was already one centre in Germany where all were concerned together in a common assignation, and where the present government of the country was established. It offered a valuable, perhaps decisive, prize to Russia in the political conquest of the whole; and in the Rooseveltian terms which governed American policy, it provided the United States with the most practical test of Soviet intentions. This was Berlin.

Chapter Two

THE RUSSIAN CONQUEST

O^N April 28th, 1945, two days after Russian troops had completely surrounded Berlin, General Bersarin issued Order No. 1 of the Occupying Forces. Although the battle for the capital had not yet been fought out, he assumed complete political and administrative authority. For two days the Russians had been occupying the suburbs against a motley resistance, consisting in part of detachments of the Hitler Youth placed in fox-holes in the path of the advancing tanks, with bazookas which they had not been trained to use. On the 29th the battle was decided, against the fiercer opposition of regular soldiers and SS, who can be seen in photographs giving the Hitler salute as the enemy tanks reached the old Pariser Platz. On the 30th Hitler committed suicide, and the Red Flag was hoisted on the Reichstag building, which stood at the heart of the last fighting. By May 2nd Russian control was complete, the German troops surrendered and the capitulation was signed.

The surrender of the German forces in the rest of the country was not to follow for almost a week. The final capitulation, on the Eastern Front, was signed on May 8th. The Russians conquered Berlin before they wrested Prague from the German occupation. The fall of the capital was not the end of the war; it was the last great Russian victory, and so the Russians saw it. An 'Information Sheet for the German Population' of May 3rd bore the announcement.

BERLIN CAPTURED

The troops of the First Byelo-Russian Front under the command of Marshal of the Soviet Union Zhukov, with the support of the troops of the First Ukrainian Front under the command of Marshal of the Soviet Union Koniev, have completed the destruction of the units of the German forces in Berlin after obstinate street-fighting; and today, the 2nd of May, are in complete possession of the German capital, the city of Berlin, centre of German Imperialism and heart of German aggression.

In fact, Berlin remained for the present a Russian prize of war, whatever arrangements the Allied governments might have reached on its future status. The victory of the Soviet forces gave them a moral mortgage on the future of the capital, which they were reluctant to abandon. The Anglo-American forces' subsequent withdrawal from those areas of the Russian Zone which they had conquered was scarcely enough to counterbalance this.

The Russian attitude was to become clearer, but it coloured the occupation from the start. The admittance of Anglo-American forces was a concession which should not be allowed to deflect the course of a wider strategy—and might even prove of some assistance. The centre of German imperialism was to become the base for the political conquest of Germany. If this could be achieved with the passive consent of the Allies, it would be the more telling; but to this end a complete system of administrative control should be established before the Allied troops arrived.

Hence, while Stalin and Zhukov pleaded the difficulties of redeployment and temporised over the entry of the Western contingents, General Bersarin's forces were rapidly creating a new political order. It seems that for the first three days after surrender most of the Russian soldiers were entirely out of hand, and the full horrors of conquest fell upon the inhabitants of the smoking city. Nor did the Russians succeed in establishing complete control at once. Even at the end of the month a warning against resistance was placarded on trees and walls in every notable street. It was signed by the new German Oberbürgermeister and laid down the penalties for arson or attempts on the lives of occupation troops or people in public office. These were to be punished by the death of the offender and of 50 Nazi hostages each time. But though isolated acts of resistance had continued, the number of people executed in this way was probably very small. The occupying forces were able to begin organising the future from the very beginning, and in general they found the population ready to co-operate. The reasons for this are clear. Two-thirds of the population were women, and with the reduction of the SS, all chances of creating a resistance movement were destroyed. The sense of intellectual liberation, particularly among younger people, was very strong, and the fatalist sufferance of the first days was afterwards animated by a sense of renewal. The first play produced in a city where less than a month before Hitler's power had still been

C

absolute was *Nathan der Weise*. The first opera was *Fidelio*. And there were urgent practical reasons. The capital was for days entirely without gas, electricity or water supplies. Communications had stopped, except by boat along the flooded Underground lines. The inhabitants were entirely dependent on the Red Army for food. Obedience in these conditions was a matter of survival—and the Soviet measures of relief were at the outset almost indistinguishable from their political organisation. The efficiency with which the army provided essential services may have induced a will to reconstruct; it certainly encouraged volunteers to give their assistance, which was often used for political ends.

In this way the distribution of rations was linked from the first to a system of supervision set up by 'People's Committees', which had appeared on the day of surrender in all parts of Berlin. *Obleute*, supervisors chosen by the committees, were appointed for every block, street and house, to distribute food, carry out the orders of the Soviet Army and create an administrative structure. The origin of these committees is confused. They seem to have been composed partly of volunteers from the older political parties, partly of men impressed on the spot by Russian officers. Similarly, volunteers were found to discharge certain public functions, even while Berlin radio was broadcasting information and calls to surrender to the remaining areas of resistance in Germany. The duties of the civil police were handed over at the very beginning to 'Anti-Fascist Auxiliary Committees', formed on very much the same basis—and the Russians were able to strengthen their authority by delegating it, even in imposing a régime that Zhukov described at a later press conference as one of the 'severest occupation'.

These were the conditions in which General Bersarin's forces installed their political machine. Its basic structure was simple. The population was organised into an alliance with the occupation authorities through an 'Anti-Fascist Coalition'. This was not originally intended to represent any of the main pre-Nazi parties, but to circumvent the need for any political parties.*

---

* This may seem to be too dogmatic, since it is generally assumed that the 'Anti-Fascist Coalition' was intended to bring the main 'Democratic' parties together. But I have not been able to find any reference to political parties, until the leading German Communists were told at the beginning of June that the

It was always spoken of as a coalition of 'forces' or 'elements' until Zhukov's order of June 10th announced publicly that new parties, including the Communists, were now to be formed. The coalition was expected to agree on a social and administrative programme which would at least ensure the 'completion of the bourgeois-democratic revolution' of 1848. This did not mean the establishment of bourgeois-democracy in Germany. The Russian and German Communists may well have hoped to circumvent this normal stage of Marxist progress, and to proceed from the completion of the revolution to the organisation of Socialism through the re-education of the workers. There is a technical difference between bourgeois revolutions and bourgeois-democratic revolutions, and the completion of the work begun in 1848 meant in fact the establishment of a system where power would be exercised by the people in a form more direct than political parties provided. This was to be accompanied by social and economic reforms which would complete the democratic structure and prepare for the introduction of Socialism. These reforms were, however, still vaguely defined, since the political leaders who returned from Russia in the wake of Zhukov's army do not seem to have been certain whether they should have been applied first to their own zone of occupation, or carried through on a national scale once the four zones had acquired a common economic and administrative system. Decision was delayed because the essential task before the implementation of any economic reforms was to secure reparations deliveries—and it was in fact the contradiction between this and the need for economic and political union which led to the division of Germany. Bersarin's system was therefore less concerned with the social reforms that were promised by the Communist Party after its formation than with the political agencies that were intended to implement them when the time came. In this, the political parties had at first no part to play.

KPD was shortly to be re-founded. Party terminology is normally explicit on such points. And though the other parties of the coalition began meeting informally about the middle of May, this was quite independently of Russian policy. It also seems doubtful that the Russian authorities would contemplate the foundation of other parties while deliberately repressing the KPD; and the change of line to which Wolfgang Leonhard refers in his memoirs of this time would seem to be rather the decision to permit the foundation of political parties in general, than the admission of the KPD to the coalition.

They were not a necessary part of the coalition of anti-fascist forces, and the decision to begin the formation of specific parties was a sudden one that seems to have taken the German Communists by surprise.

The decision is still somewhat mysterious. At the beginning of June the higher party functionaries were told that Marshal Zhukov would shortly order the formation of new anti-fascist parties, and instructed to begin work on a programme of land reform that should win the peasants and refugees of the Eastern Zone to support the Communists. The formation of a Communist Party was to be proclaimed immediately after Zhukov's order. This represented a complete reversal of their previous instructions. How did it come about? One is tempted to search for a change of policy at the highest level—to surmise perhaps that Stalin had already decided that a permanent division of Germany would be in his best interests, and that he was anxious to proceed with the organisation of a satellite state as soon as possible. But this hardly corresponds with his subsequent action in Germany itself, nor with his methods in the other Eastern European states. Moreover, Ulbricht still spoke in terms of a 'German Republic' (by which he was understood to mean the whole country) when he explained the tasks of the new party to a party committee on June 10th. A republic would be formed, he said, in which the ideological conversion of the workers was possible. He reminded his listeners that the Communists no longer constituted an opposition party, but bore the most important functions of autonomous administration. These two statements, taken together, clarify that problem, and it seems that the simplest explanation is probably the most accurate. The Soviet Army had earned much hatred during and after the occupation of Germany and was still engaged on a huge programme of dismantling. If a coalition of anti-fascist forces were to carry out the functions of administration without any political representation, it would be regarded merely as the creature of the Red Army and would hinder the conversion of the workers. If other parties were allowed to function, the Communists would obviously be indispensible, even though the anti-fascist coalition was originally conceived as an attempt to do without them. Thus, they were obliged to begin formulating a programme of economic reforms, particularly the redistribution of land, straight away, and still without knowing whether they were to be tried out first on a local scale or held in reserve for national application.

But until the political situation had been evaluated, the Soviet authorities would be forced to rely as much on the other organs of direct representation that the bourgeois-democratic revolution was to create, as on the parties themselves. They were thus to use the two forces in tactical combination until the Western Commandants refused to acknowledge the validity of the other corporations, or their right to take part in political and constitutional decisions.

These bodies were trade-union organisations, cultural unions and professional associations which attempted to unite all classes of the population in a spurious support of Russian administrative measures. Similarly, there were four parties in the original coalition: the KPD, the Communists; the SPD, the Social Democrats, who had been the largest party of the Weimar Republic, and until its last years were particularly strong in Berlin; the CDU, the Christian Democrats, who formed part of a larger German union of all Christian forces, and were to become the national champion in the fight against Communism; and the LDP, the Liberal Democrats, who claimed the inheritance of Stresemann's Liberals, and were by far the least influential party in Berlin. No others were formed for nearly a year.

The coalition was only officially constituted on June 10th although the branch organisations, such as the People's Committees, had existed from the very beginning. Now, by Order No. 2 of the Soviet Military Administration, they were brought into a more general scheme. In view, said Zhukov, of the Russian conquest's having created the conditions for a free political life in the Soviet Zone,

I order: the formation and activity of all anti-fascist parties having as their aim the final extirpation of all remnants of fascism and the consolidation of the foundations of democracy and civil liberties in Germany; the development of the initiative and independent activity of the broad masses of the population directed towards these ends is to be permitted in the territory of the Soviet Zone of Occupation in Germany.

2. . . .

3. All anti-fascist party organisations and free trade-unions mentioned

under 1 and 2 are to register their regulations and programme of activity with the municipal bodies of self-government and with the Military Commandant, and must at the same time submit a list of their executive officials.

4. During the entire period of the occupation régime, the activities of all organisations named under 1 and 2 will be subject to the control of the Soviet Military Administration and will take place in accordance with instructions issued by it.

5. . . .

Thus, all parties became willy nilly *de facto* members of the anti-fascist coalition, and the Russians may well have hoped that whatever direction they would take in their German policy during the following months, it would be closely followed by the parties in Berlin. If, in fact, the Potsdam Agreement had been observed, and a centralised political structure had been built on the administrative agencies that it envisaged, the whole country might well have been conquered. The reasons for the change of plan, and for the defeat that Soviet intentions suffered within little more than a year, will be discussed later; in this defeat Berlin played a decisive rôle, and one must first examine more closely how this system was applied to the city.

The Russians had already established a Committee for Free Germany behind their lines during the war. This was composed chiefly of old Communists who had taken refuge in Russia after 1933. It was their task to prepare for the hour of victory by broadcasting the preliminary news of Russian policy to the German population. They had to make it clear that the war was being fought not against the German people, but against its Nazi masters, as Stalin himself had already said. The liberation was to be followed by a restitution of political freedom. But apart from this, there seems to have been no political preparation at all, and indeed none was possible. When the Russian political officers entered the country, they knew nothing of its conditions. They had no idea who, among the old German Communists whose names they had, had survived the twelve years of Nazi rule, and had no means of getting into touch with them. Their instructions were of a very general nature, and their whole work in Berlin was improvised after their arrival.

Their chief assistants were the members of the Committee for Free Germany who were to be instrumental in forming the new anti-fascist coalition in Berlin. They were led by Walter Ulbricht, who had throughout been the most influential German Communist in Russia. This 'Ulbricht Group' left Moscow for Germany on April 30th. Before going on to Berlin, they conferred with the political staff of Zhukov's army, under General Galachiev, who were waiting in the small town of Bruchmühle, 18 miles away. One of their members was Wolfgang Leonhard who later left East Germany during the Jugoslav crisis and has described what happened at this time. While the political officers and committee members were conferring on the completing of the bourgeois-democratic revolution, Ulbricht visited Berlin and came back with his plans already formed. 'Our task', he told them, 'will be to form the organs of self-government in Berlin. We will go into the various Berlin boroughs and select those anti-fascist elements who agree to the new German administration. It will be best if each one of us takes over a particular Berlin borough. We will meet in the evenings and each will report on his own borough.'

Later, in Berlin, Ulbricht gave more details: only the 'reddest' boroughs were to have Communist mayors (he had discovered by this time what had happened to the Communists who had remained behind); other working-class areas should have Social Democrats, and in the 'bourgeois quarters', bourgeois mayors were to be given office. Other economic and social posts were to go to Social Democrats, and the technical administration was to be in the hands of unattached specialists. In general, at least half of all posts were to go to non-Communists.[1]

This plan was carried out as far as was possible in the very haphazard circumstances of the time—without any organised political parties, or any knowledge of what had become of the non-Communist organisations, many of whose leaders had gone into exile, and which were likely to be formed on an all-German, not local, basis. The agents of the group went each into their appointed boroughs, and found their mayors and other officers as best they could. They would bring them to the Russian commander, who appointed them. They would be responsible to him, and indirectly to the political supervisors who had placed them in office. In the eminently bourgeois borough of Wilmersdorf, which was assigned to Leonhard, he succeeded in finding an old member of the conservative *Deutsche Volkspartei* for mayor, and in placing under him a Communist deputy, a Communist head of police and a Communist councillor of education.

This was the original basis of the anti-fascist coalition. Upon it was erected within a very few days a German government for the whole of the city, the Magistrat. On May 9th and 10th discussions were held between the Russian Commandant and various representatives of political groupings for the reconstitution of the Magistrat. By the 12th, these emissaries were appointed to office and were received by Bersarin to discuss the reconstitution of the German administration. The next day Zhukov confirmed the appointments, and shortly afterwards they were publicly announced by the new Oberbürgermeister, Dr. Werner, a professor of architecture of conservative background. His deputy was Karl Maron, an old Communist who had returned from Russia at the beginning of May.

Within a fortnight the occupying forces had completed the new German administration of the city. The other departments of the coalition were simultaneously formed. Administrative and professional groups were dissolved, and then re-created under the supervision of the Magistrat. A Preparatory Commission of the Free German Trade Union Federation (FDGB) was soon established to organise the new trade unions into a body embracing the whole of the working class (partly with the help of the seized assets of the Nazi *Arbeitsfront*). On June 15th all the pre-1933 trade unions were summoned to join a new movement to liquidate Fascism and found a new democratic republic.

How far the purges and reconstitution of all the other associations were necessary to rid them of Nazism, and how far they were directed towards a future reliable front for political purposes is difficult to judge. No principles were laid down, but the later proposals of the KPD for the political representation of professional associations indicate clearly enough that the political results had already been calculated. The purges themselves were thorough and quick. The Magistrat, on the day its constitution was announced, ordered a purge of all trade and business organisations on the grounds of political reliability, technical competence and indispensibility. The next day, anti-fascist judges and advocates were assembled and ordered to set up a judiciary in all parts of the city. This new organisation began its functions on May 20th. By the end of the month, the Magistrat had ordered the withdrawal of all fascist shop-keepers' licences, and had ended the activities of all business associations, professional organisations and other economic groupings. Their functions were assumed by commercial councillors and committees, and when they were later re-established, their political tasks were emphasised.

An important potential had been created in this way, but other forces were also harnessed. At the beginning of these manœuvres, Bersarin had received the 'creative artists' who were available in Berlin, and assured them of the need to revive the city's artistic life. At the end of May, writers and journalists met to receive promises of Soviet support in the 'reconstruction' of the German Press. Berlin was now to have something more than the military *Tägliche Rundschau* which was the advance-guard of the KPD, but until October all other papers, whatever their political attitude, were printed in the Soviet sector and subject to Soviet censorship. In the cultural revival there was more than a hint of political calculation. The plays and concerts that began in the shattered city almost immediately after the conquest were freely presented and movingly appreciated. But the implications became clearer on July 4th, when the 'Cultural League for the Democratic Renewal of Germany' was formed under the presidency of the Communist poet Johannes Becher, who had just returned from Russia. This league was to be among the associations which claimed direct political represen-tation in the future evolution of Berlin.

Finally the police, still under the nominal control of the 'Anti-Fascist Auxiliary Committees', were centralised under a *Polizeipräsidium*, of which the President was Paul Markgraf, another Communist. Shortly afterwards the *Volkspolizei*, the People's Police, was officially inaugurated.

These steps had all been taken before the arrival of the Anglo-American forces in July. When they came, they were also to find that Berlin had been endowed with a new administration, whose remarkable efficiency paid great tribute to the energy and improvising ability of the Russian officers and the German officials who worked with them. This was of the highest im-portance and not only in saving the population from the acute dangers of disease and starvation which threatened for months; administrative policies were from the beginning so closely linked with political ends that they were later to become the occasion for conflict between the Allies.

Within three days of surrender, a rudimentary rationing system had been introduced, which depended for the distribution of the cards and the amount allotted to the recipient, on the House Supervisors. Food was granted in proportion to the work, health and age of the individual, and gave a vital incentive to co-operation in the immediate tasks of rubble clearance and essential reconstruction. This began at once. Some buses and tube trains were running within a few days, and electrification had so far advanced by the end of the month that trams were also started. Postal services within the city were restored, and shortly afterwards such telephones as had survived began to work—at full capacity, since they temporarily became public property, and trees in the street bore the numbers of houses from which to make a call.

The Magistrat organised city affairs with the same efficiency. A skeletal Finance and Taxation Department, set up within a month, devised methods of banking, taxation and the payment of wages. This did not involve any open link with the economy of the Eastern Zone, but it is noteworthy that both ideological and administrative necessity decreed the closure of all banks except the Berliner Stadtbank, which became a public monopoly, alone empowered to issue money and receive deposits. It had its headquarters in the future Soviet sector and it was here that the Magistrat conducted its business. This fact was to have some bearing on the subsequent relations of the occupying powers.

Similarly, social insurance was resumed exclusively through the VAB (*Versicherungsanstalt Berlin*) with its headquarters in the East. This gave added scope for economic supervision, which was now exercised on almost all levels from individual rationing to city finance.

On this basis the Soviet authorities set out to recruit a centralised labour force, which was needed for other purposes beside those of clearance and reconstruction. The first of these was dismantling, which it was apparently felt necessary to accomplish before the Western occupation troops arrived. Although Allied liaison officers had been present in Berlin since the beginning of May, and in spite the agreements being negotiated on the dismantling of installations in the Western Zones and sectors, the Soviet forces were evidently instructed to secure all that they could before the entry of the Anglo-American contingents. To this end a Berlin labour force was now formed and concentrated on the Western sectors, where perhaps 70 per cent of all surviving industry had been removed by July. Another task to which the Berliners had to contribute was agricultural work in the Soviet Zone. Rapid recruitment began in earnest in the middle of June, and on the 23rd the Soviet Command issued an order forbidding the use of the word 'unemployment' or the registration of unemployed.

In other words, no rations were to be issued after this date to those who were not engaged in active work. The next day a full-scale Labour Registration was ordered by the Magistrat. Everyone was given a Labour Book, which served henceforth as ration card and identity card as well. The grading of rations was now so strictly regulated in accordance with the manner of work, that there was a difference of over 1,000 calories a day between those of a housewife who stood at the bottom of five grades, and those of a heavy manual worker or high official at the top. These measures were successful; dismantling reached its highest point at the end of the month, with the removal of all the plant of the big electricity firms in the West—Siemens, Borsig, AEG and Osram. Such items as were not covered by the principle of reparations were often confiscated as war booty, a concept which the Soviet delegate had tried unsuccessfully to introduce into the discussions of the Reparations Commission. On July 11th, for example, Maron told the borough mayors that all motor-vehicles in Berlin were the booty of the Red Army. Such actions provided an added incentive to haste in the dismantling programme, so that Allied authorities would be unable to calculate the worth of industries and products already appropriated.

Parallel to this development was the integration of Berlin into the economic structure of the Soviet Zone. No formal financial arrangements were made, but the claims engendered by the Russian conquest were already apparent before the Western forces arrived. They were reiterated with greater emphasis after these had taken possession of their sectors. On July 21st, Order No. 9 of the Soviet Supreme Commander to the 'Zonal Administration Presidents' was also issued to the Oberbürgermeister of Berlin. It ordered the resumption of industrial production (with what was left of the city's industrial potential) and the preparation, in common with all other parts of the Soviet Zone, of an industrial plan for the last quarter of 1945. A week later, Berlin was made the administrative capital of the Soviet Occupation Zone. The Allied Kommandatura had been established twenty days earlier. The Potsdam Conference was at that moment in session.

As the Russian forces tightened their control over most aspects of the city's economic and political life, and proceeded with its integration into the Eastern Zone, its future seemed to be almost predetermined. Western representation in the city government would apparently continue to be tolerated as a formality, but the presence of Western troops was obviously not reckoned a serious hindrance to the Russian programme. It would indeed enchance its success, and demonstrate to the rest of the country that it could not hope for military protection. At the same time, the Communist Party was to work through the anti-fascist coalition to convert the working class to Socialism, and show that it offered the best prospects of social reform and economic recovery. The outcome depended on the attitude first of the Allied governors in Berlin, and secondly on the response of the other parties to the temptations of the coalition.

Little was to be expected for the present from the Allied Commanders. They attached great importance to Four Power government* in the city, and even if they had been determined to oppose the extension of Russian control, they would have been deterred by the practical difficulties of the situation, some of which they had brought upon themselves.

The most pressing of these was the question of access to the city. No guarantee had been given that the rights of Western presence in Berlin involved those of access, and though Winant, the American representative on the European Advisory Commission, had sought to raise the question, he

---

* Though France had not yet been formally admitted to a seat on the Kommandatura, French detachments accompanied the first Allied troops to enter Berlin, under Colonel Howley on July 4th.

had been overruled by the President's military advisers, who insisted that Russian suspicions should not be roused in this way.[2] Thus when General Clay and General Weeks met Zhukov to discuss the details of entry into Berlin on June 29th, they were manœuvred into accepting arrangements that gave them very little scope for provisioning the city or bringing up reinforcements. General Clay had described how this happened.

We did not wish to accept specific routes which might be interpreted as a denial of our rights of access over all routes but there was merit to the Soviet contention that existing routes were needed for demobilization purposes. . . . Therefore Weeks and I accepted as a temporary arrangement the allocation of a main highway and rail line and two air corridors, reserving the right to reopen the question in the Allied Control Council. I must admit that we did not then fully realize that the requirement of unanimous consent would enable a Soviet veto in the Allied Control Council to block all our further efforts.[3]

To this difficulty was added that of feeding the Western sectors. Immediately after their entry into the city, Zhukov told Clay and Weeks that the Soviet Occupying Power was no longer able to feed the population, and that they must now provide for their sectors out of their own zones. (Up to 1945 Berlin had depended on its immediate environment for 80 per cent of its total provisions.) This threat was overcome in an agreement reached shortly afterwards, but the Western Powers were already being forced into a position of passive dependence on Russian charity. It was specified that the agreement was to be provisional, and though all sides were able to agree on a Temporary Plan for Greater Berlin, Clay was unsuccessful in his demand for a unified rationing policy for the whole city. As a result, the inhabitants were forbidden to move from one sector to another in search of better food than was available where they lived. Apart from this problem, great numbers of refugees were passing through Berlin throughout 1945—an estimated 1½ million by the end of the year. About half of the original inhabitants had also left the city by October 1946. The constant flux of population thus made it impossible to base their calculations on accurate statistics.

For these practical reasons, and also because they did not yet appreciate all that had been done during the first two months of occupation, the Western Powers questioned none of the previous Russian measures when they established the Inter-Allied government at the beginning of July—even though it was already being made plain to them that they were only there on sufferance. The Soviet attitude was symbolised at the first session of the Allied Control Council. The Supreme Commanders were accompanied by their permanent representatives, who were to form the permanent co-ordinating committee of the Control Council. The Co-ordinating Committee would be occupied for the most part in settling disagreements among the Commandants in Berlin, and ensuring that a common Allied policy would be carried out in the city. At this meeting the Soviet delegate refused to allow the Co-ordinating Committee a seat in the Eastern sector, as had been originally agreed. But the Western Powers were at this stage anxious above all to avoid any initial disagreements.

The Inter-Allied Kommandatura was established on July 7th. This was the organ of Four-Power government in Berlin. It was not composed of individual representatives, responsible to their respective governments, as were the zonal authorities, but was jointly under the command of the Allied Control Council. Yet the delegates to the Kommandatura, though only empowered to carry out the directives of the Control Council, did have very wide areas of discretion in the government of the city, and the Western Commandants were not obliged to implement all the decisions taken by Bersarin or Gorbatov (successor to Bersarin, who had been accidently killed in June) before their arrival. But in fact the First Order of the Kommandatura, issued after the first session on July 11th, read:

The Inter-Allied Kommandatura has assumed control of the City of Berlin on the 11th of July 1945. Until special notice, all existing regulations and ordinances issued by the Commander of the Soviet Army Garrison and Military Commandant of the City of Berlin, and by the German Administration under Allied Control . . . and also the liability of the population for the violation of such regulations and ordinances, or for unlawful acts against Allied occupation troops shall remain in force.

The Western withdrawal from this almost unconditional support of the Soviet administration was slow and painful. It was with reluctance that they were forced into an alliance with the German population of the city against their Russian allies, and there was no radical change in their attitude for nearly a year. In this change the political parties in Berlin played at least as great a part as the military governments; and it was eventually the crisis of the anti-fascist coalition that provoked a crisis in the relations between the Allies.

Although the coalition officially preceded the formation of parties, German political groups had been meeting informally in Berlin for some weeks before June 10th. The first discussions for the reconstitution of the Magistrat had inevitably embraced the representatives of many earlier affiliations. But the first party to emerge in a new form was the SPD, which had formed 125 groups of old members by the middle of May. Though these were not officially recognised by the occupation forces, they set up an 'Organisation Committee of the Second International' on May 16th—some days after the Magistrat had been formed, but the day before it was officially proclaimed. The other political groups had not yet coalesced into the two parties that were afterwards to become members of the coalition—chiefly because they did not have the nucleus of opposition to the Nazi régime that the KPD and SPD had both retained throughout the twelve years of Hitler's rule. Thus, the CDU and LDP were only founded after Zhukov's order—both on June 16th. But this had a paradoxical result. Because the SPD could, like the Communists, claim a genuine inheritance of opposition, it was at the outset more disposed to join them in the policy of the anti-fascist bloc; the programmes of the other two parties made at first no mention of this. The LDP appears in fact to have waited for the arrival of the Western forces before issuing any statements at all. Its foundation manifesto was published the day after their entry. But the SPD had already met to endorse the programme of collaboration on June 17th, when Grotewohl, chairman of the party in Berlin, introduced a 9-point policy statement, based on the unity of the working class. On the same day the Preparatory Commission for the FDGB organised the first public meeting of trade union officials, urging them to combine in the common struggle. Two days later, the KPD and SPD founded a 10-member 'Commission for the Anti-Fascist Coalition', to work out agreements on a common programme, although the Communists had already issued their own party manifesto, proclaiming their intentions of working for a democratic, autonomous administration, and the creation of a national anti-fascist coalition. The Social Democrats were in this way committed to the Russian policy before the Western Allies arrived and as if to emphasise this, they held a common meeting with the KPD on July 8th to publicise their alliance in the fight against Fascism, and the creation of a democratic Germany.

Daunted perhaps by this example and the first order of the Kommandatura confirming all previous Soviet measures, the leaders of the other parties now came into line. They were in any case dependent for their survival on continued Soviet recognition, since the government of the city was based on the principle of unanimity, and they could not have hoped to lead an independent existence without it. Thus representatives of all four parties met on July 14th and agreed to form an anti-fascist bloc, though reserving the recognition of their own independence. This did not amount to much. All printing presses were in the Soviet sector, and the organs of all parties subject to Soviet censorship. Berlin radio was similarly controlled by the Russians. Political meetings were naturally supervised by Allied authorities—and in the first months it made little difference whether these were British, American or Russian. No party could hope to publicise its disagreements with the policies of the coalition. And the original 'anti-fascist forces' were still functioning in reserve, were in fact growing in strength. The *Obleute* tightened their system of supervision after the occupation of the Western sectors; the FDGB was rapidly restoring the pristine unity of the working class; and the Magistrat was still a vehicle of Soviet Zonal administration rather than a political assembly.

By July 14th the city seemed to have passed under the control of the anti-fascist coalition. The Russian conquest was complete, and the Western Allies offered little hope of a reverse. But within a year the changes and inconsistencies of Soviet policy had led to another battle for the control of Berlin, in which the Russians suffered a grave defeat. In this struggle the Western Powers joined forces with the independent political parties of the city, and the history of West Berlin began to diverge from that of the Soviet sector.

Chapter Three

THE SECOND BATTLE FOR BERLIN

T<small>HE</small> Cold War resulted from the failure of Communist policy in Europe. It seems clear today that in 1945 the overall strategy of the Communist parties of the Continent was to achieve power without revolution or international conflict— and in many countries they had unexampled opportunities of doing so. Their method was everywhere the same; they worked through a democratic alliance of anti-fascist forces, in which, thanks to their outstanding rôles in the resistance movements and the post-war need for a rapid reorganisation and redistribution of national resources, they could hope to win a predominant place. At the same time the Soviet Union was bound to the leading countries of the West in an anti-German alliance: Communist representation in the government of any country would not seem to serve the interests of a hostile great power. In this way the Communist parties of France, Italy, Jugoslavia and Norway attempted with varying success to win a share in the control of the state without resorting to frontal attack. And in Poland, Hungary and Czechoslavakia success was almost certain from the outset, since they had been both liberated and occupied by the Red Army; and national leaders were obliged to give it their co-operation on both counts. In these circumstances the reservations or commitments of their allies in the West had no significance.

But in Germany all these elements combined in a totally different situation, where Communist victory depended both on the preservation of the war-time alliance and on electoral appeal. The difficulties of the Alliance prevented a speedy unification of the country, but without this it would be impossible to establish Communist control peacefully. For these reasons Stalin preferred to wait until success was in sight before establishing a central German authority, or until failure was certain before proceeding with the creation of a separate Socialist state in the Soviet Zone. But the conditions in Germany would brook no such delay, and all the occupying powers were bound to take

urgent practical measures which demanded their full co-operation. It was practical disagreements which first threatened the
Alliance in Germany, and when the Western Communists
failed to secure power without open conflict, the new struggle
between the liberal democracies and the Soviet Union centred
on the control of Germany.

Berlin was more than a microcosm of this condition. It was
already a field of battle, before the failure of Russian diplomacy
and the internal manœuvres of the individual Communist
Parties had become apparent, or the Cold War had become an
open conflict. It offered the first strategic prize in the Russian
onslaught and the control of the capital probably represented
the indispensible preliminary for the establishment of a central
German administration. For this reason the Communist attempt
to gain political control was undisguised, and it was the
nakedness of the attack that first convinced the Western Allies
of Russian ambitions in Germany. As they took measures for
the defence of the city and the security of their own zones, the
Cold War developed from a struggle for the control of Germany
into an attempt to stabilise the situation in Central Europe. The
Berlin Blockade was Stalin's last bid to break the new pattern;
the defeat he suffered confirmed both the Western presence in
Berlin and the new order in Europe. But this stability was based
on the division of Germany; whenever it has been menaced,
whenever the Cold War has come to life again, Berlin has been
both the agent and the symbol of the threat.

Nevertheless the battle for the city was always intermittent.
It took a year of skirmishing to bring the Western Powers to
the realisation that their presence in the city implied an alliance
with the German population against their Russian colleagues,
and they were not irrevocably committed to this position until
after the elections of October 1946. Meanwhile the struggle
passed through many phases, and was fought on many levels.
The Russian attempt to gain political suzerainty before the
arrival of the Western Powers was described in the last chapter.
After the occupation of the Western sectors the situation was
complicated by the establishment of the Inter-Allied Kommandatura, which, under the Allied Control Council for
Germany, represented the government of the city. In theory
this organ safeguarded the unanimity of the occupation govern-

ment, but it soon became clear that the only measures on which all the powers could agree were of a negative and limited character, such as those of denazification. In general the Soviet member refused all co-operation in the Kommandatura, preferring to encourage the development of political responsibility in the Magistrat, which was still composed of those representatives who had been chosen before the arrival of the Western forces.

The other powers soon joined the Russians in the organisation of the city's political life, and while the manœuvres in the Kommandatura continued, the political parties which had been established by Zhukov's order competed for the allegiance of the population. In so doing they won increasing support from one or other of the occupying powers, and as this process extended, many aspects of government were rapidly transferred in fact if not in name to the Magistrat. As the Cold War began, the German parties in Berlin became for a time the protagonists of the struggle between the two blocs. By February 1946 Stalin was speaking of the irreconcilable hostility between the Socialist camp and the liberal democracies, and a decisive campaign had begun in Berlin to merge the Social Democrats and the Communist Party into a single Socialist Unity Party which should have brought the great majority of the population into the camp of German Socialism, in preparation for an advance on the rest of the country.

This merger campaign, unlike the Socialist alliances that had preceded it in other countries, was an open attack on the Western Powers, and it was clear that if the occupation were not to last for more than two years, a United Socialist government in the capital of Germany might well have ensured an ultimate Communist victory over the whole continent. Reluctantly or not, the Western Commandants were forced to oppose it, and later, when it failed, to give Berlin a temporary constitution and hold elections for a new Magistrat. After the failure of the merger attempt and the defeat of the SED at the elections of October 1946, Russian policy in Berlin was reversed: the Soviet Commandant, who had previously refused to collaborate effectively in the work of the Kommandatura, now reasserted its power and its right to veto over German elections, and it was the Western authorities who insisted on the responsibility of the Magistrat.

The battle for Berlin was thus fought on two levels: that of inter-Allied relations, which centred in the Kommandatura, and that of Allied relations with the city population, which centred in the political party battle. The political parties were established unilaterally by the Russians before the Kommandatura was formed, but their existence was scarcely independent in the first months of occupation. They acquired their importance because the Kommandatura failed to function properly, and because the Soviet authorities opposed German political organisations to the Allied machinery of government. It is in the Kommandatura that reasons must first be sought for the failure of Allied policy and the initial Russian successes.[1] But later, as the Soviet authorities used the Kommandatura to obstruct the establishment of a German government, the anti-fascist alliance that they had set up was transformed into an anti-Russian alliance.

The Inter-Allied Kommandatura, as it was originally known, was based on an agreement of 1944, later approved by the European Advisory Commission, which had attempted to ensure the smooth working of Allied government in Berlin. The Kommandatura* was to be under the direction of the Control Council for Germany, which also had its seat in Berlin, and to receive its orders through the Co-ordinating Committee of the Council. It was thus a subsidiary of the Allied government in Germany, and even if a central allied administration functioned nowhere else, it should have been imposed by circumstance on Berlin. For this reason the rule of unanimity was laid down at the beginning: the individual right of veto was held to be the price of Berlin's inter-Allied status, just as the rule of unanimity in the Control Council was a function of the Allied government of Germany. It was also for this reason that Order No. 1 of the Kommandatura confirmed *en bloc* all previous decisions taken by the Soviet Commandant and promulgated before the arrival of the Western troops.

But in practice the right of veto was completely unilateral. The Western Commandants could not fail to respect the Soviet

* The first members of the Kommandatura were: USA: General Parks; UK: General Lyne; France: General de Beauchesne; USSR: General Gorbatov. They were later suceeded respectively by Generals Keating, Nares, Lançon and Kotikov.

veto. Their Russian colleague had two means of side-stepping theirs, or preventing them from using it. Regulations to which they objected were presented at first as an extension of those Russian orders which had been confirmed at the first business meeting of the Kommandatura. Nor did the Russians always inform the Western delegates of such earlier regulations.[2] They had at first sufficient means of pressure, which have been described in the last chapter, to ensure their observance in the Western sectors without using any Allied channels.*

The second method was by the promulgation of orders through the zonal Soviet Military Administration. It was claimed that these applied to Berlin since the city constituted an indivisible part of the Soviet Zone. The first signal of this practice occurred ten days after the first sitting of the Kommandatura, when the Oberbürgermeister of Berlin was ordered to work out an industrial plan for the last quarter of 1945 in common with the other regional administration Presidents of the zone. Western opposition to this practice was long ineffective, and it remained a favourite Soviet tactic.

In effect, the Soviet Commandant therefore enjoyed a secondary veto for his own sector. He could prevent the application of unanimous Kommandatura regulations to all organisations or services in East Berlin which were considered part of the Soviet Zone's resources. Disputes arising from such obstruction could in theory be referred to the Allied Control Council for settlement; but since the unified economic administration of Germany which had been expected to follow immediately from the Potsdam Agreement was never established, there was no way of resolving disagreement at this level. It was the confusion between city and zone which enabled the Soviet authorities to restrict Western rights of access to Berlin, to obstruct the provisioning of the other sectors, and to prevent the development of common economic and educational policies for the whole city. There was no room for any such confusion in the original agreements on the status of Berlin: it was clearly an inter-Allied

---

* The Western Allies were aware of the activities of the *Obleute* and other Soviet agents in their sectors, but were for several months powerless to prevent them. No ban could be effective as long as Russian troops were allowed the full freedom of Western sectors. It was not until January 1946 that common military police patrols were established in all sectors (see Herzfeld, *op. cit.* pp. 17-18).

enclave in the Soviet Zone; but the failure to apply this agreement to concrete points of detail left the Soviet Military Governor and the City Commandant great latitude for imposing their qualifications later.

A further point of ambiguity lay in the claim of the Soviet Military Administration to exercise the legal guardianship of all the property of the old state of Prussia, of which Berlin had been the capital until 1945. Much of the territory of Prussia was coterminous with that of the Soviet Zone, and though the Soviet authorities occasionally acknowledged the limitations which the special status of Berlin imposed upon their repository powers in the city, they nevertheless claimed the exercise of those functions which had devolved on the old state capital. Though Germany had vanished, Prussia in a sense continued to exist. The question became particularly acute with the reopening of Berlin University. It was the legal pretext for Sokolovsky's refusal to place the old university under the control of the Magistrat when Robertson and Clay made this demand in October 1945, and for the formal contention at the official reopening in January 1946 that the University of Berlin was to be the centre of higher education for the whole of the Soviet Zone.

Faced with such a variety of legal impediments, which cut across the clear definitions of the war-time agreements, the Western delegates found it difficult to resist Soviet obstruction and evasiveness in the Kommandatura. Although they were quick to break away from the monopoly of control which the Russians had established over the press and radio, and the private lives of the population, they had few means of combating the formal limitations which were placed on their rights in Berlin, without provoking a crisis in the general sphere of Allied government of Germany. This is what happened afterwards, but for the first ten months the Western Powers did their utmost to avoid transferring their disagreements in Berlin to an international level. For the same reason, a number of national issues which should have been settled in the Control Council before the Kommandatura could even begin to function properly, were left open until it was apparent that there was no hope of reaching an agreement. The most important of these was the economic unification of Germany, and the establishment of a national authority to which the Council could devolve the administration of the whole country. On both counts the Russian and French delegates maintained an alliance of intransigeance against the British and Americans. The French were opposed to any form of central government, and contemplated only a highly decentralised federalism at the end of Germany's national evolution; Marshal Zhukov, and later Sokolovsky, were playing for time. The only centralised authority to which they ever agreed was a transport agency, and then in the knowledge of firm French opposition. Politically, the Soviet authorities were willing to admit the full reintegration of German life; Sokolovsky told the Co-ordinating Committee of the Control Council in March 1946: 'It seems to me that we should not raise obstacles for German democratic parties to form on a national all-German basis',[3] but there was no question of economic centralisation. Both in the Co-ordinating Committee of the Control Council, and at the level of the Foreign Ministers' Conferences of Paris and New York, the Soviet delegation insisted that there could be no economic unification of the country until the process of demilitarisation and destruction of war-potential* was complete.

Without the possibility of agreement in the Control Council, the prospect of co-operation in the Kommandatura was remote. There were three main areas of contention: the creation of a German administration for the city to replace that set up by the Russian forces in May and June 1945, and the establishment of an independent police force; the development of a common provisioning and rationing policy for the whole city; and the revival of schools and universities. In all these spheres the Western Commandants attempted to work out united policies for all the sectors, but encountered a form of Soviet opposition which seemed to be based on the postulate that each sector was in effect an extension of the occupying powers' respective zones; and which, by confusing the status of the city in the manner already described, largely succeeded in integrating the Soviet sector into the administrative and political structure of the Soviet Zone.

The administrative chain of command which the Western Allies found on their arrival extended unbroken from the Magistrat (of which about half the members were Communists)[4] through the borough committees which had been

* This obviously meant reparations.

55

formed in June 1945 to provide 'liaison between the administration and the people' to the house, street and block-*Obleute*
whose activities continued unchecked in all sectors of Berlin.
This circuit of power was reinforced in July by the Magistrat's
creation of a college of twelve borough councillors, of which it
nominated the members. Although the nomination and dismissal of the borough mayors depended on the Kommandatura,
the rule of unanimity prevented the commandants from effectively checking the activities of these agents, who had now
acquired political influence. In spite of the protests of the
Council of Charlottenburg, this system was in effect erected
into a temporary constitution by the Borough Constitutional
Statute of September. When the practical tasks of reconstruction
were so overwhelming (only about one-third of the city's
dwellings were fit for winter habitation, and the restoration of
others demanded brilliant administrative improvisation) and
while the whole administration was being purged by denazification, there was no possibility of breaking the circuit by an easy
process of replacement. *Obleute* activity was forbidden in the
American sector in August, but the ban was ineffectual, and
even in September the Magistrat passed an *Obleute* statute
assuming responsibility for their activities. It was not until the
British authorities replaced the agents with paid officials that
their control over the population in their sector was destroyed.

Nor was it easy to replace the German police force, which the
Russians had fashioned into a docile instrument before the
beginning of July. German police were essential in the energetic, repeated and sometimes effective campaigns against the
black market, which the Allied government was forced to wage
for two years after the German surrender. Markgraf's force,
though openly partisan, was not replaced until 1948. The
power it attained was demonstrated in February 1946, when
three judges in Berlin disappeared. 'They were said to have
refused to render judgement in accord with the expressed views
of the German Communist leaders',[5] and though two of them
lived in Western sectors, all the attempts made in the Co-ordinating Committee to secure an enquiry into their disappearance
and whereabouts were fruitless. One of them, who lived in
East Berlin, had been arrested openly, the other two at home
'by unknown German police' who were, according to Clay's

account, agents of the Soviet Military Administration. It is almost certain that they were acting on Markgraf's orders, and his police were involved in a number of similar cases. The Western Powers had established their own military police, who acted alongside the German force, but it was not until the city was split that a separate West Berlin police was set up, directly as a result of Markgraf's intervention in the workings of the Magistrat. The Western Allies thus created their own parallel institutions to those of the Russian authorities, but though they operated side by side for many months, they did little at first to diminish the influence of their rivals.

The development of a common economic and rationing policy for the whole city presented an even more difficult task. The Potsdam intention of creating a unified economic administration became a fiction in Berlin even before the rest of the country. There were two distinct aspects to this question: that of access and provisions for the whole of the city, and that of an equitable system of distribution between the separate sectors and the different social categories that had been imposed on the population by Russian orders.

The severe limitations which had been placed on Western rights of access in June, restricting British and American traffic to two air corridors and a main road and railway, were somewhat extended when the French acceded to a sector in the city, but they remained woefully inadequate. Although the Control Commission discussed the question on August 20th, and again on October 26th, it was unable to gain any further concessions. All that could be achieved was to rearrange the timetables and extend the train services. The final agreements on the three air-corridors between Berlin and West Germany were concluded in January, and have been in force ever since. The water traffic through Germany's extensive canal network also remained blocked: the first ship with food from the West did not reach Berlin until January 1946.

Although Zhukov's initial declaration that the Western Powers would have to feed their sectors out of their own zones was later withdrawn in favour of the Kommandatura's unified provisioning plan for Berlin, which was agreed on August 9th, and established the individual contributions from each power within a general system of calculating the immediate needs of the city, the Western Powers were still unable to bring the strictest necessities to Berlin. The British administration was estimated to need a daily supply of 600 tons of coal, all of which had to be brought from the Ruhr. It was impossible to feed the population: at the height of the food crisis in October, 650,000 people were receiving daily assistance in order to survive; and the British administration found it easier to fly starving children out to its zone than to attempt to feed them in Berlin. Sterner measures were necessary before the black market could be brought under control; the Berliners were forbidden to move from one sector to another; regular markets were set up, at which it was possible to barter for food, but outside the fixed hours and places, all bartering was forbidden; private foraging was punished under an order of the police president as 'agricultural theft'. The situation was aggravated by the return of increasing numbers of soldiers and refugees, and it was found impossible to relate the issue of ration cards to the size of the population. In these conditions, the Western Powers were extremely vulnerable to any Russian measures against them, and this may in part account for their long hesitation in opposing the political actions of their allies or in resisting the economic incorporation of East Berlin into the Soviet Zone.

This process went to great lengths before the Western Powers took any steps to prevent it. The Kommandatura had established an Allied council for production and distribution in August, but this was ineffective as long as all financial transactions were conducted through the single Russian-controlled bank. Deportations and requisitions of labour were carried out in Berlin on the orders of the Soviet Military Administration* (which it was all the harder to resist, since the Kommandatura had given first priority in the allocation of labour to the demands of the occupying powers); the land reforms of the Eastern Zone were applied to Berlin, and the Berlin parties were obliged to call on their supporters to help in the reconstruction of peasant holdings which the reform had created;† new settlers

---

* 20,000 men were requisitioned for dismantling in the Soviet zone by a single order of December 22nd. On deportations in November 1946, see Clay, p. 135.

† Statement of the Anti-Fascist Bloc of December 8th. It was opposed by the CDU which declared that the land reform retroactively approved previous seizures of property.

in Berlin were subjected to the regulations for residents of the Soviet Zone, although the Committee which supervised the matter had nominally been set up by the Magistrat. Throughout this period the other authorities continued to furnish statistics on their sectors to the Soviet Military Administration, and later to the Central German Administration which it established. It was only in March 1946 that the French military government refused to do so with an emphatic declaration that the French sector formed no part of the Soviet Zone.

If the Kommandatura proved unable, even in such clear cases of Allied competence, to withstand the Soviet process of transferring power from its own hands to those of the Russian authorities and their German protégés, it was still less equipped to go into combat on the ambiguous ground where responsibilities were shared with the German population. Although there were already indications of conflict in August, with the American ban on the *Obleute* and the dismissal of some Soviet-appointed mayors, the struggle was thrust upon the Western Allies rather than chosen by them. Eisenhower reported to the United States government on October 20th that the political bloc which had been formed in Berlin was contrary to American democratic traditions, and should therefore not be encouraged in the American Zone. In Berlin, he pointed out, all papers printed in the Soviet sector were subject to Russian censorship, as was also the case with Berlin radio. The Control Council was at present examining projects for a four-power control of the radio.[6]

The Western military governments had been conscious of these impediments all along, but they had been unable or unwilling to take any action against their colleagues in the actual circumstances, although they began from September onwards to licence German newspapers in their sectors to take the place of their own broadsheets.* They were reluctant to interfere in the nascent political life of the Berlin citizens, and had not contemplated the head-on clash which active opposition to the antifascist bloc would inevitably provoke. Similarly, at the beginning of October, the Kommandatura disagreed over the legality and functions of the leaders of the trade unions of the *Freier*

* The first two of note to appear were the *Tagesspiegel* in the American sector and the *Kurier* in the French.

Deutscher Gewerkschaftsbund,[7] since these had been appointed by the Soviet authorities, without consultation either of their Allies or the trade unions themselves. But in the early months these conflicts were confined to verbal disagreements, and the treatment of the population remained unremittingly strict. The first substantive disputes occurred in October with the British dissolution and replacement of the *Obleute*, the erection of a separate radio in the American sector (to coincide with the local elections that were then taking place in the American Zone)* and the decision in the Co-ordinating Committee to erect a special commission to supervise the security of the air-corridors to Berlin. This was after Russian charges that Western pilots were endangering aircraft in the approaches to the city. But all these measures avoided an open challenge to the Russians; and in the vital issue of education, which was also coming to a head at the time, it was revealed how far Soviet control of the Magistrat extended, how successful had been the tactic of confusing the status of the city, and how powerless the Western Powers still were in a direct conflict.

'The University of Unter den Linden', as it was called immediately after the war, began courses for new students at the beginning of September. Participants had to undergo a social and political examination before a special committee appointed by the Magistrat on the orders of the Soviet authorities, in whose sector the university lay. A month later Clay and Robertson were told by Sokolovsky in an angry exchange in the Co-ordinating Committee that the university existed to serve the whole Soviet Zone, and not merely Berlin. Before the first post-war semester began, the incumbent Rector resigned and was replaced by the more amenable Professor Stroux, while the committee which had represented the students before the Magistrat was dissolved and replaced by a new body, whose task it was to direct applicants to particular faculties and 'watch over them socially'.† At the beginning of January 1946 the new university was officially placed under the control of the zonal ministry of education. And at the opening ceremonies later in

---

* This was the predecessor of the famous RIAS, but its importance was not appreciated until the elections of October 1946.

† '*Sozial zu betreuen.*' The official name of the new corporation was *Studentische Arbeitsgemeinschaft im Jugendausschuss der Stadt Berlin.*

the month Stroux assured his audience (which included representatives from the whole of the Soviet Zone) that this was to be a real 'people's university'.

All this passed without public protest from the Western Powers, and they similarly held back for months from a dispute on the future structure of the Berlin school system, in which the Communists were plainly trying to organise the city's education on a highly central and readily supervised basis. They later responded with the opening of a technical university in Charlottenburg and succeeded in building this into an alternative centre of education. Under pressure from the old political sociologists who now led the SPD* they also reopened the old *Hochschule für Politik* as a centre for democratic education; but their general inaction was best revealed on the First of May, when the old university building was covered in Communist banners and slogans as a symbol of socialist reconstruction and education, and only the students protested.

The inaction of the Western Powers was still more marked at the beginning of the battle for direct political control in Berlin. The German parties, and particularly the SPD, were the first to offer resistance to the Russian attempt at a political *Gleichschaltung* of the system in Berlin with that of the Soviet Zone. They became for a time the champions of the Cold War. The history of the Berlin parties between Zhukov's order of June 1945 and the elections of October 1946 is one of the decisive chapters in the development of the whole struggle. The Western Powers were for long bound to quiescence in the face of the dilemma which confronted them over the whole of Germany. Open conflict with the Soviet Union would perpetuate the division of the country, which, for economic reasons, they were anxious to bring to an end as soon as possible. But a ready acquiescence in Soviet policies might prepare the way for a general Communist victory. Throughout the first year of occupation they became increasingly aware of these conditions, and by the middle of 1946 they had concluded that they would have to risk continuing the partition in the interests of the Western half.

The first move, a year after the surrender of Berlin, was

* Both Franz Neumann and Otto Suhr had been distinguished members of the old *Deutsche Hochschule für Politik* before 1933.

General Clay's decision to halt deliveries, to the Soviet Zone, of industries dismantled in the West for reparations.

This was the result of Russia's refusal to implement the common utilisation of German resources, to which under the Potsdam Agreement she was bound, in return for Western reparation transfers. The American and British governments subsequently decided to unite their zones; the French attitude was more devious. France was concerned to perpetuate the zonal division until her interests were secured by detaching the Saar from the rest of the country, but was eventually induced by the difficulties of her economic position and the clear impossibility of securing any firm commitments from Russia to accept the intentions of her other allies. Thus, Clay reported in May 1946:

> . . . If agreement cannot be obtained along these broad lines (common economic and financial policies to permit the exploitation of German resources, and prevent the imminent danger of inflation; and subsequently to create a federal German authority) in the immediate future, we face a deteriorating German economy which will create a political unrest favourable to the development of communism in Germany and a deterrent to its democratization.

He therefore proposed a merger of the British and American Zones, even if the French and Russians demurred. 'Recognising fully the political implications of such a merger it is our belief that even these implications would not be as serious as the continuation of the present air-tight zones.'[8] This report was followed in September by the famous Stuttgart speech of the American Secretary of State, Byrnes. It was important, less because of what he said, than as a declaration of a separate Western policy for Germany, which was to be reinforced by a new commitment to maintain an American army in Germany 'as long as an occupation force is required'. The speech marked a decisive change in American policy: although the punitive requirements of the military document JCS/1067 remained largely in force, it was now clear that the American government had embarked on a long-term programme of rehabilitation, if necessary in opposition to the Soviet Union. It was rapidly followed by the Anglo-American conference on the unification of the two zones (the decision for which had been taken in Paris in July), and the failure at the Foreign Ministers' Con-

ference in New York in November to make any progress towards a quadripartite administration of Germany. By the middle
of 1946, therefore, the United States and Britain had decided
on a separate policy towards Germany, and by the end of the
year, they realised that they would have to implement it.

In Berlin, however, the open battle between the West and
the Soviet Union had begun at the end of 1945, and had been
decided by October 1946. The leaders of the West were in
effect the German political parties, who were left at first to
defend their new democracy on their own. Colonel Howley
remarked that the prevailing American view during the long
struggle between the KPD and the SPD was that 'politics was
a German question and our interest was confined to safeguard-
ing democratic processes'.[9] This unconcern was shared by the
other two powers almost until the crucial stage was passed.
Although they did much to liberalise their own government—
the British introduced courts where Germans could bring com-
plaints of administrative injustice before the end of 1945—
they hesitated to take any action to defend the other political
parties from pressure and intimidation by the KPD or Markgraf's police. 'German democracy' was on its own.

The first public common meeting of the four parties of the
anti-fascist bloc was held on August 12th, at the same time as
the British and American authorities were beginning to voice
public concern at the activities of the *Obleute*, and shortly before the Magistrat began the formation of a 'Women's Commission for the Ideological Mobilisation of Women for
Reconstruction'. Under this constellation it was impossble
for the separate parties to produce any distinctive programme
or raise objections to the overall policies of the bloc. A month
later they agreed in principle to the land reform which was
designed for the Eastern Zone, in a move which was clearly
intended to merge their activities with that of the zonal anti-
fascist bloc as a whole. The process of centralisation was carried
further, when after the first general meeting of the Magistrat's
Central Women's Commission, Zhukov forbade the separate
parties to create their own women's organisations. At the same
time Grotewohl, the new chairman of the SPD, appealed to
the representatives of the Berlin *Landesverband* for the creation
of working-class unity, i.e. the fusion of the Socialist and

Communist Parties. It is hard to judge to what extent Grotewohl was already working at this stage for the merging of the two parties, but the danger to the Socialists was soon to become apparent. At a conference of Communist functionaries in October Ulbricht said that both the KPD and the SPD had the 'same interests, and therewith the basis of co-operation'. It is almost certain that the Communist leaders had already decided on the unification campaign which was to begin the next month: they were encouraged to do so by a conflict with the other parties over education reform and religious teaching in schools, which the working-class parties desired in common to forbid, against the opposition of the CDU. The CDU and LDP also disagreed in private with the land reform project, and though all parties agreed to the formation of a special commission to secure agreement on outstanding issues, it was already plain that the best hope of a Communist majority lay in the unification plans which would secure the support of the traditionally Socialist population of Berlin. If this could be done within the framework of the zonal anti-fascist bloc, it was obviously to the advantage of the Soviet authorities, since the CDU had adherents among the trade unions of the FDGB, which it was impossible to split. But the essentials were first to win support for the project of fusion in the SPD itself, and to quell any potential opposition in the CDU.

The first step in this direction was taken in the middle of November, when the two workers' parties formed a 60-man commission to examine the question of fusion. There were 30 from each party, but the decision was taken without the consent of the lower echelons of the SPD, which protested strongly five days later at the first borough conference the party had held since 1933. Moreover, the party headquarters were moved to the Soviet sector at the beginning of December, apparently with the complicity of the party leaders, so that in future all conferences would be held under the supervision of Soviet instead of American troops.

Parallel with these developments went a further extension of the powers of the Magistrat. Shortly after the SPD had moved to the Soviet sector, the Berlin parties were formed into a separate anti-fascist bloc from that of the Soviet Zone. The purpose of this move became clear when the Magistrat announced a provisional constitution, which was submitted to the city parties for approval. Only the CDU opposed it openly, arguing that the representative functions of the Magistrat should be left to the four parties, meeting in commission on a basis of parity, until a permanent constitution for Berlin could be agreed on. The SPD reserved its views for an exhaustive statement of its position; the LDP proposed some verbal changes. Though significant, these did not approach the heart of the problem, which was that the Magistrat would be empowered to represent the Berlin population for an indefinite period and without stipulating any elections. In answer to the CDU's objections, Karl Maron reverted to the tactic of the early days of the Russian conquest, which was again to be revived in the next months. He proposed that the functions of representation, instead of being entrusted to the four parties, should be exercised by the corporations of various social and professional bodies. This was the direct democracy envisaged in the completion of the bourgeois-democratic revolution: its protagonists would be such bodies as the Women's Commission, which had already been forbidden all party affiliations, the trade unions of the FDGB organised on a zonal basis and professional organisations like Johannes R. Becher's *Kulturbund*. Meanwhile the constitution was taken from the anti-fascist bloc to the borough mayors (the majority of whom were still those appointed by the Russians in the first days of May) and unanimously approved by them.

The Soviet authorities now felt empowered to move against the CDU: on December 19th two leaders of the party, Hermes and Schreiber, were summoned to Karlshorst to receive Zhukov's order for their resignation on the grounds that they were conducting a campaign of veiled opposition to Russian authority and leading the CDU into a reactionary course. The same day the Russian representative at a meeting of the CDU central committee demanded the dismissal of the two men. Although this was carried out immediately, the CDU continued to oppose the proposed provisional constitution.

Perhaps as a result of the Russian action the conference of the 60 representatives of the KPD and SPD which was held later that month in East Berlin decided on a common electoral programme to be presented to every constituency in Germany.

Although the Communist proposals for a common list, and a fusion of the constituency organisations before the official party organisations, were rejected, the SPD agreed to create a committee to examine the foundations for a united party. This consisted of four leaders from each side and included Pieck, Ulbricht and Grotewohl. On the 30th the FDGB officially welcomed the decision of the central committees of the two parties and announced its intention of supporting the united front in the coming year.

By the end of 1945 it seemed that victory was in sight. The KPD seemed to have control of the FDGB which united all trade unions in Berlin and the Soviet Zone; the fusion of the workers' parties was under way and would be certain to secure an electoral majority in Berlin, and possibly over the whole of Germany; the contumacious leaders of the CDU had been dismissed. The Western Allies had taken no action. These successes were celebrated on Pieck's seventieth birthday, January 3rd. Grotewohl spoke at a public meeting in the Soviet sector, where the honorary citizenship of Berlin was conferred upon the veteran Communist, and called upon the SPD not to stand aloof from the necessity of uniting all the workers' parties. Agitation and propaganda were thereafter conducted in all the important industrial centres of the city, and the study committee of the two parties decided shortly afterwards to create the Socialist Unity Party, the SED,* and to issue a new symbol to be worn by all its supporters.

But the first resistance was already forming and was soon to gather momentum, as the campaign for unification itself became increasingly bitter. The first reaction was the result of a decision taken in the Kommandatura. The Allied conflict of October over the structure and leadership of the FDGB had no effect until December, when the Kommandatura announced that the trade union confederation would be 'allowed' to elect delegates to a future city conference, who would then elect a central committee 'corresponding to the total membership of the organisation'. This would stay in office for one year and would within six months give the Kommandatura its proposals for a trade-union constitution. These orders contained no clear attempt to disassociate the Berlin confederation from that of the

* Originally known as the SEPD.

Zone, since the total membership of the FDGB consisted over-whelmingly of the trade unions in other parts of East Germany. But the possibility was given of electing a new leadership, even if it were to be weighted in favour of the zonal party affiliations, and of producing separate statutes for the organisation within Berlin. The elections were held on January 20th, the same day that a party functionaries' conference of the SPD met to consider the proposals for fusion which had been advanced by the joint commission of the two parties. This double event marked the first reverse in the Russian campaign to gain political control of Berlin. The party conference, though it agreed to the fusion in principle, refused to consider it until an all-German congress of the SPD had discussed the matter. The two parties were to have separate electoral lists in the meantime. They refused to wear the SED symbol and appealed to the borough organisations not to take any action which might prejudice the decisions of the all-German conference. This was a double blow to the plans of the KPD; the SPD had refused simple incorporation into the political structure of the Soviet Zone, and had asserted its solidarity with the German party as a whole—an action which the CDU had been prevented from taking at the time of the dismissal of its leaders. It had also refused to countenance any *fait accompli* in Berlin.

The result of the trade union elections was a clear victory for the KPD over all other parties; but the SPD was sufficiently strongly represented to ensure that if the party opposed the fusion, the FDGB could not be carried *en bloc* into the arms of the Communist Party. In fact, the executive committee of the trade unions in Berlin was weighted against the Communists, who held only 14 of its seats against 13 SPD and 3 CDU. With this result it soon became clear that the Soviet tactic of confusing the city and zonal organisations had turned against the KPD, for when the trade unions from the Soviet Zone held a conference in the capital in February, the chairmanship of the whole organisation was given to three Berlin leaders in a meeting where Jakob Kaiser, the first chairman of the CDU, warned the delegates that Berlin had become a political and cultural field of tension between East and West. It was no longer possible to rely, as the Soviet and East Berlin authorities had clearly hoped two months before, on the FDGB as a means of swinging the Socialists into the Communist camp.

The battle now turned on the decisions of the SPD itself. The party's central committee, which was largely composed of men favourable to the merger, announced on February 11th that a congress for the whole of the Soviet Zone, including Berlin, would shortly be summoned to decide the question, since a national congress would be 'at the present moment unfavourable'. But the general party refused to accept this decision, encouraged by the rejection in the Kommandatura of the Magistrat's provisional constitution (which was now to be prepared by a judicial committee of the Allied Powers). The SPD delegates agreed instead to submit the matter to a borough conference in April, and subsequently to a general congress, to which representatives of the Western Zones would also be invited. The next two months were occupied by a long battle between the partisans of fusion and its opponents, both in Berlin and in West Germany. Schumacher, the new leader of the Social Democrats, visited Berlin to warn the SPD there that it had no right to speak for the whole of Germany, and that the Western organisations would send no delegates to the congress in April. The fusion of the zonal parties had already been practically accomplished, and Schumacher's speech was an appeal to the Berlin party not to isolate itself from the West, or be drawn into the control of the Soviet Zone. At a memorial meeting for August Bebel, he was heavily attacked by Pieck for this reactionary attempt to split the working class. The immediate result was a sharpened response from the Socialist Central Committee, whose members now converted the joint study commission into an organisational committee for the fusion of the two parties, and instructed it to work out a constitution for the SED.

But the general congress of 2,000 party officials refused to accept this new *fait accompli*. At a meeting on March 1st, presided over by Franz Neumann, an old Socialist who was rapidly assuming the leadership of the party in the struggle against the merger, they voted by an overwhelming majority for a secret ballot of all party members, and for the first time the executive opposition declared the necessity of an independent SPD. The decision was endorsed by the borough organisations a few days later, and the ballot was arranged for the end of the month.

The KPD continued to speak as if the fusion were already accomplished, drafted with Grotewohl's assistance a programme for the future SED and attempted to steal a march on the referendum through the foundation of a united youth movement, the FDJ;* but it was evident that all hopes of imposing the merger from above had vanished. It was also now for the first time that the Western Powers began to intervene on the behalf of the SPD.[10] One official who was believed to be in physical danger was flown out to West Germany; and police reprisals against opponents of the merger were halted by Western military police. The first clear stand taken by the Western Powers was the arrest of eleven Communists in one borough for intimidation. More important, the American authorities permitted their leading sector newspaper, the *Tagesspiegel*, to oppose the merger in its columns, and the British city government made some tons of newsprint available for an independent SPD organ. These were the first positive indications of Western sympathies, and they were followed a week before the ballot by a press conference at which Clay declared that the fusion would only be recognised by the American military government if it had been agreed to by the party membership as a whole.† Although Communist propaganda was greatly increased in the next week (Berlin radio became more openly partisan than had ever been allowed hitherto, and the popular organisations, such as the Women's Commission, demonstrated publicly for the merger), and although Ulbricht told a joint meeting of the two parties that the SED would claim political power, the Independent Socialists had now been given the unofficial backing of the Western Allies in their opposition to the Soviet military government. With these developments the scale of the conflict was suddenly increased and it was impossible to present it as a purely German affair, as the KPD had hoped and the American authorities appear to have long believed. The change was sharply demonstrated by the announcement that the referendum in the

* *Freie Deutsche Jugend.*

† Davison, *op. cit.*, says that the first official American position was taken the day before the referendum 'when a United States spokesman announced that no merger would be recognised that had not been agreed to by a majority of both parties'. But Clay's press conference was held on the 23rd. I do not know who the other spokesman was.

American and British sectors would be officially protected against sabotage. In contrast the Soviet authorities claimed that they had not yet received any application for any such ballot—and although, in fact, they allowed the voting booths to open in their sector on the morning of the 31st, they quickly closed them on the pretext that certain regulations had not been observed. The referendum thus took place only in the West, and resulted in a landslide victory for the opponents of the merger. Out of nearly 24,000 members who voted, over 19,000 supported the independence of the SPD.*

This was the first decisive Western victory in the political battle for Berlin. The effect was that the concealed bid of the Russian and German Communists was now transferred to an open conflict among the Allies, which hastened the development of the Cold War over the whole of Germany. The first tangible result of the ballot was seen when the new executive of the independent SPD, under Franz Neumann, asked for Allied recognition of the reconstituted party. In the Eastern Zone formal recognition had immediately been granted to the SED by the Soviet military government, and the SPD itself had been forbidden. But in Berlin both the SPD and the SED now applied for recognition. The Russian Commandant, General Kotikov, proposed immediate recognition of the Unity Party and a postponement of decision on the Social Democrats. It was the French Commandant, General Lançon, who had in the past been subjected to unsparing Soviet pressure on the grounds that he represented a partly Communist government,[11] who first insisted that the SED was in fact merely the old Communist Party under a new name, and not a substitute for the SPD, which should be recognised as well. The dispute in the Kommandatura was referred to the Control Council, and when no agreement could be reached there, returned to the Kommandatura. Eventually both parties were recognised inside the city itself. This result illustrated the advantages which the Soviet Commandant gained from the exercise of his veto. He had pre-

* But nearly 15,000 voted for collaboration with the KPD in a further question. This figure, and the fact that nearly 9,000 members of the West Berlin SPD did not come to vote at all, suggests that the nature of the conflict was not appreciated by the majority of members, however clear the issues were to the leaders on both sides and to the Allies.

vented the referendum from taking place in his sector, and there was no basis for the existence of the SED in Berlin at all, apart from its recognition by the Zonal Military Governor. Yet unless the Western Powers were to extend the dispute to the whole question of the government of Germany, they could at best agree on a compromise which allowed the SED to operate where it had no right. Nevertheless the substantive victory was theirs. The SPD had not been absorbed by the Communists, and this failure destroyed the Soviet chances of gaining electoral victory in Berlin. And the openness of the dispute ensured that sooner or later the Western Powers would have to revise their approach to the Soviet actions in Germany: it was only one month later that Clay suspended deliveries of industrial material to the Russian government.

In Berlin the Russian response to this setback was to insist on Allied authority over the German organs of government, and to try to forestall their further development through the mechanism of the Kommandatura. But it was already too late. The Kommandatura had ordered the Magistrat to submit new proposals for a constitution on March 22nd, and these were to be ready by May 1st. Thus while the FDGB and the recognised political parties were being mobilised in the east for the First of May demonstrations in East Berlin, and even before the dispute over the recognition of the SED had been settled, the Magistrat was forced by the Kommandatura to authorise its own death warrant. Once the provisional constitution had been accepted, new elections would be certain. It was this which the KPD and the Soviet authorities had hoped to avoid, by having the original proposals accepted by their placemen in Berlin before they were submitted to the Kommandatura. They had clearly expected to achieve the Socialist-Communist merger before new elections were possible. For the same reason Kotikov had consistently opposed any discussion of an election date in the Kommandatura, and after the Magistrat's constitutional proposals were submitted, the disagreement had once again to be referred to the Control Council. This was likewise the case with the constitution, for which the judicial committee of the Kommandatura produced its own draft, but on which the Commandants failed to agree. In both cases, Sokolovsky overruled Kotikov's obstruction. Elections were finally fixed for

October 20th, after a forceful intervention from Clay; and in July the Control Council gave its approval to the draft constitution, which was to come into force the day after the elections.* The new constitution provided for a city assembly, which would elect a Magistrat. It was expected that the new governmental body would have a legislative initiative. But the constitution was brief, since undiminished authority would rest with the Kommandatura. It was important less because it wrested a high degree of self-government from the Allied councils, than because it provided a forum of debate and opinion, and of public pressure on the Kommandatura. It was not altered until the Kommandatura itself became unworkable in 1948 and the city was split by the establishment of a new Magistrat in the Soviet sector.

However, the first signs of a split were developing already. The Russians had no intention of allowing the partition of Germany to endure indefinitely, and probably still felt committed to co-operating with the Western Powers until a more favourable time for reunification should present itself. But in Berlin it was doubtful whether the SED could hope to win the city elections. It was essential to maintain such residual influence as had been left to the public organisations of the Soviet Zone, and to continue as far as possible the absorption of the city into the zone. This would now inevitably apply more to the Soviet than to the other sectors, and a certain divergence in the economic and political development of the two parts was already emerging in 1946. In June the Supreme Commander of the Soviet Military Administration ordered the unification of all important industries of the Soviet Zone and Berlin in Soviet joint stock companies. They became therewith the property of the USSR, and their proceeds were in theory counted towards the payment of reparations. These measures were also intended as a means of pressure on the trade unions and were sharply criticised after the October elections by Otto

* The fact that Sokolovsky thus twice overruled Kotikov demonstrated that however obstructive Russian tactics might be, there was no question of a head-on clash with the West at this stage. The Russian government still hoped for immense political and economic benefits from its position in Germany, and was not prepared to take the initiative in destroying them. In a sense the break was forced upon it by the Western currency reform, which prevented it from exploiting its ambiguous position any longer.

Suhr, the first president of the City Assembly and first general secretary of the Berlin SPD. However, direct expropriations only took place in the Soviet Zone and sector, and began a process of economic differentiation which was quickly extended to the political field.

When Otto Suhr demanded the release of members of the SPD known to have been arrested in the Soviet Zone, the party was accused by Sokolovsky of obstructing the Soviet administration with tacit British support. The British immediately invited an investigation, but were ignored: the real purpose of the manœuvre was to prevent the SPD from functioning effectively in the Russian sector, although the Kommandatura had recently issued a declaration of the equal rights of all parties in the coming election campaign. Later, copies of the Western newspapers, *Die Neue Zeitung* and *Der Tagesspiegel*, were seized in East Berlin, and the protests of the American and British delegates in the Kommandatura, Generals Keating and Nares, led only to fruitless discussion. As the elections approached, discrimination against the SPD was sharpened in the Soviet sector, through the impossibility of finding premises in which to work or speak, the sudden cancellation of permission to hold meetings, or the banning of SPD speakers for security reasons. These hindrances were matched by the subsidies given to the massive propaganda campaign of the SED, which distributed paper, food, drinks and coal, and was finally able to announce that it had persuaded the Soviet Military Administration to supply fruit and vegetables for the whole city.[12] In fact, this measure was the result of a Soviet-American trade agreement, and an arrangement between the British, French and Russian Zones whereby West Berlin was to be supplied with lignite, potatoes and corn in exchange for industrial deliveries from the West.

This hustings bribery was coupled with menaces designed to convince the Berliners that they were in the hands of the Soviet Union. During a period of acute electricity crises, when all passenger trains were sometimes cancelled for a day to keep industries running, the electricity supplies allotted to West Berlin from the Russian Zone were suddenly and sharply reduced; and a highly-placed Soviet official is reported by Colonel Howley to have started the rumour that the Western Powers would leave Berlin two months after the elections.[13]

The rumour proved less credible than Byrnes' speech at Stuttgart; and the other means of pressure less effective than the belated reponses of the West. A fortnight before the elections the Kommandatura announced that it had accepted the Control Commission's plans for a reorganisation of the Berlin police which was to be more closely integrated into the military government through Allied sectoral inspectors. While this only tightened the control of the police over East Berlin, it diminished, though it did not destroy, their possibilities of intimidation in the West. More, the American Commandant announced that all newspapers printed in the American sector were henceforth to enjoy complete freedom of reporting and full editorial responsibility at the same time as the Soviet Military Administration decreed a monopoly of news reporting throughout the Soviet Zone and East Berlin for its own newly established agency, the *Allgemeiner Deutscher Nachrichtendienst*.

When they went to the polls, the electors had a clear choice between two sides in what had already become the Cold War. A victory for the SED would mean the inevitable absorption of Berlin into the Soviet Zone, where the economic and political system was already totally isolated from developments in Western Germany. While the Soviet Commanders were attacking the Anglo-American plans for inter-zonal reconstruction, they continued to strip East Germany of its industries and deport German labourers to work them. While Ulbricht claimed political power for the anti-fascist forces of the SED, the SPD had been banned in the Soviet Zone. While the SED promised a speedy reunification of the capital if it won the elections, the other parties stressed their nation-wide organisation and their hopes for a democratic reunification of Germany. The Berliners are local chauvinists, and had not yet developed any warm regard for any of their conquerors; but it was impossible to choose a united capital in isolation from the rest of the country, and it was clear that their only way of influencing their destiny was to force their alliance upon the Western Powers.

On October 20th the SED received less than 20 per cent of the votes in the entire city, and less than the CDU, which had over 22 per cent. In the Soviet sector, the SPD won more seats in every borough. The traditional Berlin party was the undisputed victor, with more than 48 per cent; and even the LDP received more than half as many votes as the Communists in this predominantly working class society. The abstentions and reservations of the merger ballot in March had vanished. Over 92 per cent of the electors participated. The significance of collaboration with the SED had become increasingly clear.

The final apportionment of seats in the City Assembly was: SPD 63; CDU 29; SED 26; LDP 12. The clear majority of the 'Western' parties transformed the anti-fascist bloc in Berlin. The new alliance was anti-Soviet and already relied on the tacit support of the West. The leaders of the SED were astonished and demoralised, and it seemed for a time that the unification of the city could be accomplished under an alliance between the Western Powers and the new Magistrat. But the Kommandatura still represented the government of the city, and any such tacit agreement could be prevented by a Soviet veto. It is probable too, that the Russian defeat in Berlin and the rapid implementation of the Anglo-American Bi-Zone, as it was unhappily called, impelled a radical change in Soviet policy. All hopes of uniting Germany under a Communist-dominated government had receded indefinitely; and the Soviet Military Administration concentrated on building up the resources of its own Zone and preventing the economic unification which had been agreed on at Potsdam. It still saw great advantages in a formal observation of Allied government, notably in interzonal currency transations;* but further delay in fulfilling the Potsdam Agreement would make a split inevitable before long.

The crisis did not occur for some months. But in Berlin it was brought on by the elections themselves. It remained concealed, but the effective division of the city under the cover of Kommandatura government could scarcely be prevented. From now on the Western Powers and the German representatives were always confronted with a dilemma: whether to accommodate their Russian and East German opponents out of

---

* The economic weakness of the Soviet Zone was long covered by currency transactions in occupation marks. The Soviet authorities had been given a separate set of plates for printing these when the Allied government of Germany was established. They were thus able to produce them at inflationary rates in the knowledge that they would eventually be redeemed by United States dollars.

regard for the population of the Eastern sector, or split the city finally by resisting them. The first manifestation of the crisis came shortly after the elections when the question of an Ober-bürgermeister for Berlin arose, and it soon centred around the name of an ex-Communist who had recently returned from war-time exile in Turkey: Ernst Reuter.

Chapter Four

THE ALIGNMENT

In March 1948 General Clay wrote a special report to the Chief of Staff of the United States Army to express his concern at a change he had sensed in Soviet policy. Soviet representatives in Germany were behaving with a new arrogance and disregard for the processes of Allied consultation; and it was clear that this portended some new action in Germany. War, General Clay had hitherto insisted, was impossible. Now he told Bradley that it could no longer be precluded.[1] On March 20th the last meeting of the Control Council was broken up by a concerted walk-out of the Soviet delegation; and at the end of the month the first steps were taken to blockade Berlin.

The Cold War, which had begun in Berlin in 1946, now ranged over the whole of Europe. In Germany it had approached the point of open hostilities; and though they were avoided, a bitter and decisive struggle was soon to be fought over the original theatre of conflict. Both sides had been slow to align themselves for a pitched battle, but the nature of their ambitions in Germany and their direct confrontation in Berlin forced them to emerge in open array. The Soviet Union embarked upon the conquest of the country; the West at last joined forces with the German population in resisting her. In the country at large this decision was deliberately made; in Berlin the new allies found that the situation had come upon them almost unawares. Russia and the West had already committed themselves, probably further than they wished, at the end of 1946, and the history of the subsequent two years is one of constant attempts to improve their position without a precipitate break. Thus the Russians tried to stifle the new powers of the Magistrat through the Kommandatura, and the Western Allies attempted to oppose them without bringing the machinery of military government to a standstill. But neither side could gain its ends covertly. The people and government of Berlin were involved from the first in the tug-of-war, and Russian attacks upon their leaders ensured that they would play an important part in the

77

development of Western policy. One of the reasons for the astonishing lack of interaction between the conflict in Berlin and the situation in the rest of Germany is that the population in the capital was so quickly involved in Allied relations, and this prevented a major clash between the occupying powers directly, until the collision of their national policies.

This is not to say that Berlin was isolated from the rest of the country. Every development there was carefully followed throughout Germany; political leaders in the three Western Zones felt themselves directly involved in the events of Berlin, and the political champions of the capital exerted a strong and not always welcome influence on the national parties. But it is true that, whether consciously or not, the occupying powers restricted the scope of their conflict in the city. It was not until the Soviet Union saw an opportunity of destroying Western power and influence throughout Germany that the blockade was imposed. Until then the Russians confined their direct assaults to the German representatives. And the Western Powers, however determined they were to oppose a further extension of Soviet influence, took care not to let their defence of the German representatives hinder the possibilities of co-operation with their Russian allies. 'Western officials probably did not realise how successful they were in hiding from the Germans the basic disagreements between East and West. A high official in the city government stated after the blockade that, until early in 1948, he had believed that four-power harmony had been maintained on essential issues, and the differences between the USSR and the Western Powers were on matters of detail.'[2]

The Russian authorities were thus determined to subjugate the responsible Berlin representatives before any frontal attack on the West, and their purposes became clear immediately after the elections of October 1946. While the police continued to intimidate and kidnap opponents of the SED,* their Soviet superiors used all the powers of the Kommandatura to obstruct and reverse the promise of representative government which had been granted to the Berliners by the Temporary Constitution.

---

* The American Commandant estimated in March 1948 that 1,600 persons had disappeared in this way. The majority were city employees and borough officials.

Two points of the constitution provided them with a possibility of doing so. Article 3 laid down that the Magistrat was to be a compulsory coalition of all recognised parties—at least as far as the parties demanded representation in the government. It was therefore impossible to exclude the SED (with its 26 out of 130 seats) from a voice in all decisions. Though the Communists were slow to come out into open opposition, it was plain that here the Russian authorities had a ready instrument for preventing the Magistrat from functioning effectively. Secondly, Article 36 (for the removal of which the Berliners began to press almost as soon as the election was over) provided not only that the general administration of the city should be subject to the determining voice of the Kommandatura, but that no decision of the Magistrat could be carried through in any sector except with the approval of the Commandant. All appointments and decrees, administrative measures and constitutional amendments, all movement of personnel in the government would need the approval of the Kommandatura. In principle this was not objectionable. After twelve years of Nazi rule, experiments in self-government would have for a time to be supervised; but it imposed a heavy burden on the administrative committees of the Kommandatura; provided the Russian representatives with endless means of obstruction; and concealed from the German public the interest that the Western Allies had assumed in protecting its independence. Above all, it enabled the Soviet authorities to prevent a purge of the administration that they had appointed in the early days of 1945, and of which the reform had now become an acute political necessity.

In this situation it was certain that either the organs of self-government in Berlin would have to bow to Soviet pressure, or that a major crisis would quickly develop. It was not long in coming.

In November the City Assembly had met and elected Otto Suhr to be its president. A few days later, at the beginning of December, the new Magistrat was elected from among all the parties represented in the House. The Oberbürgermeister was Otto Ostrowski of the SPD and his deputies were Ferdinand Friedensburg of the CDU, Heinrich Acker of the SED, and Frau Louise Schroeder, again of the SPD. Otherwise the three non-Communist Parties occupied most of the key posts, the

SED having only three in a total of seventeen. Ostrowski's inaugural speech emphasised his socialist and democratic beliefs, and announced his intention of pursuing a middle course between the opposing tendencies in Berlin. The first priority was to be given to the reconstruction and restoration of the city. In addition to a conciliatory and sincere mayor, people of great gifts represented the city in other leading positions. Otto Suhr, whose earlier years had been spent in the pre-Nazi trade-union movement and in political and economic scholarship, had retired from public life during the Nazi period and had emerged afterwards as an economic administrator, first in the German Central Administration of the Soviet Zone and then in the Economic Department of the Magistrat. He had a keen understanding of the political possibilities of the new situation, as well as of the motives and methods of the Soviet authorities. He refused to be intimidated. Professor Friedensburg was likewise an economist and came late to politics. But he had a clear grasp of the position in which Berlin was now placed, and understood better than most the dangers of a permanent split along the sector border. Throughout his period as mayor, and later in the forum of the CDU, he tried to prevent the split from becoming definitive, in opposition first to the SED, then to those of his fellow citizens who identified themselves too readily with the Cold War. Frau Schroeder was soon to show great courage and endurance in fulfilling the duties of Oberbürgermeister during the first great crisis between the Allied Powers.

These people were not anxious to force a showdown with the Russians. Ostrowski indeed went out of his way to avoid it in an honest endeavour to prevent the already split city from being even more sharply divided. But his sense of political realities was miscalculated, and on his own initiative he attempted to strike a bargain with the SED. His action was undoubtedly sincere, but he was also impelled by ruthless Soviet pressure. He was summoned to Soviet Headquarters several nights a week and alternately cajoled, interrogated and blackmailed. In February 1947, confidential conversations were held with a view to compromise in the local and personal political issues which had been raised by the attempt to reform the administration, and the Kommandatura's refusal to countenance any far-reaching measures by the Berlin government. His efforts were by no means unsuccessful. The SED consented to the removal of five leading Communists from the administration—on condition that the two 'workers' parties' should present a common programme for the next three months. These terms were, from the SED viewpoint, extremely reasonable. Their motives can only be guessed at; it is possible that had they been accepted, the Soviet authorities might have provoked some kind of constitutional crisis, after which the SED could have attempted to come to power within the three stipulated months—with the help of the SPD. Any coalition of this kind would inevitably have been dominated by the Communists. In fact, the crisis was to come immediately. Ostrowski's bargain, however reasonable on the limited scale he intended, was a dangerous reversal of the gains of the previous year. The SPD was, after all that had passed, committed to a Communist line, and the mayor himself emphasised the significance of the arrangement when defending it to his party: the only way to exercise the powers of government was by co-operation with the Communists.

All the non-Communist parties attacked Ostrowski severely. Franz Neumann, the chairman of the SPD, objected not only to the Oberbürgermeister's handling of the matter, but even more strongly to the constitutional absurdities which made it necessary. He demanded that the result of the elections, not the ordinances of the Kommandatura, should provide the guiding principles for the government of Berlin. The crisis, he declared, was not centred on the action of the mayor, but on the constitution itself. In April in the City Assembly Neumann submitted a vote of no confidence, which was carried by a large majority against the opposition of the SED. Ostrowski submitted his resignation to the Kommandatura, and the crisis began.

The pattern of coming developments was already apparent from the manner in which Ostrowski's resignation was received in the Kommandatura. The Western Commandants acknowledged that it was a perfectly constitutional procedure—though Neumann's declaration of a 'constitutional crisis' might have given ground for holding that it was a deliberate attempt to extend the competence of the Berlin authorities beyond the prescribed limits of the constitution. But it was sharply attacked by Kotikov as an unwarranted submission to anti-Soviet initiatives. The Kommandatura was unable to approve the resignation unanimously—and the matter was referred to the Control Council.

This was the first time that the Soviet veto had been used to override the decision of the Magistrat and the concurrence of the Western Commandants at the same time. Ostensibly it was used in support of a Berlin official, but its significance was clear; and in fact Kotikov's attitude gave the Berliners added incentive and opportunity for asserting that they should have more than a passive voice in the management of the city. It soon became known that the SPD had decided on a new candidate for the office of Oberbürgermeister, and that the CDU and LDP were determined to support him. He was an outspoken opponent of the SED and of Soviet attempts to force Berlin into the Communist domain, and as an ex-Communist was well-qualified to lead the SPD in this struggle.

Ernst Reuter had recently returned from Turkey, after an absence from Germany of more than sixteen years. Except for one brief period, his political life had not hitherto been of any great significance—though as a student he had joined the SPD and worked for it until he was conscripted during the First World War. He was little more than seventeen when he was carried wounded into a Russian field hospital in September 1916. This was the first decisive event of his life, for it was as a prisoner of the Russians that he abandoned the doctrines of the SPD and began to envisage a 'revolutionary solution' to the problem of war-time Germany.*

After the February Revolution he began Socialist courses for German prisoners of war; and after the Bolshevik Revolution he was taken to Moscow as chairman of a prisoners' committee, where he met Lenin, Trotsky and Stalin. In 1918 he served, under Stalin, as Commissar for the Volga Germans and was the essential agent in the foundation of the Volga Republic, which became one of the Russian Federal Units. Before he was nineteen he had become one of the most important international

---

* Reuter's conversion to the Bolshevik theses on war and revolution was not the result of indoctrination or education. His biographers remark the deep impression made on him by the 'Russian people', and it was the fall of the Russian monarchy which disposed of the SPD's original arguments for supporting the war. Reuter's way to Communism lay through the pacifism of 1917. See Willy Brandt and Richard Lowenthal, *Ernst Reuter*, pp. 80-84.

converts to the Bolshevik cause, who were later to return to organise the revolution in their homelands. (Others, prisoners like him, were Tito and Béla Kun.) On the outbreak of the German Revolution he returned to Berlin and became, first, secretary of the *Spartakusbund*, later, after the formal establishment of the German Communist Party, its secretary in Berlin, and finally in 1921 secretary-general. He was thus about to become one of the key figures in German politics, but later that year he formally left the KPD and returned to an insignificant position with the Social Democrats. The occasion of the break was one of the decisive episodes in the history of German Communism. The party split over the possibility of the formation of a 'popular front' of all working-class parties in Germany to withstand the dangers of a reactionary putsch. The advocates of this course came into conflict with the Leninist centralism of the Comintern and were expelled—originally with Reuter's support. It was on this occasion that he was elected secretary-general; but when the murder of Erzberger revealed the growing danger of a putsch, he vigorously opposed this sacrifice of a proletarian movement to the rigid discipline of the Third International. In spite of a personal, though public, appeal from Lenin and the Bolshevik leaders he left the party. One of his chief adversaries in this contest was Wilhelm Pieck, who was to lead the campaign for proletarian unity in Berlin in 1946. The importance of this episode in Reuter's political development was vital: he realised that German Communism could no longer be regarded as a weapon of the German working class but as an instrument of the Russian government; that its aim was not to bring the proletariate to power, but to seize power itself. His struggle here, though ostensibly the opposite of that which he fought in Berlin a quarter of a century later, was essentially the same. It was to save Socialism in Germany from the dictatorship of Russian Communism.

Reuter never lost this idealism, almost a controlled naïveté, which was to become eloquence in his public speeches. But with it he allied a shrewd political realism, which he had opportunity enough to cultivate during his long and seldom important service with the increasingly ineffective SPD of the Weimar Republic.

His rôle in the party before the Nazi seizure of power was

never very powerful. For a time he was editor of the SPD news-paper *Vorwärts*, later a member of the Berlin City Assembly, where he became Senator for Transport. His attempts to ex-tend the underground system—partly intended as a public works programme after the crash of 1929, but which accorded ill with Brüning's stringent economic orthodoxy—and the dis-closure of a financial scandal in the city administration exposed him to the combined attacks of Pieck and Goebbels, leaders of the Communist and Nazi parties in the Assembly. When the Conservative Parties joined these attacks, and the SPD com-mitted itself to the support of a 'non-political' mayor, Reuter left Berlin to become Oberbürgermeister of Magdeburg. He returned as a member of the Reichstag in the elections of 1932; but the Weimar Republic was coming to its end, the SPD had virtually collapsed, and in January of the following year Hitler came to power. He was stripped of all his offices by the Nazis, and twice arrested; in 1935 he left Germany.

This was the third decisive episode of his political life. At the end of its existence, the Weimar SPD refused to support the Enabling Act conferring full power on Hitler; but it was then too late to resist the advent of the Nazis. Reuter was henceforth determined to oppose from the beginning any form of compromise with totalitarian threats, and it was this deter-mination which made him a natural choice for the office of Oberbürgermeister in Berlin when he returned from his un-eventful exile in London and Turkey. He had never held high office in the SPD, but his evident resolution and the ability to manoeuvre without compromise which he had learned from the party's mistakes in the Weimar era fitted him for its leader-ship in Berlin. It was this same ability which was later to clash with the much more downright attitude of the party's national leader, Kurt Schumacher. His return had not been easy. In spite of his protestations from Ankara, and the intervention of Schumacher on his behalf, he was long refused Allied permis-sion to go back to Germany—apparently on the grounds that he was too anti-Russian.[3] It was only in July 1946 after the personal intervention of Philip Noel-Baker, that he heard that the British government had now granted him permission to return. He reached Berlin in November, to experience the bitter cold spell that presaged the hard winter of 1947. It was under these exceptionally difficult conditions that he was to lead the inhabitants of the still ruined city in resistance to their Soviet overlords.

The SPD immediately elected him to the Magistrat (again in charge of transport), which brought him into repeated conflict with the Allied administration, and particularly with the Soviet Commandant. The SED was indeed well aware of the danger which Reuter's presence in Berlin would mean. While he was still on his way back, *Vorwärts* (now Communist) had begun to attack him under the headline 'A Turk for Mayor?' What it had feared now came to pass.

In April the SPD announced that it intended to put forward the name of Ernst Reuter for Berlin's next Oberbürgermeister. This step was taken in conscious defiance of the Soviet Commandant, and indeed of the Kommandatura as a whole. It was the first Berlin *démarche* in the 'constitutional crisis', for Kotikov had finally agreed to accept Ostrowski's resignation only on condition that the next mayor would have to be approved in advance by the Allied Powers. This was clearly beyond the provision of the Constitution and was rejected by the Western Commandants, but finally approved in the Allied Control Council. The SPD, and the CDU and LDP which gave it this support, knew quite well that Reuter would never be approved by the Soviet authorities, but insisted on asserting their legal power. As many Berlin papers[4] emphasised during April and May, while the matter was being examined in the Control Council, the SPD had no intention of being diverted from this deliberate defiance by the open threats of the Eastern press—which were too reminiscent of the treatment given to the opponents of Communism in Hungary and Vienna.

The first aspect of the crisis lay precisely in this native resistance—the first effectual opposition in a Soviet-occupied territory that the Communists had encountered. The Berlin representatives were well aware of this rôle in the European conflict and were not to be deterred by the appearance of passive complicity which the Western Allies sometimes seemed to have—as when the Kommandatura forbade the City Assembly to comment on the Moscow conference of March 1947, or when they acquiesced in a Soviet demand for the removal of an SPD councillor (Dr. Nestriepke) who had shown too much independence in the reorganisation of his department.

The feeling that Berlin must stand on its own in opposing Soviet pressure was heightened by a number of other developments: the apparent inability of the Western Commandants to curb the powers and interventions of the police; separate conflicts with the Western authorities over dismantling or distribution of food and fuel; Reuter's own personal relations with the Allied representatives, which were not easy at the highest levels, although the obstinacy with which they encountered each other appears to have given place to a more friendly collaboration with junior officers and officials—at least among the British and Americans.

The second aspect of the crisis may be seen in the wider field of relations between the Great Powers, which took a decisive turn for the worse in 1947. When Marshall replaced Byrnes as Secretary of State in January, he was already aware that a struggle was about to begin along the whole perimeter of Soviet power.[5] Acheson told the Senate Foreign Relations Committee at this time that Soviet policy was 'aggressive and expansionist',[6] and the Truman Doctrine, which promised the support of the United States to all free people struggling to maintain their independence, was promulgated at the same time as the disastrous Moscow Foreign Ministers' Conference in March. On this occasion Molotov raised all the Soviet demands that had been put aside at Yalta and Potsdam in a manner apparently designed to convince his colleagues that he was encompassing the downfall of Western Europe: in particular full reparations (at a moment when West Germany could only be saved from starvation by American and British food supplies) and a Russian share in the control of the Ruhr. At the same time he refused all further discussion of the Oder-Neisse Line, on which it was claimed agreement had been reached at Potsdam. With these demands he also advocated a more highly centralised government for Germany than any the Western Powers were now prepared to consider. To accede to his programme would have meant unconditional surrender. In fact it seems clear that Stalin regarded the Moscow conference as nothing more than the preliminary skirmish to a pitched battle for Germany—though it is doubtful whether he had yet considered what form this should take.

But whether or not he had decided on his next course of action, he had evidently not abandoned the policy of delay that had informed the Soviet attitude in all discussions of Germany throughout 1946. Molotov had refused to discuss the question at the Foreign Ministers' meeting in Paris; and in New York at the end of the year he had succeeded in avoiding concrete proposals by advocating the appointment of a commission of deputies.[7] It was after four months of consideration by this commission that the Foreign Ministers now met in Moscow. But instead of going forward to the establishment of Central German agencies as had been proposed (and as would have been a necessary preliminary to any realistic policy of reparations) Molotov reverted to the original Soviet demand for reparations, and added as a limit of concession that any central agency which might be established could be overruled if need be by the individual zonal commanders.

The open contempt which the Western delegates encountered in Moscow was hard to interpret. It is possible that at the time the Soviet government was thinking in terms of a definite division of the country—of the erection of a separate Communist state in the East, from which the Western Zones could be subverted at leisure. It does not seem likely that the Soviet Union was yet prepared to risk an open conflict with the Western Powers, or hoped to defeat them on their own ground —if only because she was incapable of herself maintaining a starving Germany.

If this was true, it was rapidly changed—by Marshall Aid. Marshall's announcement of an American plan for the economic restoration of Europe in June 1947 was followed with startling speed by the Paris Marshall Plan Conference of July. This was probably the turning point in the post-war relations between Russia and the West. Until then the conflict could be concealed by more or less plausible pretexts. The Soviet refusal to allow its new satellites to participate in the conference was an open challenge.[8] Europe was now effectively split in two. But the Soviet Union had no intention of letting matters rest there. If Marshall Aid could be quickly implemented, if Western Europe could be set on the path to recovery, her value as a prize would be enormously increased. And there was every reason for optimism. The Communist Parties of France and

Italy would certainly be able to seize power if they were assured of Russian support, and the whole of Europe would then be at the mercy of the Soviet Union. But the condition for success lay in Germany. As long as the Western Powers maintained their position there it would be impossible to gain quick control of the country: at some stage they would have to be driven out.

They could not be openly attacked without the risk of a nuclear bombardment of Moscow, but it would perhaps be possible to inflict on them a defeat so decisive and so humiliating that the population of West Germany would be driven to an alliance of despair with the Communist régime in the East.

The conditions for such a national surrender were already being prepared. Before the Foreign Ministers could begin the next round of negotiation over Germany, the various organs of 'direct democracy' in the Soviet Zone were being incorporated into a single national organ—the 'German People's Congress', which convened in Berlin at the beginning of December. The London Foreign Ministers' Conference—the last before the blockade—was taking place at the same time, and a week later Molotov tried to persuade the Council of Foreign Ministers to receive a delegation at the Conference. If they had agreed, it is likely that he would have renewed the demand Sokolovsky had made earlier in the year—though at that time as a pure propaganda move—for an all-German plebiscite on reunification. In any case the People's Congress now concentrated its energies on campaigning for a plebiscite and collecting signatures throughout Germany—though it was officially forbidden in the West. Its purpose was obvious from the beginning: in March 1948 it established a People's Council in East Berlin, which became a kind of Constituent Government-in-Exile, and busied itself with discussion of a peace treaty, constitution and national policies. It was clear that in the event of a Western defeat in Berlin, the Soviet Union would have a ready German instrument to exploit its success throughout the country and to secure Communist victories in subsequent elections.

The struggle in Berlin thus acquired a totally new significance in the middle of 1947. There was no sudden break in continuity: the Cold War had been fought there from the beginning of 1946. But the city suddenly became the focal point of

European history, and this coincided with the final and most decisive phase of the 'Bürgermeister crisis'.

In spite of the open opposition of the SED, whose representatives in the Assembly threatened that the election of Reuter would end all co-operation between the workers' parties (i.e. that the Communist would go into open opposition, with the support of the Soviet veto in the Kommandatura to make Berlin practically ungovernable), and private Soviet pressure on the leaders of the LDP and CDU notwithstanding,* the City Assembly elected Reuter Oberbürgermeister on June 24th by a majority of 89 to 17. The whole city had thus joined the SPD in the defiance of the Soviet Army and its German representatives. Naturally, this gesture also represented an open challenge to the West: during the weeks when, according to the agreement reached with Kotikov, the confirmation of Reuter's appointment was being discussed in the Control Council, the Marshall Plan Conference was meeting in Paris. The intransigeance of Russian hostility was clear to the world; and the symbolic action of the Berlin representatives demanded at least some symbolic support from the Western Powers, wavering between their uneasy alliances—their official commitments to Four-Power government, and their tacit obligations to the city's population. If they were unable to support Reuter, they could have used the occasion of the dispute to demand a radical reformation of the organs of Communist power in the city— notably the police and the trade unions. In the end they proved unwilling to force any showdown, and the impression was allowed to gain ground that in a conflict of wills, the Soviet Union would emerge victorious.

On August 18th the Kommandatura announced that it was unable to support the nomination of the elected mayor. Although Frau Schroeder, the new deputy,† carried out her duties courageously, undaunted by increasing ill health, the

---

* Davison, *op. cit.* p. 50, remarks that the LDP leader, Karl-Hubert Schwennicke, was opposed in his stand against Soviet inducements to vote against Reuter by his colleagues in the Soviet Zone and that this lay behind the later split between the Berlin and zonal organisations of the LDP. It should, however, be noted that Schwennicke's abstention from the debate of June 24th was due simply to a Soviet veto on his participation.

† Friedensburg was in fact first deputy mayor. But he stood aside for Frau Schroeder, to allow a Social Democrat to represent Berlin.

city was left without an ultimate authority to represent it to the Western Allies.

Instead it was subjected to repeated pressure from the entenched power of the Communist organisations. If they could not govern the city themselves, they were making it impossible for anyone else to exercise effective control. In particular the power of the police continued to grow throughout 1947. While he insisted that he was responsible to the Kommandatura alone, and refused to account for the activities of the police to the Magistrat, Markgraf instructed his subordinates in May to avoid any appeal to Allied authority in any proceedings against German officials to which they might be ordered. In case of disobedience to police orders, it was the German *Polizeipräsident* and not the Kommandatura which was to be informed. This dispensation gave him unquestioned power and a test at the end of November served only to confirm it. After the notorious kidnapping of a journalist on *Der Abend*, the Assembly passed a resolution of no confidence in the police but they were not disturbed. As long as the police headquarters remained in the Soviet sector, there was no way for the Magistrat to by-pass the provision that each Commandant should have final powers over appointments and dismissals within his suzerainty.

At the same time the Soviet authorities began to get rid of those political representatives and party leaders who stood in the way of the SED. They began with the most vulnerable: in May student members of the CDU were expelled from the university. Then, after persistent Communist agitation, Ella Kay, the SPD mayor of the borough of Prenzlauer Berg in the Soviet sector, was removed for 'economic sabotage and provocation', and the case became the occasion for further fierce debates between the two parties along the whole range of economic and social policies—which also meant in effect the question of Soviet control over Berlin's future.[9] More far-reaching in its consequences was the removal, by order of the Soviet Military Administration, of the chairman of the zonal CDU, Ernst Lemmer, and Jakob Kaiser.* They had succeeded the original chairman, who had been dismissed in 1945;[10] but this time the

* Both men later became prominent in the governments in Berlin and Bonn. Both were to be Federal German Ministers. Jakob Kaiser died in 1961.

Soviet action was the preliminary to a more radical attack.

They were removed for opposing the People's Congress, and it soon became clear that the zonal authorities were determined to stamp out any organisation which could provide an alternative to the SED and the organs of 'direct democracy'. Shortly afterwards a Soviet officer forced delegates from the CDU in Berlin to leave a congress of the Zonal organisation; the party in the capital was impelled to declare that co-operation with that in the zone was impossible, and broke off formal relations. The same thing happened in reverse with the LDP: the Berlin branch was formally expelled by the party headquarters in the Soviet Zone.

There was then no further connection between political life in Berlin and in the rest of East Germany, where the SPD had of course been banned from the beginning. The democratic forces in the zone were completely isolated, and the parties that remained there were rapidly reduced to side organisations of the SED, which were used to prop the façade of people's democracy in East Berlin when the city was finally split.

Similarly the FDGB, on whose executive committee only 13 Communist trade unionists had sat before the SED merger campaign in 1946, had now been brought under complete Communist control, and functioned as an ancillary organ of the People's Congress. Early in 1948 it looked as if Berlin, for all the brave resistance of the SPD and the other democratic parties, was coming increasingly under Soviet domination, and that opposition to this process would result in the definitive division of Germany. From the Hanover headquarters of the SPD it appeared to Schumacher that this was above all the danger to be averted. He maintained that it was the primary duty of the German working class, and of Germans in general, to unite in winning independence from all the occupying powers. But to Reuter and the leaders of the Berlin parties it was evident that unity could now only come at the price of communisation; that at best, resistance to Soviet pressure was bound to involve some abandonment, for the present at least, of the East German population; and that the problem before them was not to save the country from the Allied occupation, but to save West Germany through collaboration with the Western Allies.

If there were signs of hope that the new alliance was taking shape; if Frau Schroeder had been able to carry out her duties in relative freedom from the kind of pressure that had been put on Ostrowski; if Reuter had been allowed to broadcast his defiance over RIAS; if the censors of the West Berlin press had permitted it to voice the hopes and fears of the population, i soon became obvious that real success would exact a heavy price. On February 17th delegates from Poland, Czecho-slovakia and Jugoslavia met in Prague to protest against Western policy in Germany, and particularly against the provisions o: the Marshall Plan. A week later the Prague coup brough· the Czech government under total Communist control. The tragedy of Czechoslovakia emphasised the fate that would await a prematurely united Germany. If it lay behind the sudden determination of the Western Powers to construct a strong Western German state as quickly as possible, it also explains the acquiescence of the German politicians in a policy of tota collaboration, and the increasing realisation in West Berlin that its future lay not in union with the other half of the capita under Four-Power control, but in identification with the Western half of Germany.*

The new Allied programme, and the participation in it of West Berlin representatives, also do much to account for the new determination on the part of Russia to force a showdown as quickly as possible. It was at this time that Clay wrote o: sensing a new attitude behind his encounters with the Russians and it is probable that the decision had now been made to blockade Berlin.

In the city itself there were many signs of this reappraisal Reuter, who a year before had insisted that it would be 'naïve speculation' to hope for advantages from differences between the Allies, and that Germany's future depended on nothing more than 'honourable co-operation and true understanding with the Russian people; who had still hoped to differentiate between the Soviet Union and the German Communists;[11] now recognised that Germany had been split by the action of the East and told a demonstration of all democratic youth organisa-

* It was primarily the SPD leadership which established this view. The CDU and the Assembly seemed to accept it much more reluctantly. See Davison, op. cit pp. 78-79.

ions: 'The conditions for all political dealings and all real political life, for the individual as for the whole nation, is to win freedom and independence. . . . Let us not be distracted from the heart of the matter by any words, any fog of propaganda or any agitators. . . . National unity without true freedom in every corner of our land is Utopia. . . . We have known unity in slavery long enough.'[12] That the other parties shared these views was demonstrated by their new offensive against the Communist claim to speak for all Germany. In February 1948 all three collaborated in the foundation of a new trade-union organisation to provide an alternative forum to the now flagrantly Communist FDGB. The UGO—the Independent Trade-Union Opposition—under the initial chairmanship of Ernst Scharnowski, became a non-party focus for the population's resistance, still symbolic in form but increasingly articulate and determined, to withstand the open Soviet threat to incorporate the German capital into the Eastern Zone. (In February Sokolovsky had told the Central Council that Berlin was part of the Soviet Zone, and that the Western Powers were endangering their right to stay there by 'abusing their position'.)

On the hundredth anniversary of the 1848 revolution, the UGO and the three democratic parties called a West Berlin demonstration on the Platz der Republik,* in answer to one that, true to their original directives, the SED and the People's Congress were holding in the East. Here Reuter told a crowd of 80,000 that after Prague, Finland and Berlin were next on the Communist list, but that the 'Communist flood would break on their iron will'. The world must know that it could not leave Berlin in the lurch. The demonstration proved to be the prelude to a bigger one on the First of May—the first time that the population celebrated Labour Day by demonstrating against that unity of the working class which the Communists had been trying for over two years to impose on them. In East Berlin the FDGB, the FDJ, the SED and the Volkskongress brought brigades of members onto the streets for a march-past—the only effective way of ensuring that a demonstration would continue as planned for the required length of time. The two rival demonstrations, the assembly on the Platz der Republik, and the march down

* In front of the Reichstag building.

93

Friedrichstrasse to Marx-Engels Platz* have taken place on May 1st ever since.

By then it began to seem credible that 'the world would not leave Berlin in the lurch'. Up to 1948 the development of Western plans for West Germany had given no indication that they also implied a commitment to defend West Berlin. Nor could this be so until the Three Powers, and primarily the United States, publicly recognised the eventuality of splitting the country and proceeding with the creation of a separate West German state. Although General Clay and the American ambassador in Moscow, Bedell Smith, had both separately warned Washington in the summer of 1947 that a conflict with the Russians was bound to come, such a public declaration was not made until March 1948—perhaps because they had added that in this case it was likely that Berlin could be blockaded. In the city itself the alignment was far less definite than on the international plane. The Western representatives there had not, and in view of their position could not have, decided on a course of action to protect the inhabitants and their spokesmen against Russian encroachment. They could not demand a purge of the FDGB without raising the whole question of the political future of Berlin and the different zones, which was being discussed throughout the year by the four Foreign Ministers. It was impossible to forbid Markgraf's police to operate in West Berlin without accentuating the split in the city which they were trying to avert. But on a more mundane level, it would have been possible to treat the elected deputies with more sympathy, and to have given them private assurances of the Western commitment to the city. They could have shown more energy in ridding the administration in the Western sectors of known Communist agents—(of which three were dismissed from influential positions in 1947). And they were unwise to accede to Kotikov's demand that the city mayor should have to be confirmed in office by the Allies in the midst of the crisis of confidence which had been provoked by Ostrowski's resignation. Reuter, Suhr and Lemmer found sympathy and understanding among the junior officers and administrators of the British and

---

* Since 1950, when the old royal palace at the end of Unter den Linden was pulled down to make room for a square for speeches and demonstrations. The original demonstration was held in the old Lustgarten.

American governments; but they could not judge to what extent this attitude was shared in London and Washington, and as the crisis approached, many of the city's leaders wondered how far the allies were determined to support them in the eventuality that they feared the most: a systematic sabotage of the democratic government that after eighteen months' struggle was just beginning to assert its own identity. It was not easy to tell: hitherto the Western Powers had shown great resolution in creating representative government in Berlin; in endowing the city with a constitution; in protecting the largest democratic party from enforced communisation, and in ensuring free elections. But where these achievements were undermined through the organs of 'direct democracy', or where their representatives had been threatened by Soviet brow-beating, as in the cases of Ostrowski and Reuter, the Three Powers seemed helpless or reluctant to protect them, particularly when German protests and Soviet tactics succeeded in confusing the issue with the different question of the authority and limitations of the Berlin government.

The final break with the Russian authorities in Berlin and the incorporation of West Berlin into the Allied plans for Western Germany arose not out of political determination but economic necessity. Up to 1947 the city's economic relations with Western Germany had depended largely on independent initiatives of the Magistrat, which had been greatly encouraged by the formation of the Anglo-American Bi-zone. Frau Schroeder and the other representatives of the city who travelled to the Congress of German cities* were able to lay before other delegates the particular economic needs of Berlin, and have them brought to the attention of the economic administration of the Bi-zone. The greatest success of such indirect methods was to have the Western sectors of the city incorporated in the operation of the bizonal Joint Export-Import Agency.† If the productive capacity of the city (whose production index still stood below 30)‡ were to be restored, it was essential that it should have this purchasing power behind it. Before the war one-third of Berlin's products had gone to the German territories which later fell to Poland and the Soviet

---

* *Deutscher Städtetag*, which met in Goslar in 1947.
† Established for the Bi-zone in January 1947. ‡ 1936 = 100.

Union, one-third had remained in Berlin and one-third had gone to the area of the present Federal Republic, or abroad; and even in 1953, the internal purchasing power of the city was less than half of what it had been in 1936. The conditions in Berlin in 1947 were demonstrated by the fact that there were more than twice as many deaths as live births.[13] In these circumstances, it was imperative for the survival of the Western sectors that their economy should be fused with that of West Germany. Economic failure here would have meant total political defeat, perhaps in the country as a whole, and when they were considering the future of Germany the Western Powers and the German ministers recognised the necessity of incorporating Berlin into the economic structure of the Western Zones. But they were hesitant about the extent to which they could do this immediately. They did not feel confident enough to introduce Western currency into Berlin, in case this should raise further local obstruction by the Russians. But at the same time they were determined to proceed with the reconstruction of Western Germany, to which they knew the Russians were implacably opposed. This inconsistent situation was the immediate background to the blockade.

After the breaking-up of the London Foreign Ministers' Conference in December, it was evident that the Soviet Union would never accede to a unified administration of the country unless she was certain to gain control of it. The economic situation demanded immediate action, however, and all attempts made during 1947 to work out a common economic programme in keeping with the Potsdam Agreement had failed. The essential to recovery was the reform of the now completely worthless Reichsmark, which no longer permitted any rational investment or export policy,[14] and kept the internal price structure artificially isolated from the international market. At the beginning of the year the British and American military governments decided to move ahead with the beginnings of German government in their zone, and, after a last attempt at agreement on currency reform in the Control Council, to consider the whole future of West Germany in conference with France and the Benelux countries. At the start of the conference in February, the French delegation agreed to proceed with a West German currency reform without discussing the future political structure of the country or the other French demands. In so doing, they tacitly admitted the unrealistic nature of French zonal separation, and in effect committed France to collaborate in the rebuilding of Germany. It was currency reform, in fact, which brought about West German unity.

A month later the Marshall Plan states, meeting in Paris, established the Organisation for European Economic Co-operation, to which the French Zone was invited to adhere. German experts, who already formed the Economic Council of the Bi-zone, now represented this country in OEEC. These were the preliminary steps to the London Recommendations issued by the Six Powers on June 2nd. Henceforth the economic policies of the three zones would be co-ordinated, West Germany would be fully incorporated in the European Recovery Programme and the German state authorities could begin to draft a constitution for the Federal Republic.* Western Europe had begun to take shape, and Western Germany had been created.

The Soviet authorities had not waited for these developments before making their replies. While the Marshall Plan Conference was taking place, they had set up their own 'economic commission' for the Eastern Zone, and it seemed for a time that they would be content to develop an East German parallel to the West. But their next action demonstrated their intention, not of proceeding with the separate erection of an East German state, but of bringing the Western Powers to surrender by pressure on Berlin. Three days after Britain, France and the Benelux countries had signed the Brussels Defence Treaty, one month after the coup in Prague, one month before the Italian elections, Sokolovsky demanded that the Control Council be given a full report of the decisions of the London Conference. When he was told that the discussions were private, and that the outcome was not yet ratified, the whole Soviet delegation walked out, and Sokolovsky declared that the Allied Control Council had ceased to function. A few days later the meaning of this step was made clear, when the first four trains on their way to Berlin were stopped and turned back.

* The Ruhr was to be internationalised under the control of the Six Powers and Germany herself.

Chapter Five

THE BLOCKADE

THE Berlin Blockade was in Russian eyes a substitute for war. It was a deliberate attack on the whole Western position in Germany and on the American commitment to Europe, which the Soviet policy of the preceding three years had brought about, but which was nevertheless unexpected. But in Western eyes, the issue was by no means so clear. The blockade took a long time to develop (the first moves were made in March, but the final measures were not imposed until August), and the Western governments wavered in their appreciation of its significance even while they were organising the airlift. They were united in their determination to remain in Berlin; at the same time they could hardly believe that the Soviet Union was really trying to force them out. Thus, though all would have agreed with Clay's famous words in his teletype conference of April 16th: 'When Berlin falls, Western Germany will be next. . . . If we withdraw, our position in Europe is threatened. If America does not understand this now, does not know that the issue is cast, then it never will, and communism will run rampant.'[1] There was nevertheless a strong disposition to regard the blockade as an instrument to force negotiations, not as a decisive battle in the Cold War. Negotiations in Berlin and Moscow continued at intervals until September; only after that did a finally united West resign itself to an indefinite contest of strength and will. But it was also at this time that Russian purposes changed. During the autumn the Soviet government realised that it could not hope to force a retreat or change Western policy in Germany without war. A decision seems to have been taken in September to make the best of the alternative: without abandoning their long-term aims, the Communist Allies in Russia and Germany set about creating an East German state with East Berlin as its capital. Whether they could have made such a clean break in Berlin without the cover of the blockade is hard to judge; it is certain that they hoped at first to intimidate the Magistrat and

98

Assembly into choosing a united, though Communist, city rather than face the consequences of a split. They failed, but the price of Western victory was the complete separation of the Soviet sector from the West, and the emergence of two Berlins, one embedded in the Communist bloc, the other tenuously attached to the new Federal Republic one hundred miles away. The mass of political and human problems which this situation created for the inhabitants of Berlin was to have tragic results in 1953 and 1961.

The history of the blockade is, therefore, not that of a clear and continuous struggle. Three periods may be discerned. From April to June, as the siege was progressively imposed, Russia expected to intimidate the West into abandoning its policy in West Germany, while her German supporters attempted to persuade the Berliners to oppose currency reform and 'maintain the unity' of the city. In this, they had some success: Western councils were divided and confused; most of the Berlin leaders were anxious and uncertain of their power to resist. In the second period, from June to September, the full blockade changed the situation. The city's population was united in resistance, the Allied Powers introduced currency reform to Berlin and improvised the airlift, but at the same time made constant attempts to negotiate. At this stage, both Russia and the West were convinced that resistance could not continue indefinitely. After September, the unexpected success of the airlift persuaded the West to hold out and Russia to change her plans. The city was finally split.

Western victory in the face of overwhelming odds has since that time come to be taken for granted. But when the first threatening moves were made in March, it was by no means certain that the Three Powers would resist at all. In public, the American and British governments insisted that they would defend their position in Berlin, but

There was a lack of consensus among Western officials in Berlin on whether the Soviets would in fact attempt to impose the full blockade on the city, and whether in such an event it would be within the limits of possibility for the Allies to remain. Colonel Howley came to the conclusion that the Soviets would attempt to drive the Western Powers out of the city, possibly by a blockade, and he proposed a plan to meet this eventuality.

His conclusions, however, were not fully shared by General Clay's political advisory staff or in other quarters. The French sector commandant, General Ganeval, with whom Howley discussed his plan, did not believe the Russians would do such a cruel thing as to blockade the city but thought of it as a possibility for which it would be well to be prepared. General Herbert, the British sector commandant . . . did not think it likely that the Soviets would blockade the city; but he believed that if they did the Western powers would have no choice but to leave. As far as can be determined, no top-level decisions about what to do in the event of a Soviet blockade had been made in Washington, London or Paris.[2]

In fact, as April passed, the apprehension of March seems to have given way to a mood of uncertain optimism, both among some politicians in Berlin, and in the political staffs of the military governors. They may have felt that the immediate threat to the city was now past, and there was certainly little general appreciation of the connection between Western plans for Germany and Russian intentions in Berlin.[3] In this they were certainly encouraged by the SED, who began to press during those weeks for greater co-operation between the parties in preserving the unity of Berlin, for the prevention of 'industrial emigration', and for greater efforts to maintain the city's economy.[4] These manœuvres were not ineffective: even such an unwavering opponent of the SED as Otto Suhr was able to express his belief, in the middle of April that tensions among the occupying powers had decreased, and that an opportunity had arisen to co-operate in a free and united administration of the capital, as a step towards the speedy establishment of German unity.[5] The constitutional debates in the Assembly seemed for a period in April to confirm this conclusion.

But as currency reform was discussed among the council of German and Allied experts in Bad Homburg near Frankfurt, it was realised more clearly on all sides that the dangers were increasing. It would be a challenge that the Russians could not ignore, and they would choose their own response. Berlin could then find itself in a desperate position—the more so as the Allies originally had no intention of applying the currency reform to Berlin. They were still reluctant to provoke a struggle for power in the city, and had few expectations of winning it if they did. Among the leaders of the political parties, there were two opinions. The majority of all three parties counselled caution: in May and June, representatives of the Magistrat made approaches to the Kommandatura to remonstrate against a hasty currency reform in the West, which would expose Berlin to grave political and economic dangers. Their attitude was understandable: even after the incidents of March, few thought in terms of a blockade, but rather of the form of political sabotage which had already persisted for two years and which they had with difficulty survived. They had not been able to count on unequivocal or enduring Western support, and now Berlin was to be cut off from Western Germany by economic measures which would invite the Soviet authorities to intensify their pressure. Their misgivings were well-founded.

If they temporarily ignored the real nature of the struggle before them, it is also true that the American, British and French authorities had shown a similar inconsistency. If the Berliners who had demonstrated against Soviet pressure on May 1st later opposed the London Recommendations, they also knew that the Western Powers, who had announced their intentions of remaining in Berlin, had made no plans and saw no way to feed the civilian population.[6]

But there was also a more resolute reponse to the situation, and its protagonists were determined not only to resist the Russians but to force the hand of the West. Two members of the Magistrat, Reuter and Klingelhöfer, the Economics Senator, opposed all compromise. They rejected equally the Western plan of continuing with the Reichsmark in the 'Four-Power city', and the proposal put forward by a large group of politicians for a special 'Bearmark' for Berlin.* They were fully aware that for Berlin to rely on any currency which the Soviet authorities controlled could lead to its eventual incorporation in the Eastern Zone; and the economic division of the city was by far the lesser evil. In May the Magistrat sent a delegation, to which both men belonged, to the Economic Council of the Bi-zone in Frankfurt. Berlin was henceforth to be represented in a special committee of the Council, but the delegates were immediately told that at first it would be excluded from the provisions of the currency reform. The Director of Economic Administration, Professor Erhard, supported this decision. Though he expected to grant increased economic aid, he did

* The bear is the symbol of Berlin. The name of the city is popularly supposed to originate from a Teutonic heraldic emblem, the *Bärlein* or little bear.

not believe it possible to include the city in West Germany'
financial system.[7] But the leaders of the Berlin minority found
that they had the unanimous support of the Prime Ministers of
all German states in the Bi-zone. A meeting of the *Länderra*
(the council of state ministers which the American and British
authorities had established as a first step to a German government) telegraphed the military governors: 'On the eve of the
currency reform, the prime ministers . . . ask that they may
express their apprehension that it will probably not be possible
to bring about an all-German solution to the currency reform
In this case, they regard it as self-evident that the three Western
sectors of Berlin should be included in the currency reform for
the three Western occupation zones.'[8]

This unanimous support from Western Germany was more
powerful than could have been any pressure from Berlin, where
the Communist members made it impossible even to discuss
the matter in the Magistrat. Moreover, Frau Schroeder had
been forced by exhaustion to go on holiday, and the acting
mayor was now Dr. Friedensburg. He was above all concerned
to maintain the unity of the capital which he feared currency
reform would finally destroy. Only Reuter and Klingelhöfer
among the leaders of the Assembly were prepared to champion
Berlin's inclusion, and their cause depended ultimately on
West German support. The British and American military
governments were not convinced, but agreed that if a separate
Eastern currency were introduced after that in the West, Berlin
would have to be included in the provisions of the reform. In
general, the British political and economic advisors were the
more inclined to take this step, and in the coming weeks they
showed the most considered support of the German view.[9]

As the Allied intentions of proceeding with the creation of a
West German state became known, tension had begun to
mount. In March the Russian authorities turned back four
Allied trains* in response to the Marshall Plan Conference. At
that time they had demanded the right of inspection and control, in clear violation of the oral agreements reached with
Zhukov in 1945. Thereafter, as the Western Powers continued
their discussions the campaign of threats continued intermittently. It was decreed that no freight could leave Berlin by

* Two British and two American.

rail without permission from the Russian Commandant, and trains began to return empty to West Germany. Later, outgoing passenger trains were halted, sometimes for a day or more. Allied signal corps were then expelled from East German territory. Although a small and unpublicised military airlift had now begun, these steps did not yet indicate a full blockade. They were designed rather to isolate the Western Powers from the civil population, and impress them with the potentialities of the Soviet weapon, and the difficulties they would have to surmount in pursuing their present policies. In this, they were successful at first; in April and May tension and relaxation followed each other so rapidly that the Allied authorities continued to assume that they could ultimately depend on Russian grace in supplying the population. General Clay seems to have been alone in prophesying a full blockade.

But while the discussion on Western Germany progressed, the incidents increased. In the middle of June came the announcement that the Elbe autobahn bridge was in need of repair, and traffic would have to be diverted. It was the first of the famous series of technical hitches which were soon to put Berlin in a state of siege. To underline the significance of this declaration, and ensure that the Western delegates should have no chance of direct appeal or negotiation in Berlin, the Soviet authorities now formally withdrew from the Kommandatura. It had ceased to function in March, but its existence had hitherto implied certain Soviet obligations towards the Allies, which were now in effect denounced.

The signals of an impending blockade were now plain, but neither the Allied authorities nor the Berlin representatives had decided whether to extend the currency reform to the city, in case of conflict with the Russians. The Western Powers had been discussing a series of alternative solutions (including the introduction of Eastern currency) with financial experts, who reported afterwards that they were frightened to realise how much the Americans in fact favoured this way out of their difficulties. Clay and Robertson also told the representatives of the German Economic Council that the Bi-zone, America and Britain, would have to subsidise West Berlin—if necessary every inhabitant, if necessary for the next twenty years—in order to maintain the Western position there without war.[10]

This course of action would have made the Western position untenable within a few months, if the Soviet Union had been prepared to take the ultimate risk of war. Nothing could have been more calculated to assure the city's inhabitants that the West was not in the end prepared to defend its position. In this sense the blockade was the salvation of the West. It revealed that Russia was not prepared to risk war, and it finally encouraged the Western authorities to make up their minds, and include Berlin in the economic structure of West Germany.

On June 18th it was announced that currency reform would become effective in West Germany two days later: Berlin was excluded. The immediate Soviet response was to promulgate further restrictions on travel between the German zones, and new measures of inspection for all freight between West Germany and West Berlin. This step was intended to impress upon its inhabitants the city's isolation; Sokolovsky went further the next day and made public the claim he had advanced in the Central Council the previous February. The currency reform, he declared, was not extended to Berlin because it 'formed part of the Soviet Zone', and subsequent Soviet notices of a new currency for East Germany took care to include Berlin specifically. But it also became clear that Sokolovsky had not yet been instructed to impose a full blockade; under cover of the threats which they had made intermittently since March, the Communists still hoped to gain control of West Berlin through political pressure. Frau Schroeder had just told the Assembly that the city government would continue as before. Now she and Friedensburg were summoned to Sokolovsky's headquarters and instructed that the Eastern currency reform would apply to the Western sectors of Berlin too. It was this event which proved decisive: there could be no hope of compromise with a power which had plainly decided to bring the whole city under its exclusive control. The Western Allies were under virtual blockade already, and it was evident that their Soviet partner intended to drive them out. The blockade was only extended to the civilian population when other Russian pressure had failed: it is possible that had the Western Powers foreseen the course of the next week, they would have decided to withdraw. But for the moment they were the only victims of the threat; they hoped to ride this situation out, and they realised that their only course was a public commitment to the German inhabitants.

On the 23rd, five days after their original order, the Western Powers gave instructions that the Soviet decree applied only to the Eastern sector. West German marks were to be introduced into the rest of the city forthwith, and both East and West marks would be accepted there as legal tender. The West was now committed. The final decision lay with the City Assembly itself; if it had bowed to Sokolovsky at this point—if it had maintained the previous view that a unilateral Western reform would be disastrous for Berlin—the Russian triumph would have been complete. But it would also have been impossible for the Assembly to give open support to one side in an inter-Allied conflict: it could have provoked direct Soviet military intervention. Instead, the Magistrat gave a lead to the Assembly by passing a formal reassertion of the Four-Power status and the city constitution. This was not, and could not be, a firm statement of support for the Western Powers; it was an attempt to prevent the final division of the city while admitting currency reform. Reuter summed up the position of the Magistrat in a statement that the two currencies would circulate side by side, and the administration would continue as before.* But it did mean that the city government had formally defied Sokolovsky, and refused to be blackmailed into a renunciation of their underlying solidarity with the Western Powers and West Germany.

On the afternoon of June 23rd, the City Assembly met at the old Rathaus in the Soviet sector to ratify their decisions. They were confronted with a carefully organised Communist demonstration, which had taken possession not only of the streets but also of the galleries inside the building. Loudspeaker vans were broadcasting speeches by Ulbricht and Grotewohl. Members' calls for police protection were ignored, and for two hours the meeting was prevented from convening. The incident was a demonstration of Soviet power, intended not to prevent the Assembly from functioning, but to cow it into support for Sokolovsky. After what seemed a sufficient demonstration, the mob withdrew at the sign of an SED member.[11] The City Assembly listened to the Magistrat's decision, and the SED's

* The SED members of the Magistrat naturally voted to implement Sokolovsky's order.

arguments against it, notably a threat to block the bank-accounts and social insurance funds which the Soviet 'City Bank' still exclusively held—and then voted overwhelmingly to support the Magistrat. As they came out, members of the three democratic parties, and particularly the SPD, were attacked by the demonstrators on the street, with the active connivance of the police.*

The same night all the electricity supplies which West Berlin had hitherto drawn from the Soviet Zone were cut off; and the next morning it was announced that technical difficulties on the railways between Berlin and West Germany had forced the Soviet authorities to close them down 'for a long period'. The blockade was now almost complete. All civilian and military passenger traffic had already stopped; this new attempt to sever the supply lines of food and fuel was expected to accomplish what the other demonstration measures had failed to do. The Western Powers and the City Assembly would be forced to capitulate within a few weeks.

There were good enough reasons for these hopes. Apart from any other necessities, Berlin only contained enough food and fuel for six weeks.[12] It was scarcely conceivable that even the best improvised air-transport would be able to extend the period of grace for much more. No one could foresee that a population of over two million† could be sustained for months from the air. These considerations aroused immediate mis-givings in the Allied advisory staffs,[13] and in the three Western capitals. In London, from what is known of the Cabinet discussions, Aneurin Bevan advocated a tank break-through from West Germany to Berlin, in the certainty that Russia was not prepared to risk war. But it was hard to imagine that Berlin could hold out for a long period by purely passive means of resistance.[14] Only two men had at that time concluded that Berlin could be saved by an airlift: Colonel Howley and General Clay. The airlift was essentially Clay's creation. He began its initial organisation, and he pressed Washington to extend it. When, on June 24th, Truman decided to place it on a regular basis, he was only registering Clay's achievements.

* Jeanette Wolff, an SPD member, who had already experienced a Nazi concen-tration camp, was particularly severely beaten.

† The population at the end of the year was 2,108,000.

The response in the city itself was immediate defiance. The SPD called a demonstration on the 24th which was addressed by Reuter, Neumann and the vice-chairman of the national organisation, Erich Ollenhauer. In their speeches the change in emphasis from the Magistrat discussion two days earlier was marked. It was no longer a financial question, Reuter declared, but a struggle between two opposed political systems. Berlin was threatened by the fate of Prague, but would not succumb. Neumann appealed to the democratic world for support, without which freedom in Berlin could not survive. The questions of currency reform and the status of Berlin had, through the Soviet action, suddenly become a world-wide struggle, in which the defeat of the West could have changed the course of European history. But it was equally clear that the people of the city were determined to resist, that Russia was not prepared for war; and that resistance could perhaps be successful.

These were Clay's arguments in his teletype conference with Washington on the 25th. The Department of the Army had suggested slowing down the introduction of Western currency in order to avoid armed conflict. Clay replied: 'If Soviets want war it will not be because of Berlin currency issue but because they believe this is the right time'. The German leaders had courageously expressed their opposition to Communism, and this confidence could not now be destroyed.[15] The same conclusion was reached by the British government the next day, and it officially proclaimed its determination to stay in Berlin in spite of Soviet attempts to gain political victories by 'a campaign of starvation'. It was the same day that the airlift was placed on a regular basis.

The first American aircraft with food for the population had already landed on June 25th. They were small transport planes with a cargo capacity of two and a half tons. There were only 100 available to the American forces, and the British resources were still more limited. It was estimated that the absolute minimum required in an airlift would be 4,000 tons a day for the population, and five hundred tons for the Allied forces.[16] The outlook was desperate, particularly as the ultimate measure of blockade—the severance of the remaining road and canal connections—could be imposed at any moment. For this reason the British and French governments advocated a final attempt to negotiate. It was only at this time that the airlift came to be looked on as a regular weapon in the struggle for Berlin, and even afterwards, it was regarded primarily as an instrument to gain time for negotiation.[17] American aircraft resources in Europe had been reinforced from the United States, and at the end of June the RAF had joined the daily service; but it was still not considered possible to supply Berlin indefinitely by air. On the thirtieth day of the airlift, after Clay had held a telephone conference with the American Air Force Commander in Germany, Curtis E. Le May, coal began to arrive in Berlin by plane. Such deliveries were soon able to augment the electricity supply; but they gave no indication of success in providing fuel for the city throughout the winter, or in enabling industry to continue without electricity from the Soviet Zone.

The morale of the Berlin population was certainly better than that of the Allied authorities throughout the first month of the blockade; but when the initial technical difficulties had been overcome, when aircraft began to land at Tempelhof at the rate of one every five minutes, and when the capacities of Tempelhof and the more rudimentary British airport at Gatow were augmented by the construction of a new French airport at Tegel, they realised that Berlin could be held by these means alone throughout the winter. This new appreciation, common to both sides, emerged in August and September. It was then that Stalin decided to break off negotiations, and instead of attempting to drive the Western Powers out of Berlin, to use the situation to split the city definitively and create an East German state.

The most remarkable feature of the German population's attitude throughout this period was their refusal to be influenced by the fact of negotiations between the Four Powers. Their resistance to Communist attempts to destroy their morale was unwavering, and seems to have been inspired entirely by the visible success of the airlift.[18] Soviet efforts to tempt the people into buying food in the East sector failed completely,* and the West mark soon rose to three times the value of the

* About 1 per cent of the West Berlin population registered in the East for food supplies between July and September. The proportion in September rose to 2·2 per cent.

East mark in the open market. While the broad public hesitated to commit themselves to an open choice between Soviet and Western political organisations (in paying their trade-union subscription to the UGO rather than the FDGB, for example) a hard core of organised SPD supporters was ready to resist any eventuality, even that of a Communist putsch. Their ability was soon to be severely tested.

During August the Magistrat was slowly brought to a halt. By the most persistent, ruthless and even infantile personal pressure, Soviet officers attempted to wear down the resistance of the ministers in the city government, with the ultimate intention of inducing them to hand over the function of the Magistrat to a more 'directly democratic' body. Frau Schroeder's health again broke down at this time, she had to leave for West Germany and Friedensburg now became the regular acting mayor. If his health or nerves had given way, he would have been replaced by the third deputy, a member of the SED. This would certainly have given the opportunity for a putsch, and like his subordinates, Friedensburg was subjected to midnight interrogations, the constant presence of Soviet liaison officers in his office, and smear campaigns in the East German press. But like them, he was fortified in his determination by the open Russian expectation that he would give way.

This vindictive pressure was the result of some notable victories for the Magistrat. At the end of June the representatives of the city had already responded to the Soviet attempt to isolate them by a direct appeal to the United Nations. This demonstrative action was followed up by more radical measures, measures which the government would scarcely have been able to take before the break-up of the Kommandatura. Communist officials were dismissed, and attempts were made to reassert the powers of the Magistrat over the police. When Markgraf responded by moving all the chief offices to the Soviet sector, Friedensburg, acting within his constitutional powers, temporarily suspended him;* and appointed his deputy, Dr. Stumm

* The history of the Magistrat's attempts to gain control over the police is still somewhat obscure. In the circumstances, Friedensburg's action was certainly audacious; he was not of course empowered to dismiss Markgraf without the unanimous approval of the Kommandatura. An account of the general measures of the Magistrat is given in Plischke, *op. cit.* pp. 78-81.

of the SPD, to take his place. Kotikov immediately reprimanded him, and, in an order signed 'Military Commandant of the City of Berlin', instructed Frau Schroeder to reinstate Markgraf. This was the most open challenge to their authority that the Western military governments had yet had to face. They declared Kotikov's order invalid, and recognised Stumm's authority. But the result of this first open clash was that henceforth two police headquarters operated in the city. Although the majority of the police now followed Stumm to the West, Markgraf was left with the substantial minority who had preserved his power hitherto, and his writ ran undisputed in the Soviet sector.

Neither the Magistrat nor the SED desired such a split. The one was still fighting to preserve the unity of the city, the other hoping to gain complete control. But the struggle was bound to divide Berlin still further, even though neither side yet wanted it. As long as Soviet attempts to gain control of individual departments persisted, the Magistrat would have to establish them anew in the West. This was particularly the case with the Food Department, whose head, Paul Füllsack, was subjected to an outstandingly cruel campaign of intimidation and obstruction before he finally moved his office to the British sector.[19]

Two key departments of the city administration had thus been split through pressure from the Russian authorities, though against their will. A third, the Finance Department, nearly suffered the same fate before the campaign was temporarily abandoned. The failure of these tactics now impelled them to made a frontal assault on the Assembly, particularly as the negotiations in Moscow seemed to be nearing success. On August 26th the City Assembly was due to meet in regular session at the City Hall. The events of June now seemed to be repeated: a large and well-organised mob prevented members from taking their places, and some hundreds forced their way into the chamber. But there was a vital difference: this was not an attempt to influence the proceedings, but to disperse the city government on the spot. It was a last effort to take power through the organs of 'direct democracy', and the intention was proclaimed by an SED member who told the crowd that the session was cancelled and read a motion proposing that a mixed body of 'citizens' and members should take over the functions of the Magistrat. Karl Maron, who was now chairman of the Berlin SED, also spoke after an interview with Friedensburg. The Magistrat, he declared, was unable to continue, and decisive things would happen in Berlin.

To those who had read *Neues Deutschland* that morning, his meaning was ominously clear. An SED conference the day before had decided to put through an 'Immediate Programme' with the help of the masses (since the Magistrat was no longer capable of fulfilling the needs of the population). This programme comprised a unified administration, a unified currency and a unified police force.[20]

The leaders of the SPD were fully aware of the significance of these remarks. The Magistrat was now going to be taken over by force, and it was possible at any time in the next few days that West Berlin would share the fate of Prague. A march of demonstrators, supported invisibly by Soviet troops, could have been the occasion for a putsch, which it was hopeless to resist by military means. The whole success of the airlift and the resistance of West Berlin depended on avoiding a military confrontation.* To test their readiness for a putsch, Reuter and the SPD had called a lightning demonstration that day without prior warning; and as the streets in front of the City Hall in the East filled with SED supporters, a crowd of 50,000, representing the hard core of the Social Democrats, gathered on the Platz der Republik to hear Reuter warn the communists that any attempt they might make would be opposed.[21]

These days were decisive. The Assembly did not convene that afternoon but met again the next morning. Under the leadership of a Soviet liaison officer, the demonstrators again broke the meeting up as soon as it began,[22] and Kotikov returned an openly contemptuous answer to the President, Otto Suhr's, request for police protection. Although the President refused to accept defeat and announced that the Assembly would meet again on September 3rd, it was already understood in West Berlin that this meeting would not take place.[23] There was no chance that the Assembly and Magistrat could continue to govern Berlin from the Eastern sector, and all the hard-won

* There were less than 6,000 Western, and about 18,000 Soviet troops in Berlin apart from the large Soviet units in the immediate vicinity.

victories of the last three years could now be lost in a few days. If the people of West Berlin ever had reason to tremble for their future, it was at the end of August 1948; for it was also at this point that the Moscow conferences had reached an 'interim agreement'. The four military governors were now instructed to make arrangements for introducing the East mark to the whole city, and ending the blockade. There can be no doubt that had this been allowed to happen, Berlin would have very quickly come under total Communist control. The Western delegates might have remained, but their military presence would soon have had no more significance than that of other military missions from countries which had been at war with Germany. Whether or not the Kommandatura continued to function would have been of no importance: the democratic city government had already come to a halt, and once the Soviet authorities acquired economic control, neither the population nor its political leaders would have been able to withstand Soviet pressure any longer. They were well aware of this; Neumann who had led the original resistance to the SED, now warned the West that if it agreed to introduce the East mark, it would be the beginning of the end.

The best that they could hope for would be a continuation of the blockade. It was impossible to tell as the autumn began whether the success of the airlift could continue; it still depended largely on slow C-47s with a limited cargo capacity. They were not entirely replaced by the giant American transports, which ensured an adequate daily supply, until October. The recognised daily minimum of 4,000 tons took no account of winter fuel, and double this amount was needed to maintain more than a subsistence economy.[24] It was by no means sure that the limited resources then at the disposal of the airlift could meet these demands, and as victory seemed to come in sight, the East Berlin press mounted a campaign, supported by an array of apparently credible figures, to convince the population that the operation could not go on.

It was in these circumstances that the representatives and leaders of the city fought to preserve the government and the Assembly. They needed great physical and moral courage to continue meeting in the Soviet sector at all, and could never be certain that if they did meet it would not serve as the pretext

or a putsch. As had been foreseen, they were forced to postpone the meeting of September 3rd for lack of assurances from
Kotikov. The occasion was seized by the SED to demonstrate
the existence of a 'Berlin Democratic Bloc' which met in the
City Hall, with alleged representatives from the other three
parties, and delegated a commission to negotiate a virtual take-
over with the Magistrat.[25] Otto Suhr responded with one last
attempt to preserve the unitary government of Berlin—though
it was already clear that the most that could be achieved would
be a demonstrative gesture—a refusal to let the Magistrat
yield by default and leave the way clear for a catastrophic concession by the Western Powers. The Assembly met on
September 6th—only to experience even more violent intervention from the proletarian demonstrators, who were this
time openly directed by a Russian liaison officer in collaboration
with the leaders of the SED. The Assembly was again unable
to convene, and volunteers from the West Berlin police who
had come to guard the proceedings were beaten up or arrested.
It was impossible to continue this series of grotesque and tragic
incidents, and on the same day the city was effectively split.
The Assembly met in extraordinary session in a student house*
in the British sector, to register a protest, which was more than
a formality in the state of Four-Power relations at the time, at
the sabotage of the government. The SED meanwhile continued to sit in the City Hall and voted a 'winter emergency
programme' consisting almost entirely of propaganda against
the airlift and the Magistrat.

Henceforth there were to be two German governments in
Berlin. The rest of the history of the blockade was one of growing Western confidence under the unceasing roar of the aircraft
engines over the city's three airports, and of the virtual acknowledgement of failure by the Soviet authorities. At this moment
they might still consider that they had won, and the next day,
they sealed off the City Hall to prevent the Assembly meeting
there. But as the negotiations in Berlin broke down because of
Sokolovsky's exorbitant demands for the complete control of
the city's trade and inspection of air traffic, demands to which
the apparent success of their campaign had doubtless impelled
Stalin and Molotov, Soviet objectives were abruptly changed.

* On the Steinplatz, the main residence of the Technical University.

East Berlin was now endowed with its own government, and the foundations of the East German state were laid.

The public embodiments of this change occurred very soon. After negotiations had broken down on September 7th, nineteen police volunteers (who had taken refuge with Western liaison offices in the East) were arrested as they left—in spite of a personal guarantee of safe conduct from Kotikov to General Ganeval, the French Commandant.[26] That this was a deliberate affront, intended to emphasise the new split, is apparent from *Neues Deutschland's* comments on the preceding events, which appeared not after the day of the City Hall meeting, but after the arrests. Here it was asserted that the other three parties had deliberately sabotaged the economic life of the city in order to split Germany, and present the powers with a *fait accompli* before the Moscow talks could be concluded.[27] If this report sounded like the uncomfortable echo of a change of line, it was to be noticed that in future the organ of the SED concentrated its exhortations not on the united proletarian aspirations of the people of Berlin, but on the need for building up a strong workers' state around the new capital.

In response to these events, the inhabitants of West Berlin attended a mass demonstration on the Platz der Republik. Some 350,000 people came to the biggest demonstration since the war.[28] It nearly ended in catastrophe. After listening to impassioned speeches from Reuter, Neumann and other party leaders, a section of the crowd surged to the Brandenburg Gate nearby, tore down the Soviet flag* and burned it. At this, Russian soldiers fired, killing one person and wounding others. As Russian reinforcements arrived, and East Berlin police vehicles were overturned by the crowd, there was a real danger that the incident might become a massacre—or a military clash. It is impossible to tell what results this might have had. The situation was only saved by a number of British officers and men who succeeded in separating the two sides, and inducing them to retire—the East German police with a number of prisoners.

These events marked the definitive division of Berlin. Reuter and Suhr were now determined to consolidate the government

* The Brandenburg Gate stands a few yards behind the boundary of the British and Russian sectors.

nd administration of West Berlin, and ensure its continued
ntegration with West Germany and the rapidly forming
Western alliances. Friedensburg, with lonely courage, refused
o admit that the emigration of the Assembly to the British
ector could be more than a temporary solution. He and other
members of the Magistrat continued to cross over to the City
Hall, and tried to go on working there in an effort to preserve
ts position as seat of the administration until a united government could be restored. But one by one the departments of the
Magistrat were split by Soviet action. Reuter and Klingelhöfer
were 'dismissed', other non-Communist leaders were obliged
o reconstitute their offices in the West, and at last on December
st the acting mayor of Berlin was prevented by the East
Berlin police from entering the City Hall.

This had become the seat of government in East Berlin the
day before, after an SED Congress had resolved to create a
new Assembly. The resolution was put into effect by a four-day
programme of action by the Democratic Bloc. On November
26th a women's organisation, factory representatives and other
groups met and expressed their spontaneous desire for a new
Assembly. On the 30th, the militants of the Democratic Bloc,
including representatives of all three parties in the Soviet Zone,
members of the mass-organisations and delegations from
factories in Berlin, met in an 'extraordinary session' of the City
Assembly in the Admiralspalast near Unter den Linden, while
a massive demonstration marched past outside. Here the
Democratic Bloc, consisting for the moment of 26 SED
deputies, put forward a motion for the dismissal of the Magis-
rat, and a new Magistrat was immediately unanimously
elected. Friedrich Ebert, the son of the first President of the
Weimar Republic, who had been interned in a Nazi concentra-
ion camp for a short period and had joined the SED on its
foundation, became the Oberbürgermeister of Greater Berlin;
and the other heads of department were all unanimously elected
after presentation by Hans Jendretzky, chairman of the SED and
he Democratic Bloc. All the parties in East Germany and East
Berlin* had posts in the new Magistrat, and others went to delegates of the Democratic organisations for whose representation

* Including the East Berlin SPD, which was of course banned in the rest of the
Soviet Zone.

in the Assembly and Magistrat the Soviet authorities had
striven for so long. These included the FDGB, the FDJ and
the Kulturbund.

The chairman of this City Assembly addressed a letter to the
four commandants the same day, asking for their support for
the 'newly elected' provisional Magistrat whose members
would remain in office until free, city-wide and democratic
elections were held in Berlin:* The Western Commandants
refused, calling the establishment of the new government a
flagrant violation of the constitution and all existing quadri
partite agreements; but on December 3rd the Soviet Kom
mandatura recognised 'the provisional democratic Magistrat
of Greater Berlin, elected in the extraordinary session, as the
only legal organ of the city government' and declared it would
'lend to the provisional democratic Magistrat all aid and sup
port required for exercising its functions for the welfare of the
people'.[29]

Ebert had already outlined these functions. They included
additional rations for West Berliners who supported the democratic Magistrat, and the immediate drafting of a new progres
sive constitution and new election regulations. Elections based
on these would establish a new city government. In fact the
new constitution never appeared, the need for it having been
superseded by the creation of the German Democratic Republic
in 1949. Although no official steps were taken to incorporate
East Berlin into the Democratic Republic until 1956,† no
separate elections to the government of East Berlin have ever
been held.

But some steps towards the democratic constitution were
taken in the definition of the competence of the new Magistrat
which was granted power to issue decrees and ordinances with
the force of law. Broader legislation has normally been taken
over direct from the legislation of the GDR, or more often the
resolutions of the SED are enshrined in legislation by both
governmental bodies. As an executive, the Magistrat is officially
subject to the control of the SED.[30]

* Elections were due in Berlin on December 5th, but did not qualify. See
below.

† Until then East Berlin was the seat of government of the GDR, but officially
claimed to be the capital of the whole country.

With the creation of the new Magistrat, the history of East Berlin was finally separated from that of the Western sectors.* These were already establishing their own government. The constitution of 1946 was amended to give it increased responsibility, and West Berlin has become in effect if not in name a Land of the German Federal Republic. At the same time, the legal fiction of Four-Power status has been preserved and, until 1961 at least, has enabled the Western authorities to protect the city from the encroachments of the GDR, the inhabitants to maintain personal contact with those of East Berlin, and has given the government in the West the legal right to represent the whole city.

One of the points on the Assembly's agenda for the end of August had been to fix a date for the next elections, which were soon due under the 1946 constitution. It is understandable that in view of the reverse it had suffered two years before, the SED should be anxious to gain control of the Assembly before these could be held. Failing in this purpose, they had decided to complete the division of the city government before the elections could be held. These had been set for December 5th. Friedensburg's stubborn insistence on maintaining the administration in the East Berlin City Hall, and Soviet reluctance to dismiss the elected heads of department without some pretext, almost prevented the SED from achieving this aim in time.[31] After they had established the new Magistrat, and so confined the elections to West Berlin, the SED still did all that was possible through propaganda and more or less direct sabotage to disorganise them. Apparently for the sake of doing so: there was never any suggestion that the election could influence the new situation in the city; nor could they hope to induce the West Berliners to vote for the SED, which had officially boycotted the campaign. Possibly they hoped, by inducing a high proportion of abstentions, to foster Allied doubt on whether to proceed with a unified administration of West Berlin. Certainly they hoped to intimidate the population from

---

* One judicial link between the two halves remained for a few more weeks. The *Kammergericht* or supreme court retained its seat in the East, until the President was arrested on February 4th, 1949. Thereafter the court and office of public prosecutor were transferred to the West, and People's Courts introduced into East Berlin.

voting for the clear programme of integration with the West which Reuter and the SPD had now adopted. In the circum stances of the blockade, they might still expect West Berlin t wither slowly away. A victory for the SPD would deny them any chance of taking it over in the foreseeable future.

The results put an end to all these hopes. The proportion o the electorate which voted—86 per cent—was astonishingl high, in view of the number of old and sick who had to queu in the cold, and of those who commuted to work in the Eas and were prevented from reaching the polling booths. The SPI emerged as overwhelming victors; their supporters had in creased from 51 per cent in 1946 to 65 per cent. The LDP ha also gained; the losses were borne by the CDU, whose initia reservations about currency reform, and later action in attempt ing to preserve the Magistrat in the East, were interpreted a unwillingness to withstand Soviet pressure. The elections wer welcomed throughout Germany as a victory for Berlin. Reute had emerged not only as the champion of the capital in it struggle with the Soviet Zone, but as the international spokes man for the whole nation. His re-election as Oberbürgermeiste was a foregone conclusion, but the old Assembly went througl the symbolic formality of electing him before it was dissolved He took the oath before the new in January 1949.

In the new Assembly the Social Democrats had 76 seats, o which 16 belonged to the East Berlin members whose term were renewed without election. The CDU had 26, of which equally dated from 1946.* The Christian Democrats at firs refused to join the new Magistrat. It was Reuter who insistec on a coalition, as the only possible government for Berlin; anc without it there was in fact little hope for success in the enormou tasks which it now faced. Ultimately an all-party coalition wa formed again. Friedensburg remained deputy-mayor, Otto Suh president of the Assembly.

The most urgent task for the new government was the recon struction of an efficient and reliable administration. The olc system had almost entirely broken down, first through the pre sence of Communist functionaries in every department, ther

---

* This system affirmed the City Assembly's constitutional position as the sol representative body for Berlin. The 11 SED seats of the 1946 election wer naturally left vacant.

through the vacuum left by their dismissal in the last months. The situation was complicated by the duty, which Reuter accepted, of continuing to employ large numbers of men and women who had shown the courage to resist Communist pressure in their previous positions, but who had become frankly superfluous in the reduced and divided city. Not all the leaders of the SPD agreed with this policy,[32] but he insisted successfully on maintaining it. A high proportion of these redundant civil servants were absorbed in the next months in the re-creation of departments which the division of the city had temporarily crippled—notably banking and insurance, where the Soviet threat to freeze the bank monopoly in the East had been carried out; and fuel, where such irregular supplies of electricity from the Soviet Zone as had continued were now finally cut off. Under airlift conditions new sources were gradually found in the stocks of coal which were flown in, and used to generate electricity from a large new power station which was built in the West to render it independent of Soviet action in the future.

The city government had also to deal with economic difficulties of staggering complexity. The circulation of two currencies in the city, of which one sank to a fifth of the other's value by the end of the year, had forced the Magistrat into a system of subsidies which threatened to swamp the city budget. No one could receive more than a proportion of his wages in West marks; and pensioners and landlords were paid entirely in the Eastern currency. The whole population was anxious to exchange East for West marks at the best available rates on the black market, and a rapid inflation of the first set in, while the second became increasingly dear. The Soviet authorities played a conscious part in this process, exchanging their funds for West marks at every opportunity before the city was split. And since all governmental rations were paid for in Eastern currency, which the Magistrat could not or would not afterwards exchange, it soon began in effect to feed the whole population free. There was only one solution: to have the East mark banned as legal tender altogether, and the Magistrat, under Klingelhöfer's leadership, was already pressing the Western Commandants to do so before the events of December strengthened their case. After the creation of a separate East Berlin government, there could in fact have been no further objection to adopting the West mark as the sole currency for the rest of the city. But it was precisely at this time that, on the initiative of Trygve Lie, the United Nations had set up a commission of experts to examine the whole currency question and mediate between the two sides. Nothing could be done while these deliberations were in progress, and West Berlin was still tied to a dual currency system until March 1949.[33]

It could not in any case have survived without massive external aid; but during this period the Magistrat and the Oberbürgermeister had to direct an inordinate amount of time and energy to negotiations with American and West German representatives over the modalities of aid and forms of expenditure. The monthly income of West Berlin at the time was about 70 million West marks. Almost the whole of this went on immediate expenditure or emergency programmes, such as the building of the airport at Tegel. It was supplemented by 40 million from the Bi-zone, which had imposed a special tax for the relief of Berlin, and about 50-60 million from American sources.*

With these means[34] the Berlin government had to continue its programme of reconstruction, maintain over 100,000 unemployed (the total reached 113,000 in December) and attempt to rebuild the city's industry—which could, however, scarcely gather any momentum until the new power-station was completed in the summer of 1949. Nor was it feasible to create a rational balance of exports and imports with West Germany until the blockade was ended. In fact, the city's dependence on West German aid increased during the period in spite of the growing supplies of the new gigantic airlift. (The daily amount delivered after the introduction of the C-74 Globemaster reached a record of 13,000 tons at one point, and the daily average rose from 5,000 to 6,000 tons as the winter ended.) With the end of particular construction programmes, the number of unemployed increased, and in the first half of 1949 Berlin's economic life was almost entirely passive. Only with its full incorporation in the planning of the European Recovery

* This does not include the GARIOA fund (Government Aid Relief in Occupied Areas) which the American government had established in the summer of 1948, and of which a large but variable proportion went to Berlin. A substantial amount of the direct subsidy was absorbed in airlift expenditure.

Programme and a special German measure of 'blockade assistance' in June did its production capacity show a real increase; even then private investment was slow, in spite of the release and revaluation of pre-war savings, which had since 1945 lost all their value.*

West Berlin's greatest internal difficulties had been surmounted by the end of January. Social assistance and the distribution of food were maintained with remarkable efficiency from the Rathaus Schoeneberg, the new seat of government, in the American sector; the administration of the three sectors was closely integrated in a manner that ensured the uniform authority of the Assembly and Magistrat throughout the whole city, but left enough scope for private initiative in the city's new bureaucracy' to deal with the daily emergencies of the situation.[35]

The endurance and solidarity of the population during this winter were wholly admirable, particularly as it was now universally realised that the blockade could continue for months, and that all would certainly have to survive until spring with a coal ration of 25 lb. a month for each household. It is a startling tribute to the Berliners that in temperatures which often register 30° of frost, in conditions where neighbouring families were forced to share each other's kitchens in turn to eke out the fuel, the whole population upheld the rule that only alternate trees on the streets could be cut down for firewood—on occasion against the insistence of Allied officers.†

They were fortified in their resistance by the visible success of the airlift, and the growing knowledge that the Western countries' blockade of deliveries to East Germany was seriously affecting economic life there. These counter-measures had been imposed in the summer, but were hardly effective at first. Their success was always greater in the American than in the British Zone, largely because the British military government paid undue heed to the protests of the smaller European countries at this interruption of their trade. During the autumn

---

* The contrast with the rate of recovery in West Germany was startling. Some phases of the European Recovery Programme for West Germany were 20 per cent complete by October 1948. See Davison, *op. cit.* p. 251.

† Most of the trees in the Tiergarten had either been burned in the war, or used for fuel in the winter of 1947. It was cultivated for vegetables at this time.

and winter, however, they were progressively tightened until n
important industrial supplies were allowed through. Thes
restrictions coincided with the break-through of the airlift. I
the early months it had barely succeeded in maintaining Berlin
now, in the middle of the winter, it regularly began to bring i
more supplies than had previously arrived by rail. The demon
strative success of the American and British air forces ha
begun with an audacious gesture of the French Commandant
General Ganeval. Tegel Airport, on which work had begun i
September, was completed by the beginning of December. It
effectiveness was hindered by the tower of Radio Berlin, whic
had been in Soviet hands ever since 1945, and was administere
as an enclave in the French sector. On December 16th, afte
the Soviet authorities had—understandably enough—refuse
to remove the tower, Ganeval had it blown up. It was a satisfy
ing symbol of the counter-offensive that the airlift had nov
become.*

In the early months of 1949, West Berlin was taking shap
as an independent and self-contained city. Though it depende
entirely on outside help, it had begun to construct its own ad
ministration and economic and social relief systems. One aspec
of this new independence, however, deserves a particular ac
count; it had begun entirely on the initiative of the German
themselves, before the city was divided, and its success was th
most striking witness of the new character of West Berlin: th
Free University.[36]

The idea of creating a new university in the West had bee
discussed since 1946, when the *Gleichschaltung* of the old wit
the zonal educational system was finally pushed throug
Throughout 1947 the cause had been strongly advocated b
the *Tagesspiegel*, and the SPD and CDU student organisation
had been studying ways of expanding the Technical Universit
in the British Sector into a full university. But opinion an
action among the students at this stage was confused, partl

---

* When the Soviet Commandant asked him how he could possibly do such
thing, Ganeval replied, 'With the help of dynamite and French sappers'. The con
struction of Tegel Airport had its tragic consequences. In 1945 the Sovie
military government had given the outlying village of Stolpe to the French secto
in response to a French claim for space for an airport. After December 16th th
French had no choice but to return it. Ninety-three per cent of its inhabitants ha
just voted for the three Western parties in the elections. See Davison, pp. 236-237

because a high proportion of them had been accepted as 'victims of fascism' who had been prevented from studying during the Nazi period, and had nowhere else to go. A number of these nevertheless led the opposition to the rapid 'Marxisation' of their courses, and worked for the independent student journal *Colloquium* which was licensed and published in the American sector. The moves which led to the creation of the Free University began with the introduction of an obligatory political science course, 'Introduction to a political and social understanding of the present'—which had to be successfully completed before any further studies were permitted. It was still not easy to see what action should be taken: after the purges of the student body in 1947, two-thirds of the remainder were party members. At least half of these had joined for practical reasons, but the same considerations would prevent them from joining a Western university. A rival in the West would only attract a minority of the present students, and would end all forms of opposition among the rest. For the first months of 1948, Soviet response to public opposition was still comparatively mild, largely because the contemplated blockade was then expected to succeed, and the SED continued to hope until May that it could win the city over to support their programme.

But in April the most active contributors to *Colloquium* were expelled. From that moment onward, the latent determination to found a new university became public. A mass protest meeting was held in the West—just outside the Soviet sector—and the Western Commandants, and Clay himself, were later approached with requests for assistance if a new university could be founded. Material help was eventually promised; moral support was harder to give at a time when the prime objective of German and Allied policy was to preserve the unity of Berlin. The City Assembly voted unanimously (except for the SED) that the university should be removed from the zonal administration and placed under the authority of the Magistrat. This was a purely symbolic demand—the students themselves had to take the next step. In January the Student Council* staked everything on one action. It resigned in a body. From

* Under the German university system, a Student Council has certain rights of participating in university administration.

that time it received the active support of the Allies—particularly Clay, Howley, and an American journalist, Kendall Foss—and of a German committee headed by Reuter and one Professor, Edwin Redslob. On July 24th, a public appeal was launched 'in the spirit of independence with which the city rose against the blockade'. The new university was to be the spiritual centre of free Berlin, and so serve the recovery of Germany.

It was not an exaggeration to say that it served this end. For the first time, the German intellectuals who had been thrust out of public affairs since 'the German catastrophe' of 1933, found a new focus of intellectual and political activity. Friedrich Meinecke, perhaps the greatest historian of the twentieth century, became the first Rector of the new university, and the links between the university and the city government have always been peculiarly close—perhaps because it is freer than any other university in Germany from official control or financial pressure. West Berlin is often called a city without a centre, since the whole historical complex of the old city lies in the Soviet sector. But it is West Berlin that has developed a rich and energetic cultural life which is intimately bound up with its political determination, and the university has played a great part in preserving this sense of purpose. It is East Berlin that has no centre.

When the first lectures began in November, students had already been improvising their education for months, beginning with two rooms and the books they had brought with them. For a whole year the university depended entirely on American financial support. But if any event marks the point where a new and independent city was created out of the Western sectors, it was the opening ceremony of the Free University.

From the turn of the year it was apparent that the blockade could not endure much longer. The West had already won the battle, and the result could not be reversed without war. After negotiations were broken off in September, contacts between the two sides had been maintained; but these never amounted to more than a restatement of their positions. When the matter was laid before the United Nations, time was already working in favour of the West—and the protracted debate at Lake Success probably did more to lengthen the blockade than any residual Soviet optimism. In spite of buzzing and artillery practice in the air-corridors, stocks in Berlin were increasing daily.* At the end of January Stalin hinted to a Western journalist that the currency question was no longer an obstacle to negotiating the end of the blockade. Six weeks later Malik confirmed this in conversation at the UN, and negotiations were thenceforth conducted largely by confidential talks, first between the American and Russian representatives there, and then between those of all four powers. In effect, the Soviet Union offered to lift the blockade if the whole German question could be discussed by the Council of Foreign Ministers, thus abandoning the whole policy Molotov had represented until the end of 1947. Although the blockade had been conducted with unremitting severity throughout this period, and the East Berlin government had followed an unhappy course between imposing new restrictions on its own subjects and attempting to win over the West Berliners,† rumours began to circulate in the West that negotiations were now nearing a successful conclusion. To those who followed fluctuations in the SED line, this seemed to be confirmed by the behaviour of the East German press which, in keeping with that of all the Cominform countries, was now engaged in a massive peace campaign.

All the misgivings that had been felt in Berlin at the mention of negotiations throughout the months of the blockade had now been dispelled. In part this was due to Reuter's triumphant tour of the Western capitals in the new year, and to Attlee's visit to Berlin in March—when he was able to witness a constant stream of aircraft landing at Tempelhof. But the chief ground for confidence lay in the second currency reform. It may be significant that the West did not take this step until Malik had let Jessup know that Stalin no longer attached importance to the currency question. In West Berlin, however, this represented economic salvation. The order of March 21st which

* Exports by airlift were also showing a marked increase. Their value rose from half-a-million marks in January to over one million in March.

† As well as making many attempts to assert its authority over the whole of Berlin. Apart from posters and offices erected in the West by the Eastern Magistrat, factory inspectors were occasionally sent over as a gesture. At one point, the East Berlin press even announced a mass-meeting in the Western borough of Kreuzberg, to elect a new mayor there. Police precautions prevented this, but raids and kidnappings still occurred. See Davison, *op. cit.* pp. 258-259.

recognised the West mark as the only legal tender in the city, finally assured its future. It could no longer be subjected to the economic pressure of the Soviet Zone, and its effective integration with West Germany was now secure. More, it represented a political guarantee in perpetuity—and the Russian announcement a few days later that Marshal Sokolovsky would return to the Soviet Union looked like an admission of complete defeat.

A month later negotiations between the Four Powers were publicly made known, and on May 5th simultaneous statements in the four capitals announced that the blockade would be ended on both sides on the 12th. The airlift had already achieved its record success. On April 16th almost 1,400 aircraft landed in Berlin. The average daily deliveries at the time were well over 8,000 tons, including more than 5,000 tons of coal. These achievements were to be maintained and even increased in the next two months, until stocks were high enough to prevent any emergency arising from a sudden renewal of the blockade. In the end about 2·3 million tons were delivered to Berlin by air. The United States Air Force accomplished two-thirds of this enormous operation, the RAF the rest. Seventy-nine British, American and German pilots and groundsmen lost their lives in defeating the blockade.

The barriers over the land routes were lifted at midnight on May 11th. West Berlin celebrated the end of the blockade in a special session of the City Assembly, in the presence of the Western military governors and West German representatives. According to the Four-Power agreement, the Council of Foreign Ministers was to discuss the whole German question in a few days. But the Western victory was already won. There could be no further question of driving the Western Powers from their position in Germany by pressure on Berlin.

'Without the bold initiative and admirable devotion,' said Reuter, 'of all those who created the airlift, and co-operated in its development, Berlin could not have withstood the pressure; it would have disappeared in the Soviet Zone. The consequences for the whole world would have been incalculable. . . .'

Chapter Six

THE CITY AND THE WORLD:
ERNST REUTER

On the day that the Russians lifted the blockade of Berlin, the draft of the Federal German constitution was completed. The blockade had hastened by years the development of West Germany to a point where it could again become an independent state, and had ensured that its future would be intimately linked with that of West Berlin. It was not an easy condition and was sometimes regretted by politicians of both sides; but in a divided Germany each needed the other to fulfil its national rôle. If Berlin depended for its survival on the material assistance of the Federal Republic, it was also the custodian of the national future. Bonn without Berlin, as the very choice of this market-town capital implied, would have been nothing but the administrative headquarters of a European province, subject to the control of its powerful allies until the national identity could be restored. If West Germany has become a leading political force in the West, this is not due merely to her economic strength (the control of which could quite well have remained in the hands of an international consortium) nor to her military potential, which remained a potential throughout the 1950's and is entirely subject to supranational control. It was because the Western Powers were permanently committed to upholding West Berlin, and because Berlin, according to the faith of the whole Alliance as well as the belief of the Germans, would again become the capital of Germany.

The outline of the future was already discernible before the blockade was lifted. On April 4th, 1949, the North Atlantic Treaty was signed. This was a new development in American policy. Hitherto the United States had consciously maintained a distinction between its two main overseas commitments, the European Recovery Programme, and the Mutual Defence Assistance Programme, so that she need not become automatically committed to European conflicts. But when she accepted a Canadian proposal that all parties to the North Altantic Treaty should consider an attack on one of their number as an attack on themselves, she had in effect decided to amalgamate the two policies into a comprehensive system of European security, involving her full participation in a peace-time military alliance.

The Mutual Defence Assistance Programme had already been undertaken in 1948 under the stimulus of the blockade. 'This was the summer of 1948,' wrote Truman.[1] 'Berlin was blockaded, and it was not yet at all certain that the airlift would succeed . . . the main purpose of this aid proposal was to make sure that we did not have another tragic instance of "too little and too late"—the kind of thing that had helped Hitler subjugate Europe.' With the creation of NATO, the scope of the programme was greatly extended. The United States, Canada and the Brussels Treaty countries now decided to build a balanced force for their common defence. And they were well aware that this would be impossible without German participation. Not only the United States, but also Britain was from the start anxious to rebuild Germany as soon as possible, and Bevin was convinced that this could only be done through an Atlantic security system.[2] If the French leaders were reluctant to commit themselves, it was largely because they foresaw no effective means at the time to ensure that German forces would remain under international control.

Without the blockade, it is doubtful whether the leaders of West Germany would have finally consented to this degree of identification with Western policies. The London Recommendations were not popular in Germany[3] and the strongest advocate of the creation of a West German state in the summer of 1948 was not Adenauer but Reuter, who travelled repeatedly to the meetings of the *Länderrat* and Parliamentary Council to urge this course upon the prime ministers of the eleven states that had been created by the military governors. He had had few supporters at the time: only Carlo Schmid, the foremost constitutional lawyer and political scientist in the SPD, worked as consistently as he did for unanimous acceptance of the Western plans. The common attitude was to demand full sovereignty or refuse all co-operation. In some respects this was understandable. Both American and French interventions in the

constitutional debates of the time were deeply resented, and
none more so than the attempt to secure the financial autonomy
of the individual states from the Federal government.[4] This ran
counter to the political and economic policies of the CDU and
the social philosophy of the SPD, and was a barely-concealed
attempt to assure the permanent weakness of the future state.
But the German response to this intervention was often short-
sighted and unduly intransigeant. It was only as the success of
the airlift was demonstrated, and as the defence programmes of
the Western Powers took shape, that the attitude in the newly-
established provisional capital in Bonn changed. Nor were the
Western leaders at first convinced of the need for rapidly
establishing the West German state. They only decided to take
the ultimate step when the North Atlantic Treaty was signed,
and the end of the blockade was in sight. Immediately after
signing the treaty, the three Western Foreign Ministers agreed
at a meeting in Washington to the principles of unification of
the three Western Zones, and the text of a modified occupation
statute. On April 14th the military governors handed these to a
delegation from Bonn with a pressing request for a speedy conclusion to the labours of the Parliamentary Council.[5] Resistance flared in the SPD at the last minute; but Reuter's
mediation was more effective with the Parliamentary Council
than Schumacher's denunciation. The constitution was completed by the time that the blockade came to an end.

Thus, three separate developments had decided the future
of Germany in the early months of 1949. The emergence of
West Berlin; the rise of a West German state; and the creation
of NATO. None could have succeeded without the others, and
Reuter's rôle in these events was greater than that of any other
German statesman. He had become not only the foremost
representative of Berlin, but the most forceful exponent of the
new Germany's integration with the West. At the beginning
of its existence, the voice of Germany was not Adenauer's but
Reuter's; and while he headed the government of Berlin his
words carried to the city and the world.

This new era for Berlin began with the NATO treaty, just
as the years of resistance had been ended by the currency
reform. Article 6 of the treaty defined armed attack on the con-
tracting parties to include any attack on their occupation forces

I   129

in Europe, while Article 5, the kernel of the agreement, embodied the Canadian proposal that an attack on one should be regarded as an attack upon all. Berlin was thus undoubtedly covered by the provisions of NATO: 'a definitive recognition of the fact', declared Reuter, 'that we here in Berlin are a part of the West, regarded as such, treated as such and esteemed as such'.[6] The Western Foreign Ministers, meeting in New York, had confirmed the declaration by sending symbolic contingents of tanks to Berlin to emphasise that any attacks there would begin a general war. Their purpose was fulfilled in 1961.

At the same time as the Western Alliance was formed, the Soviet government abandoned its expansionist strategy in Europe. Zhdanov was sacked, and his place was taken by his old rival Malenkov. The Four-Power Paris Conference, which followed the end of the blockade, began, as promised, with a discussion of German reunification. But when Vishinsky demanded a 'return to Potsdam', and a dismantling of the structure of the West German state without renouncing the corresponding creation in the Soviet Zone, both sides soon reached a tacit agreement to let the conference 'fail', and in effect to put the division of Germany on ice. The Soviet Union would not renew her threat to Berlin, the West would not press for German reunification. The energies of the Soviet Union were now concentrated on advancing from post-war reconstruction to a new phase of industrial development, and on consolidating its Eastern European empire. Henceforth, the Cold War conferred an uneasy stability on Europe, while the new victories of Communism were sought in the Far East, in China and Korea. Berlin no longer had to fear direct Soviet pressure; but it was faced with a new problem in East Germany. Shortly after the new constitution was promulgated in Bonn, the German Democratic Republic was proclaimed from Pankow. The task of the West Berlin government was now to maintain its close relations with West Germany without promoting a crisis in East Berlin; just as in a wider sphere it had to preserve its special relations with the Western Allies without compromising the diplomacy of Bonn. These interlocking problems occupied the last years of Reuter's life, and dominated the history of Berlin until 1953.

There were many difficulties. They might perhaps have been

reater if Schumacher had come to power in the general elections which followed the promulgation of the new German
onstitution. The leader of the SPD had spent twelve years in
oncentration camps and was already a sick and crippled man
n 1949. For these reasons, perhaps, he was an outspoken and
mpatient patriot, his national feelings not attenuated by any
ersonal sense of guilt, his anxiety to see Germany reunified
mbittered by distrust of his political opponents.* Adenauer,
vhom, in a famous apostrophe, he accused of being the
Chancellor of the Allies', did not share his views. He was con-
erned above all to re-establish one German state, and had little
ope that its independence could be extended to the Soviet
Zone in the foreseeable future. For this reason he now worked
vholeheartedly for Germany's full identification with Western
Europe and the Atlantic Alliance, and was as desirous as
Schumacher was reluctant to foster the revival of a German
rmy within this framework.

Schumacher's accusation could just as well have been
evelled at the Prefect of Berlin, as he sarcastically called
Reuter. Their differences were equally fundamental, arising
rom opposite analyses of the blockade. Schumacher was all
long convinced that it represented a Russian plot to ensure
he definitive division of Germany—and its outcome naturally
eemed to prove him right. But Reuter had realised much more
learly that it was originally intended to secure the ultimate
onquest of the whole country, and concluded from the outset
hat the only salvation lay in alliance with the West. It was
natural for him to greet the Atlantic Treaty on the day of its
publication with the hope that the common determination of
he Western nations could lead to a change of Russian policy,
and eventually bring about a true international co-operation
n constructive work.[7]

Thus Adenauer and Reuter were agreed on essentials and
vere prepared, after the former's narrow election as Chancellor, to work together for German sovereignty within the
Western Alliance. But there were many obstacles to such col-
aboration, which arose from more fundamental causes than

* Alfred Grosser interprets Schumacher's attitude as a form of 'preventive
nationalism', designed to forestall a return to the temper of the early Weimar
Republic. See *L'Allemagne de l'Occident*, p. 255.

their political differences. The greatest lay in the legal position of Berlin. Since December 1946 a committee of the City Assembly had been working on a new constitution for th capital. It completed its work early in 1948, and it had seemed for a while that agreement could be reached among the fou parties;* but the SED finally rejected it, and the discussion in the Kommandatura, which broke down first over the aboli tion of Article 36,† were abruptly terminated by the Sovie walk-out. After the division of the city, the new Assembly had again submitted the proposed constitution to the tripartit Kommandatura, but no action was taken on it until Octobe 1949, in the hope that a Four-Power administration migh eventually be re-established. All that the city gained in th interim was a new occupation statute, permitting a greate latitude of control over its own affairs, and the acknowledged right, after the adoption of the West German constitution, t send non-voting delegates to the Bundestag to participate in co ordinating the development of West Berlin with that of Wes Germany.[8]

This right, however, was the beginning of the city's sub sequent difficulties. The Assembly and the Allies would soor have to choose between Berlin's incorporation into the Federa Republic as a twelfth Land, or preserving the legal fiction of it Four-Power status. Reuter firmly favoured the first course and was supported in the SPD press,[9] but the whole security of the city depended on the preservation of the Four-Power status East Berlin had not yet become the legal capital of the GDR, and a unilateral violation of the war-time agreement would have left the Allies in an indefensible position, legally as well as militarily. The majority of the Assembly were aware of the danger of too close or sudden a policy of integration, and though they took steps in October 1949 to co-ordinate the proposed constitution with the Basic Law,‡ they delayed for almost a year before declaring the identity of the two. First, a further attempt was made to hold new elections throughout the city. When this was rejected by the Soviet Commandant, the Assembly adopted a revised draft of the 1948 constitution and forwarded it to the Commandants for approval. Berlin was now

---

* This was in April. See above, p. 100. † See above, p. 79.
  ‡ I.e. the West German constitution.

leclared a West German Land—though only in principle; in
he interim period the constitution and other laws of the
Federal Republic were considered binding on the city. But
either the Kommandatura nor the Allied High Commis-
ioners in Germany accepted these provisions. They could not
olerate any such infringement of the Four-Power status, and
aid down instead that any Federal Law could only apply to
Berlin after it had been passed again in the City Assembly.*
This is still Berlin's constitutional postion today—though the
machinery for the adoption of Federal laws has been stream-
ined to a point where it is almost automatic. For practical purposes it has become a German Land; but its legal position is
till that of an occupied territory. Nor are Berliners officially
German citizens, though they acquire citizenship immediately
hey settle in Germany. This situation has had odd consequences. A prominent Berliner, son of one of the leading statesmen of the Weimar Republic, who became an American
citizen during the War, has been living for years in his native
city. Threatened with the loss of his nationality for returning
o his country of origin, he was able to defend himself successfully on the grounds that Berlin does not form part of Germany.

The maintenance of the city depends, in fact, on upholding
an ambiguous position. On one hand its political and economic
survival depends on the closest possible integration into West
Germany. On the other its ultimate security can only be assured
by the protection of the Western Allies—acting not on the
basis of the NATO treaty (whose provisions they would undoubtedly invoke to demonstrate that any attack on Berlin
would lead to general war), but on that of war-time agreements
with their Russian partners which alone established the Four-
Power status and their right of armed presence in Berlin. If the
difficulties of this situation account for the apparent immobility
of the West when confronted with subsequent crises, they also
led at the time to immediate conflict between Berlin and Bonn.

There was a certain disposition in the new German government to regard Berlin as a purely Allied concern, and to cultivate an attitude of careless indifference towards the new
state that had been created in half a city. There were strong

* Known after the adoption of the new constitution as the House of Representatives. The Magistrat then became the Senat.

diplomatic reasons for this: Adenauer undoubtedly desired to emphasise that German reunification was a task for the Four Powers. He did not wish to condone or deepen the division of Germany by too close an association with one section of its former and future capital. His immediate desire was to build up West Germany's economic (and, as soon became evident, military) strength to a point where she could become an equal member of the Western Alliance, and impose her own terms for a European settlement. The essential was to ensure that reunification would not be bought at the price of an American withdrawal, or before West Germany had been able to construct her own defences. His diplomacy, whose long-term consistency enabled him to seize unexpected chances whenever they occurred, can best be likened to that of Cavour. And at times he seems to have suspected Reuter of a Garibaldian impetuosity, although their fundamental approach remained the same. There can be no doubt that in a sense he was right: Reuter's insistence on the identification of West Berlin with West Germany was damaging to the eventual attainment of Germany unity.

But while this diagnosis underlay Adenauer's sarcastic reply to Reuter's message of congratulation on his election to the chancellorship (it was at present, he declared, a more urgent task to ensure the stability of the currency than work for reunification[10]) it does not fully account for the open negligence, almost contempt, with which Berlin was treated by the first Bonn government. Possibly, the maintenance of the Four-Power status, and the Berlin leaders' consequent right of direct access to the Allied authorities were felt as a challenge and an obstacle to the central government's function of representing the nation to the Western Powers. Possibly too, it was felt that the prolongation of a direct occupation status in that city which the Bundestag had just acknowledged to be the only true capital of Germany implied certain Allied obligations which the German government was not required to share. Certainly, a coalition dominated by the Socialists in Berlin was an unwelcome object of expenditure for the *Soziale Marktwirtschaft** policies of the CDU coalition in Bonn.

* 'Social free economy', Professor Erhard's economic policy of directing a free economic system to include social benefits without imposing rigid controls.

At all events, West Germany seemed for a time to go back on its earlier commitment of economic support for Berlin, at one moment suggesting that the city should after all adopt a special currency, at another, informing the Magistrat that all Marshall Aid funds for 1949-50 had already been allocated and could not be redistributed.[11] The Berlin government found more open understanding and less equivocal support from Howley, Ganeval and the new British Commandant General Bourne, than it received from Adenauer or Erhard. The British High Commissioner, Sir Brian Robertson, is reported to have warned the German government that he would not tolerate being forced to justify 'an insufficient engagement of Bonn for Berlin'.[12] This attitude may also have lain behind the American decision to withdraw direct GARIOA aid to Berlin, and so force the German cabinet to more incisive support. This certainly caused greater unemployment in Berlin (the number rose to 279,000 during 1949), but it also played a part in inducing the Bundestag to place aid to Berlin on a more permanent footing than the blockade assistance programme of 1949. Early in 1950, the city was declared an 'emergency area'* of the Federal Republic, and aid of about 60 million marks a month continued to flow in.

At the same time, the Allied High Commissioners agreed (at last) to end all dismantling in Berlin. Though this had by now become more of a threat than an operation, it had prevented the resumption of production in the heavy industrial plants. It was not until April 1950 that steel began to flow again in the Siemens works, and the highest post-war unemployment figures (306,000 in February) were passed.

If the city's economic problems were aggravated at first by the difficulties of its relationship to Bonn, they were also fostered by the government of East Berlin. A symptom of these troubles was the strike of the city railway workers immediately after the end of the blockade. The employees of the Eastern *Deutsche Reichsbahn* which ran the railway were paid in East marks. Those who lived in West Berlin struck to secure payment in the new exclusive Western currency. The situation was complicated by the refusal of the Eastern authorities to negotiate with UGO, by the impossibility of direct contact

* *Notstandsgebiet.*

between the Magistrats in East and West, and by the fac
that Howley was basically not sorry to observe the propagand
effects of workers' strikes against a Communist government
At one stage the *Volkspolizei* occupied the railways in Wes
Berlin to protect Eastern strike-breakers against the Western
population—an action for which there was some justification
in the temper of the people. When these were relieved b
Western police after American-Soviet negotiations, the Eastern
Magistrat imposed a form of intra-city blockade, which pre
vented travel to the Soviet sector, and imports of fresh food
from the Soviet Zone, which had just begun again. The whole
episode, which lasted several weeks, revealed how vulnerable
West Berlin could be to pressure from the German Communis
government, even without any Soviet intervention. It was
finally settled by an agreement that the Western workmen
should receive 60 per cent of their wages in West marks, which
were to be financed by the payment of fares in the same cur
rency throughout West Berlin. The Magistrat was to change
a further proportion at 1 : 1. This system prevailed until 1961
it illustrated in itself the financial burdens West Berlin had to
shoulder in a city through which two currencies continued to
circulate.

When a food crisis in the new German Democratic Republic
supervened in this situation, the economic prospects of Berlin
appeared darker than ever—and reinforced the reluctance in
Bonn to 'throw good money after bad'. To the constantly
rising number of unemployed was now added a flow of refugees
from the Soviet Zone. Over 17,000 came over between September and December 1949.[12] The total shrank during the
winter months, but increased again in spring, as a new State
Security Service* began to work in the GDR, and the non-
Communist parties were purged in preparation for the forthcoming People's Chamber elections. In 1950 over 60,000
people crossed into Berlin. The city government was responsible for their maintenance until they could be flown to West
Germany, and in the first year they might have to wait for
months until the overstrained social services and rigorous employment policy of the German economy could cope with them.
(Later a definite quota system was established, whereby each

* SSD: *Staatssicherheitsdienst.*

state guaranteed to take a fixed proportion of refugees. Berlin then retained about 20 per cent of those who registered there—something less than 10 per cent of the total.*)

Thus, though Berlin was just beginning to enjoy the miraculous appearance of prosperity which had followed overnight upon currency reform in the West, the city government still had exceptional burdens to bear. If they were shouldered by American or German organisations, this still meant a diversion of capital from the industrial reconstruction in which the city lagged conspicuously behind the Federal Republic. Until 1953 it was hard to believe that a viable economy could ever be restored, and long-term investments, which were its sorest need, were frightened off by political and economic uncertainty.

The most tragic aspect of this uncertainty from the Berlin viewpoint lay in its political effects. It is hard today to realise how openly and completely the political life of the Federal Republic was dominated in these years by economic considerations. All the disasters of German history since the First World War were attributed directly or indirectly to economic factors. If democracy in Germany were going to survive now, it had to be assured first on the economic plane. More, Adenauer's primary concern with foreign policy could only be pursued on the basis of a sound economic structure at home. For these reasons the government had from the beginning, rejected the possibility of a coalition with the SPD, whose social philosophy it regarded as a dangerous luxury† which could reduce Erhard's carefully balanced economic programme to incoherence.

The government in Berlin, on the other hand, was dominated by political considerations. It was already an all-party coalition, and felt it was essential that the central government should also have a broad 'national' basis. Equally, Reuter was convinced that Berlin should be reconstructed as a full component of the Federal Republic and focus of national unity as quickly as possible. Only if this were first achieved could there be any hope for a change of Soviet policy in the Eastern Zone. As long as Berlin remained economically unstable, and its political

* This is only an estimated average. Naturally it varied widely from year to year.

† The Düsseldorf Programme of the CDU, presented before the elections, had been violently attacked by the SPD on social grounds.

destiny uncertain, Ulbricht's government could hope to gain eventual control over the whole city. Thus he desired a full economic engagement as the basis of a political coalition in Bonn—in which it was no secret that he wished to become Foreign Minister. He needed a rapid economic programme to realise long-term national aims, and was bitterly disappointed at the grudging attitude displayed in Bonn.

While these conditions lasted, Berlin's rôle was reduced to a form of defensive coexistence with the East German régime, while its differences with the central government were increasingly accentuated. The divergence was common not only to the SPD, but to the Berlin coalition in general: one of the most pronounced critics of the CDU was Friedensburg. And Reuter differed as sharply from the policies of national SPD as he did from those of Adenauer. Carlo Schmid had summed up the party's position in the Bundestag's first foreign policy debate. The SPD, he declared, was as anxious to create a united Europe as the government: 'but not a Europe of the Holy Alliance, nor the Europe of a joint-stock company, but an authentic Commonwealth, a Federal European state. . . . This Europe can only be the whole of Europe, and not a little Europe; for a little Europe could be nothing but an American bridgehead, or a temptation to the East.'[13] In other words, Western integration would have to wait upon a Russian withdrawal from the East—for which the essential condition was German reunification. But while working towards this aim, he insisted that Berlin should be treated as the twelfth Land, whatever the juridical position of the Allies.

This was the fatal flaw in the SPD's position: it was impossible to absorb Berlin into the Federal Republic without accentuating the division of Germany, at least in the short run. Yet the party had no choice but to support the government in Berlin, even including Reuter's demands for full Land status. Notwithstanding these contradictions, they continued to attack German participation in the Schuman Plan, as aggravating the division of the country in the interests of a 'Christian Democratic Europe', and were still more violently opposed to German rearmament, as destructive of the last chances of reunification.

Reuter was more logical. When Adenauer visited Berlin in

April 1950 he reproached him as openly as he dared for his reserved and hesitant attitude to the city, and though he was anxious that his words should not be interpreted abroad as evidence of a squabble between Berlin and Bonn, he privately accused the Chancellor of obstructing the integration of the city with the rest of the country.[14] But at the same time he was anxious to pursue Germany's integration into Western Europe as far as possible, and in particular to bring about a permanent partnership between Germany and France. In this he stood opposed to his own party, but regarded Western European unity as the only method of inducing a change in the Soviet attitude or of promoting international co-operation throughout Europe. He insisted in public speeches and private conversation that European unity could only be brought about on this basis, and that Berlin was the point of departure for the whole journey. Beyond this, however, he seldom formulated his ideas. Though his correspondence and his international visits won him a numerous and influential audience—particularly on his journeys to the United States—he seems to have confined himself to stressing the natural unity of the whole of Europe and the vital importance of Berlin at its heart. For this reason he welcomed the Schuman Plan, but attacked the 'Western Europe' idealism which informed it in France. 'Germany,' he remarked in an article criticising the French High Commissioner, François-Poncet, for this attitude, 'will never be healthy or recover her basic balance until Berlin is truly recognised as a part of Germany, and until it is realised that Berlin is the gate to reunification with East Germany, momentarily suffering under a foreign yoke. There can be no security in the West alone! There can be no security for France without the restoration of a free and united Germany.'[15]

His approach to German rearmament was more complex. Adenauer's secret memorandum to the Western Powers after the outbreak of the Korean War, which offered a German contribution to the defence of the West, in case such a situation occurred in Europe, was warmly welcomed in America. In September the North Atlantic Council, meeting in New York, made mention for the first time of an eventual German army within the framework of a European defence system—the forerunner of EDC. The Berlin SPD had already been discussing this idea, and in contrast to Schumacher, favoured rearmament on these terms. 'Since the nations in the Atlantic Pact are protecting West German territory from aggression,' wrote the *Telegraf*,[16] 'the Germans must make their contribution to defence.' But, it warned, this could only come about within a European framework. Otherwise the officers of West Germany would join hands with their old comrades in the *Volkspolizei* to subject the nation again! Reuter was concerned with a different danger: the growing tendency towards neutralism in the SPD. A few weeks earlier he had declared himself against rearmament—'but not because we are neutral, or because we afterwards want to play the supreme arbitrators between Stalin and Truman.'[17] But he soon changed his mind, partly because precisely this form of neutralism lurked behind part of the opposition of the SPD,* partly because of a long interview with the American High Commissioner John C. McCloy† (perhaps the only man in Germany who had the full confidence both of Adenauer and Reuter). While still opposed to any idea of a national German army, he came out in favour of a German contribution to a unified Western army, with a unified General Staff

This was one of the possible forms of German rearmament which was being discussed in this period. In October it was broadened into the Pleven Plan for a European Defence Community. But the British and American governments feared that it would delay German rearmament,[18] and soon began parallel discussions in Bonn to explore the possibilities of a direct German contribution to NATO. Though these failed, it was by no means clear before July 1951 what the nature of German rearmament would be. As the delays increased, the debate in Germany became more intense (the issue was even brought before the constitutional Court at Karlsruhe, because the SPD claimed that it conflicted with the Basic Law). The position of those in the SPD who supported rearmament was more and more embarrassing, the more so as there was a certain revival of right-wing nationalist activity at the time, and it was felt that all democratic forces should unite to resist the dangers of renewed militarism.‡ Reuter skilfully defended his position by

---

* Though certainly not Schumacher's.   † Clay had left Germany in 1949.

‡ Feelings, and suspicions, ran high over this in Germany as elsewhere. I have been told of one occasion in Berlin where a number of German agents of the

appealing to the Social Democrat demand for 'equal rights' for Germany in the Western Alliance. 'In Berlin', he told an SPD meeting, 'we have equal rights, in Berlin we are allies, and the others are our allies . . . we have daily made a practical contribution' to our defence.[19] But these arguments cut no ice, as long as it was known that NATO had no intention of defending German territory in case of conflict. The NATO 'forward strategy' was only adopted after Schumacher's death, and he was able to concentrate his demands on a stronger NATO commitment to Germany, without which he refused to countenance a German contribution.

Obviously, the second was a condition of the first. In 1950 NATO had 14 divisions with which to oppose about 175 on the Soviet side. Schumacher shrugged off the weaknesses of his argument by refusing to give any figure of what he thought American strength should be before he could support German rearmament. Nevertheless, his views prevailed in the SPD so long as EDC was not ratified. There was always a deep, though usually submerged, conflict between the national party and the Berlin SPD on this matter. But at the end of 1950 Berlin found itself in a critical position. The leader of its government was known to be deeply dissatisfied with the support it received from Bonn; there was a marked divergence in the views of all the party leaders in the two 'capitals' (if Reuter was something of an anti-pope to Adenauer, Jakob Kaiser, who was now Minister of All-German Affairs, was regarded as a heretic by the Berlin CDU for his support of the official government policy); Reuter himself was torn between his loyalty to the Western Allies and his solidarity with the SPD; and the economic situation was only just beginning to improve. The Western Alliance was still desperately weak on the continent of Europe, and while there was little expectation that war would break out there, the Berliners had good reason to fear that the East German government would take advantage of any opportunity it had to seize control over the rest of the city.

It had already demonstrated its intention at Whitsun that

American, British and French military governments, and of the Berlin police, met in a *Bierkeller* to hold a reunion, each under the impression that the rest were Nazis. But there was a real danger of a swing to strident nationalism, particularly of course, in the Saar.

year, when a mass rally of the FDJ was held in Berlin. Thousands of young men and women were sent to the Western sectors to create disturbances wherever possible—presumably to give the *Volkspolizei* a chance to intervene. This experiment backfired: the food crisis in East Germany was at its height, and the Berliners had the spectacle of the blue uniforms in long queues before Allied soup-kitchens. But on occasion the police had had to turn hoses on motorised squads, and mount strong guards on the sector boundaries. The possibility of new disturbances remained.

To set against this, Reuter had had one success. Though he was further from his aim of seeing Berlin become a full Land than he had been at the beginning of the year, the practical incorporation of the city into the legal and financial structure of the Federal Republic had made important advances. At the beginning of the year the Federal Republic had designated a plenipotentiary in Berlin. At the time this seemed to emphasise the division between the two; but as the year progressed it proved to be the prelude to a closer co-ordination of their policies. A *Bundeshaus* was established in Berlin to co-ordinate action in governmental departments;* the administration of justice and the courts was unified; Berlin sent delegates to the Bundestag, and though they did not vote, they had the right to speak, and work in committees. Like the other Länder, it also sent delegates to the upper house, the Bundesrat. Finally, Reuter succeeded in inducing Erhard to grant Berlin a subsidy of 550 million marks to undertake industrial reconstruction. This was largely the result of the Federal Court of Audit's examination of the Berlin budget: at least it demonstrated that the money was not wasted, and that bigger immediate grants were needed to avoid unnecessary expenditure in future. With this, the number of unemployed began very slowly to fall, though at the end of the year it was still over 286,000, or more than 25 per cent of the labour force.

It was this record which the population had to judge when the first elections under the new constitution were held in December. The issues were confusing. The voters were choosing between different members of a coalition that was almost certain

* It has now the more symbolic purpose of housing actual departments of the Federal administration.

o continue, and Reuter, though he did not lead the SPD as a party to the polls, was bound to remain *Regierender Bürgermeister*.* The voters essentially had to judge two matters: the national policies of the opposing parties, and the relations between Berlin and West Germany. On both counts the CDU made significant gains; and the FDP† nearly doubled its seats. This was clearly a vote for the Bonn coalition of the two parties. The SPD, though still the biggest single party, was now in a minority, with 61 seats out of 127. Yet there is no evidence that Reuter's personal popularity had decreased. The result could in a sense be interpreted as a vote for him and against his party, for it was the SPD which against all evidence was regarded as lacking in national spirit. There was, however, a certain justice in it: it was also a vote for the Allies, and for the German Government's 'Western' orientation—influenced perhaps by the consideration that the CDU might have a greater success in integrating Berlin with the rest of the country.

Whatever the motives of the voters, they enormously complicated the task of the new Senate. In the first place, the local issues which had been raised in the campaign now made it almost impossible to agree on the composition of the government, so that at one point Reuter considered the possibility of resigning and leading the SPD in a loyal opposition. But not only did the mass of voters and even the newspapers of other parties[20] declare that this was out of the question; the leaders of the FDP and CDU openly favoured a continuation of the big coalition'. Nevertheless, it seemed impossible to agree either on local issues, or on the election of a mayor for both Reuter and Schreiber, the leader of the CDU, received 62 votes when the House of Representatives met. In the end, they agreed between themselves to continue the coalition, with Reuter as mayor and Schreiber as his deputy.

That they succeeded in spite of deep differences over educational, social and administrative questions is a tribute both to

* His new title since the 1950 constitution came into force. It signified the change from a municipal government (where he had been Lord Mayor) to what was in effect the government of a semi-autonomous state where he was now Prime Minister.

† The LDP, too, had changed its name, in an attempt to emphasise its independence rather than its continuity: FDP—Free Democratic Party.

their political agility and their sense of the situation. Above all it was a sign of the position which Reuter had conquered: it was not easy to win the co-operation of the CDU in expanding social services further than was done by the government in Bonn,* nor to restrain the SPD from demanding more. But in every Senate crisis, of which the papers for the next two years were carrying monotonously frequent reports, it was clear that Reuter was considered indispensable. Primarily, this was because he above all represented Berlin abroad; and in America at least was the unrivalled spokesman for the whole country. But it was also true that no one else could hold such an evenly balanced coalition together.

In fact, this situation meant that Reuter was exposed to increasing criticism from his own party. Too often a controversial question in the Senate would be resolved by a personal vote of confidence in the Ruling Mayor which failed to produce agreement on policy, angered the SPD and embarrassed Reuter himself. In April 1952 he demanded a vote on the maintenance of the coalition: all parties split to provide it with a narrow majority. But the occasion brought the internal crisis of the SPD to a head. Neumann now led those who accused him of continuously giving way to his coalition partners and of using his external importance to cover his internal weaknesses. When the matter came to a vote, he won again, but by a small majority. This was also the first occasion on which he put his young collaborator, Willy Brandt, forward as his political heir. Brandt, at the age of thirty-nine, already secured a third of the votes for chairman of the party and thereafter he and Neumann were to be the chief contenders for the leadership. Reuter's victory was partly due to the unwavering support he received from Schumacher. Whatever the differences between the two, Schumacher had complete trust in him as leader of Berlin, and never failed to plead the cause of the capital in the Bundestag. The government was prodded into occasional demonstrations of solidarity, raising the number of Berlin delegates to the Bundestag—to which it naturally had less objection after the 1950 elections.[21]

Schumacher died in September 1952. There was some

* Though it was more urgent in Berlin than elsewhere. Its former position as capital had left it with a number of unemployed and aged officials, who depended on government support.

peculation that Reuter might succeed him—but never within he SPD. The party as a whole did not support his views on the outstanding international problems, and least of all on German rearmament. The successor was the deputy leader, Erich Ollenhauer, who had led the party in exile in London during he war. Although he managed to preserve the external unity of the SPD, he lacked Schumacher's iron determination; nor had the time come when it could be adapted to a new national rôle. It was only after the unquestioned success of Adenauer's government in building up a strong national state as one of the most important members of NATO that the SPD was able to challenge it, and then chiefly on its own ground. Under Ollenhauer the divergencies within the party increased, particularly as the fundamental question of reunification again appeared to become a practical possibility.

After 1951 the history of Berlin developed along three lines: he fast developing rhythm of reconstruction; the growing ension in East Germany; and the international debate over the future of Germany.

The government of Berlin was fortunate to plan its reconstruction programme under the direction of Paul Hertz, who returned to the city in 1949. During the Weimar Republic, Hertz had been secretary of the Parliamentary party of the SPD, and later emigrated first to Prague, afterwards to New York. Here Reuter met him on his visit to America during the blockade, and asked for his help in Berlin. He became first a liaison agent between the city government and the Marshall Plan representatives, and in 1950 Senator of Economic Affairs and Credits. He was fully conscious of the need to convert transient unemployment relief into an economic industrialisation policy, and was able to do so on the basis of a 'Four-Year Investment Programme' prepared in part by an American economic commission and a Senate commission on the possibilities of expansion.[22] He was able to invest about 230 million marks in the manufacturing industry in 1950, and guided it to a point where it could compete for orders in West Germany. Thus, though unemployment declined very slowly, the forms of production which alone could provide a long-term employment policy increased rapidly in the next two years. For the same reason, the rate of building rose as unemployment fell.

This was natural since any large scale building programme had to wait on the preparation of an economic infrastructure, particularly fuel and transport, which was not adequate for these tasks until 1951. Thus, only some 4,000 dwellings were completed in 1950, when unemployment was at its height; the total rose by 1,000 in 1951 and approached 8,000 the following year. In 1952, it nearly doubled, reaching well over 15,000. The first years after the war were naturally spent primarily on restoring damaged dwellings.

The main source of investment was Marshall Aid, and the so-called counterpart funds which were paid by the West German government from the Mark reserves created by the sale of imports of American aid. This was in effect a continuation of GARIOA aid, though now under German as well as American responsibility. The greater part of these were invested in the public sector until 1952; thereafter the rate of investment in industry increased rapidly, reaching 700 million marks in 1953.

Parallel to this, Hertz directed an emergency programme, intended to provide some thousands of unemployed with real work for some months of the year. The public works on which they were engaged—traffic through-roads, afforestation, clearance of wasteland—have done much to make Berlin one of the best-planned and most spacious cities in Europe.

The production statistics of the restored city provide a truer indication of the extent of recovery in these years than the unemployment figures, which were naturally continuously swollen by the number of refugees who remained in Berlin. From the beginning of 1950 to the end of 1951, the monthly industrial deliveries rose from 96 to 225 million marks; monthly exports abroad from 3·8 to 28·4 millions. The production index which stood at 23* in January 1950 attained 50 over the following year, and mounted to 67 in 1953.[23]

This rapid advance was largely achieved through a decisive step which the Bonn government had taken in January 1952. This was the *dritte Überleitungsgesetz*—the 'third transference

---

* 1936 = 100. The Berlin production index shows a more remarkable recovery than that of West Germany, where the production per head was much lower than in 1936 long after it had passed 100. In Berlin, on the contrary, the population had considerably declined.

ıw'—which enabled Berlin, like other Länder, to claim a cover
or its budgetary deficit from Federal funds. Such a scheme
vas clearly more necessary for Berlin than any other state,
ince its financial fortunes were, to a large extent, beyond its
ontrol; but even here the government at first refused, and only
•owed to the Bundestag after the representatives of the Berlin
oalition had converted the most influential men in all three
nain parties to their cause. From this time on, Berlin in return
•aid Federal taxes—to the dismay of the Allied authorities
vho regarded it as an infringement of the Four-Power status.

In 1953 Berlin began to achieve what is known in Germany
s 'economic normalisation'—though the greater part of the
wentieth century has been a succession of economic disasters
or the country. It was perhaps three years behind the Federal
Republic, and hundreds of thousands still depended on public
ssistance. But prosperity was coming to be taken for granted,
t was beginning a flourishing tourist trade, and the city was
naking great efforts to become a national and international
:ultural centre, a *Weltstadt*.

In East Germany the 'transition to Socialism' had begun.
The monthly number of refugees had fluctuated wildly, but
ıad shown a strong overall increase. In the summer of 1950,
•ver 20,000 people escaped every month; again the average
ıad risen from some 14,000 in 1951 to 16,000 in 1952.
Tension had increased almost daily since the People's Chamber
:lection of August 1950. It soon became apparent that this
)arliament was summoned to support a number of measures
lesigned to ensure full governmental control of the whole state.
Action began with a thorough purge of the SED, which was
ollowed up by a Law for the Protection of Peace, a form of
Enabling Act conferring wide arbitrary powers on the government. Thereafter the state was engaged in two crash program-
nes, one economic and one military. The first, which began in
he middle of the food crisis, was an attempt to raise industrial
ıorms through propaganda campaigns, and the announcement of a severe Economic Plan. The second, which followed
ı plebiscite against West German rearmament, was to provide
he country with armed forces. The *Volkspolizei* were re-
:quipped with Soviet arms, and a new recruiting system was
:stablished for the police, the para-military Labour Force, and

the Pre-Military Training Corps. To ensure that these mea
sures were carried through, the zonal border was closed, the
evacuation of the neighbouring population began and the court:
were given power to administer 'political justice'; student:
were put on public trial, and SED members themselves were
arrested with increasing frequency. Finally, as the food crisi:
reached its peak, collectivisation was extended from industry
to agriculture—and to mark the end of the era of 'land reform
which had been instituted in 1945, the Minister of Food wa:
arrested, and the Ministry of Supply was purged.

In a sense the most intimidating aspect of these develop
ments was the purge of the SED itself: a certain minimum o:
security could previously be bought by passive conformity to
the party. Now this was shattered, and the population exposec
to the arbitrary pressures of a naked dictatorship, which wa:
also beginning a calculated onslaught on the last organ of
resistance—the churches.

The refugees now came over in floods.[24] Peasants joined the
industrial workers for the first time, and as the *Hausobleute*
were given new powers over the inhabitants, whole households,
and even villages, made for West Berlin. In 1952 nearly
118,000 crossed the sector boundary.* The sense of urgency
was heightened by the knowledge that the surrounding country
was now finally closed to the inhabitants of Berlin. The perimeter of the city was unceasingly patrolled, and there were
recurrent fears that the internal borders might be closed as
well. The broadcasts of the Western stations in Berlin, particularly RIAS, seem also to have been particularly influential
at the time: their detailed reports of the situation in East
Germany encouraged those who could to leave. At all events,
over 22,000 crossed in January, 32,000 in February, almost
59,000 in March, the highest total for any month before or
since. For the next three months it fluctuated between 35,000
and 40,000. Nearly all these refugees came to Berlin.† Conditions in the refugee camps were catastrophic. Although
West German firms sent agents to recruit skilled labour from
the Zeiss works, or the textile and electricity industries, most

* Compared with 54,000 who crossed to the other centres in West Germany.

† The total figure for Berlin for 1953 was 297,000, compared with 34,000 in
the other centres.

people had to remain encamped under the most primitive conditions for months. They were still there when the revolts in East Berlin, Leipzig and Jena broke out in June.

The rising of June 1953 marked the end of an epoch for Berlin. Until that time it had stood in the forefront of international politics. Since 1945 every development in Berlin had been of international significance, and the fate of the city had likewise mirrored international relations. In June 1953 this came to an end. This was so, because the events of June 17th again reflected relationships between the great powers, and the immobility of their position in European conditions. Attempts had been made on both sides in 1952 to change the pattern which the Cold War had imposed on the continent. It was now revealed that they had failed, and their subsequent meetings only confirmed this failure.

In 1952 the Supreme Commander of NATO forces in Europe had been elected President of the United States. The problem of German rearmament had now become almost as urgent as that of bringing the Korean war to an end; the two were interlocking links in the Western barrier against further Communist aggression. In his Inaugural Address, Eisenhower recognised the necessity for quick decision in Europe, urging the leaders of the NATO countries to 'make the unity of their peoples a reality'. The new British government, too, had for six months been pressing for a speedy conclusion to an interminable round of discussions on EDC. It was now nearly a year and a half since Pleven had proposed his plan to the French Assembly, and no progress had been made.

There was one essential difficulty. French opinion, and the French Assembly, refused to contemplate any form of German rearmament which might subsequently revert to national control. They did not regard EDC as it stood as an adequate safeguard, and came increasingly to demand British membership, or at least a strong British commitment to maintaining its integrity, as the price of ratification. For military and political reasons this was unacceptable to both Britain and the United States at the time, and Eisenhower was convinced that to recast the whole organisation in this manner would only delay German rearmament still further.[25] Yet without such a commitment it was impossible to persuade the French Assembly that Russia was a greater long-term threat than Germany. In spite of Schuman's firm adherence to EDC, the parliament wavered continuously in its appreciation of the relative dangers and as German rearmament approached there was a growing inclination to attempt a new political settlement with the Soviet Union first. For other reasons the smaller Brussels Treaty countries also favoured such a move: they feared that if EDC were ratified, the American forces in Europe might eventually be withdrawn. Inside Germany, the official policy of the SPD naturally supported this current of opinion, though both Reuter and Brandt spoke against it at the party congress of 1952.

There was, therefore, at the beginning of the year a strong swing in Europe towards the resumption of discussions with the Soviet Union for a settlement of the German problem. An opposite tendency was equally strong in Britain and the United States—an impatience to get EDC settled, and to begin building up NATO's strength to the level recommended at the Lisbon conference that year: 96 divisions. It was still thought possible to match the Russian army on the Continent, and this mould of thought was also producing more determined views: Acheson, Dulles' predecessor as Secretary of State, was widely if foolishly attacked in America for the limitations of the policy of containment. Dulles was determined on more positive action, and though it is hard to tell how far this was a legend emanating from his election speeches, it was believed in Europe that if he came to power he intended to drive the Russians back behind their borders.* This belief also coloured the outlook of those who advocated negotiations with Stalin.

The West was thus caught in an impasse. There seemed no way to rearm Germany without EDC—Adenauer himself had never advocated an independent national army, and at the same time the implementation of the treaty was likely to give added strength to the demand for new negotiation. It was a favourable moment for Stalin: while offering concessions, he could yet seem to be 'negotiating from strength'. Whatever the outcome, he would certainly succeed in postponing the rearmament of

* But almost anything was believed of Dulles. Within a year, he was thought to be preparing the abandonment of Europe, and again his speeches lent colour to the legend.

Germany—while at the same time Ulbricht was beginning to build up a considerable force in the East. The two were permanent motives of Russian policy for three years, and long seemed effective. West Germany was not incorporated into NATO, and the whole country, if not reunited on acceptable terms could be kept weak until there was a better opportunity.

On March 10th the Soviet government handed Notes to the three Western Powers, proposing that all should 'discuss without delay the question of a peace treaty with Germany' and 'examine the question of the conditions favouring the speediest formation of an all-German government expressing the will of the German people'.

There has been much discussion of the ambiguities of this Soviet prose. It was regarded at the time, and certainly by the three Foreign Ministers, as a clumsy manœuvre to delay the final signing of the EDC treaty. It has since been cited as an example of Russian willingness to reach agreement on Germany if only the country could be 'neutralised'. It is clear that Stalin had no intention of abandoning East Germany, which was at that moment conducting a propaganda campaign against the Federal Republic, and calling on the SPD and the trade unions to rebel against Bonn. Possibly, he hoped that if a peace treaty could be signed, the myth of working-class unity could be revived as a political weapon; and that Germany, once deprived of the protection of NATO, would choose unification on terms which would allow a Communist take-over. He may have felt there was some support for these views in the current temper of the SPD. Whatever his motives, this was the beginning of a long Soviet campaign to delay German rearmament by offering a peace treaty, and for a moment after his death it seemed that it might work.

The response of the Western Powers, then as afterwards, was to demand free elections throughout Germany as a condition for signing a treaty with a national government. They were in any case determined that this initiative should not postpone the integration of Western European defences—or German rearmament.[26] Later in an exchange of notes, which continued throughout April and May, they stipulated that a German government must be free to choose its own alliances. This was in accordance with the spirit of an agreement which had just been reached on the new status of Germany; and there was certainly little wisdom in hoping that any agreement with Stalin would offer hope of stability in a neutralised Germany; but with this declaration the Western Powers had in effect fixed their position for all time. It was never renounced, and they never took the chance, even the outside chance which they later had, that an adequate agreement could be reached on the status of a neutral Germany.

On March 5th, 1953, Stalin died. Reuter, who had for months been insisting on the signs of a growing weakness in the Soviet régime, now advocated that the West should seize the chance of Malenkov's offer of a 'peaceful solution to all outstanding conflicts'. He is believed to have urged Eisenhower to meet Malenkov in Berlin,[27] two months before Churchill's 'summit' call in May, and he declared over RIAS in April that peace would be impossible without a solution of the German question. It is scarcely conceivable that at this time the new Russian régime was prepared to revolutionise its European policy. It was going through a certain upheaval, as the world realised when Beria was executed, but there is not the slightest evidence for the suggestion that is occasionally heard, that it was prepared to give up East Germany in exchange for a European settlement. What does seem possible is that it might have considered a security treaty between the Great Powers, on the lines that Churchill proposed. There was equally some support for this proposal in America—Dulles is said to have considered it at the time—and also from Adenauer, though he was at pains to stipulate that it should only follow German rearmament. What could perhaps have been achieved in the first months after Stalin's death was some form of mutual guarantee which allowed the withdrawal of a large proportion of the Soviet divisions in East Europe. Even such a limited agreement would have been difficult: it implied Western acquiescence in the division of Germany, and there was not yet any suggestion either that the West would give up its proposal for free elections, or that Russia would agree to it. Perhaps it might have been possible to arrange an interim settlement if the Soviet Union had agreed to a change in the régime of East Germany. The state seemed to be on the verge of collapse,

nd Ulbricht had clearly become a liability to the Commun-
st empire. This one slender hope lay in the formation of a
ew government with genuine representation of other parties
esides the SED. This hope was shattered by the rising of
une 17th.

This date, which is now observed throughout Germany* as
ne Day of German Unity is one of the most tragic in the post-
var history of Europe. Not only because of the hopeless resis-
ance which the young workers and students put up against
oviet tanks, but because the rising itself destroyed all chances
f a change. On June 15th there were signs of improvement:
ne radio announced that inhabitants of East Germany would
ow be allowed to travel 'without bureaucratic delay' to the
ther zones. The news was heard in an atmosphere of great
ension, since a few days before the Central Committee of the
ED had issued a public self-criticism, announcing that the
empo of the 'transiton to Socialism' was 'false and damaging'—
nd hindered the chances of German unity. It was believed that
 radical change of line had succeeded the party purges of the
receding months, and that the régime was being liberalised
rom above. But the next day, in a summer temperature which
vas nearing the 80's, *Neues Deutschland* carried renewed pro-
aganda for raising the norms in all industrial work. This was
robably the decisive mistake: norms had been consistently
aised ever since the New Economic Plan was announced.
The population was already tired out from overwork and lack
f food.

The first reaction came from a group of workers on the
uilding sites of the Stalinallee. A few at one site downed tools,
efusing to work to the new norms. How spontaneous this
ction was is hard to say: it is remarkable that a banner sud-
enly appeared, demanding the abolition of the norms. With
his, the group began to march down Stalinallee to the Alex-
nderplatz, joined on the way by workers at all the other sites.
3y one o'clock this procession, which the passers-by seem at
irst to have taken for an SED demonstration, had changed the
vhole situation. It turned into a march on the government.
The first intention was to present a petition against the norms,
ut when the crowd of about 5,000 reached the 'House of the

* And in some American states.

153

Ministries' in the Leipzigerstrasse, they began to shout f
Ulbricht and Grotewohl. The crowd was still confused and u
certain. They demanded a sight of Pieck as well—who ha
disappeared for some months, and was thought to be a victi
of an SED purge.* It was only when Selbmann the Minist
of Mines began to speak to them (Ulbricht and Grotewo
having crept into the cellar, from where they were later to di
appear by a side-entrance), that the demonstration became
revolt.

The Government put up a grotesque performance. As tl
minister spread his arms and began to speak—'My de
colleagues, I, myself, am only a worker',—a loudspeaker va
drove up with the news that the norms 'would be reconsidered
The crowd suddenly roared with laughter, and one of tl
builders jumped on to the table on which Selbmann w
standing, pushed him aside and demanded free elections.
was the signal of revolt. From this moment the government w
bound to use force—and there was nothing the population cou
do. They did not occupy the buildings, from whose entranc
the *Volkspolizei* had disappeared; they could not hope to ga
control of the city. They had only one weapon—to proclaim
general strike and hope that it would be followed througho
the Zone. They stood for an hour in front of the building, wai
ing for Ulbricht to appear, decided on a general strike for tl
next day, and dispersed in groups.

There was little sleep, but little activity, during the nigh
The whole of Berlin knew of the general strike, and a demo
stration was organised for seven o'clock the next morning
but as they turned out into the rain, no one knew what to d
They chanted slogans† as about 100,000 marched through th
streets, but refrained from provoking intervention. A numbe
attempted to storm the Economic ministry, but were repulse
by the rubber truncheons of the *Volkspolizei*. The rest turne
towards the Potsdamerplatz, and it was here that the *Volk
polizei* opened fire.‡ It was a concerted action. Twenty Russia

* I was told this by eye-witnesses. It did not appear in the press.
† 'Es hat keinen Zweck, der Spitzbart muss weg.'
　'Nieder mit der SED.'
‡ Some only, others had thrown down their arms and crossed the border
seek the protection of the West Berlin police.

anks began to clear the Lustgarten at the same time; tanks then
ppeared in all parts of the city, patrolling Unter den Linden,
'riedrichstrasse and Leipzigerstrasse. In the Friedrichstrasse a
ew youths climbed to the turret of a tank, and a single shot
vas fired. But it was not the tanks which suppressed the revolt:
t was the *Volkspolizei** who shot demonstrators with machine-
juns as they ran before the tanks. At the Brandenburg Gate,
Russian soldiers shot and killed a group of demonstrators who
vere trying to hoist the black-red-gold flag of the Federal
Republic in place of the red banner which had already been
orn down. Tanks also opened fire on groups of young people
vho tried to stop them by throwing stones into the tracks. But
n general, the Russians confined themselves to clearing and
)atrolling the streets; the real shooting came from the *Volks-
)olizei.*

The clashes lasted all afternoon. The police barracks were set
)n fire. Spokes and bits of piping were strewn over the Pots-
lamerplatz to prevent the approach of tanks, and now the
)olice stood helplessly by while the Café Vaterland and
Columbus Haus went up in flames. The government buildings,
nore heavily protected, escaped with broken windows. The
ittacks of the demonstrators were symbolic: at no point did
:he revolt turn into a revolution. But the government, which
had apparently hoped the day before that it would blow over,
1ow requested Soviet help. The Soviet Commandant had, unknown to the mass of demonstrators, proclaimed a state of
emergency as the tanks began to move. By nine o'clock, the
streets were almost clear, and a curfew was imposed. Any
issembly would be punished by court martial. At the Brandenburg Gate, Russian patrols fired a warning salvo from time to
time to keep back the crowds from West Berlin. But there
had never been any danger of intervention; groups had crossed
and recrossed the border during the day. Some were killed,
others burned the demarcation signs. A crowd of 12,000 steel
workers had been cheered on their way through the French
sector to the 'Walter Ulbricht Stadium' in the north, where they
tore down the SED banners and the gigantic portrait of the
First Secretary. That was all.

By nightfall the Soviet army was in complete control. The

* I.e. the *Kasernierte Volkspolizei*, in effect the East German army.

border was closed, and constantly patrolled with tanks and armoured cars. Next day troops had taken up positions in the ruins, and on the roofs of public buildings. The streets were completely deserted. The East German radio announced that a West Berliner, Willi Göttling, had been shot by court martial for provocation. The general strike was still complete, but it could not last more than a few days; it was a matter of holding out without food. All shops were shut, and most were empty anyway. There was no prospect that the rising would spread, or the strike succeed. On the 18th and 19th, work stopped in all the towns and cities in East Germany; there were demonstrations in Magdeburg, Halle, Leipzig, Brandenburg, Jena and Görlitz. Political prisoners were freed, where they were known to be imprisoned. But they were already succeeded by new arrests, which continued throughout the country for a month. Norms were soon to be raised again, and a still harsher economic plan introduced. No one knows how many people were killed in East Berlin. The number of dead was probably not very high, but several hundred were wounded. All chances of a change in the régime had been destroyed, and Ulbricht was secured in power for years to come.

As the news of the rising went round the world, the first reaction in the West was apprehension. This was the opportunity for Dulles to fulfil his election pledge and 'awe' the Russians back behind their frontier. But within a few hours it was clear that he could do nothing of the kind. Once Russian tanks appeared on the streets and the repression began, the obvious fact was demonstrated that the new Soviet régime could not bow to force, and that the United States was no more willing now than it had ever been to risk war for the liberation of Eastern Europe.

In Berlin there were other expectations. On the afternoon of the 17th, the SPD had published an appeal to the Western Powers to begin immediate negotiations with the Soviet Union to end the 'intolerable conditions in the Soviet Zone'. This showed more political wisdom than any other Western reaction. It was the last hope of saving the situation, and it was repeated in the following weeks, particularly in an appeal to the Federal government to intervene in this sense. It was probably a lost cause already, but there was a faint possibility

hat in the month before Ulbricht had regained complete
control, the new men in the Kremlin may have been looking
or another way out of their difficulties. But it was ignored.

The Western Allies protested to the Russians, and America
offered free food deliveries to East Germany. Molotov rejected
his with contempt, declaring through Semeonov, the Soviet
High Commissioner, that it was a deliberate provocation.

Reuter was in Vienna when the rising happened. He was on his
way back from holiday in Italy, and only heard of the events in
Berlin on the night of the 16th. He spent twenty-four hours trying
o get a flight back, first through civil flights to Munich, then
oy an American military aircraft, which was refused him. He
lid not arrive until the evening of the 18th, and immediately
elephoned the American Commandant, General Timberman,
oegging for an intervention with Dibrova (the new Soviet
Commandant, who had ordered the execution of Göttling) to
end the reprisals in the East. There was obviously nothing that
he General could do without higher authority, and the
Western Powers had already committed themselves to a studied
non-intervention. The West made no approach to the Soviet
Union for a month. A Note then proposed a Four-Power
conference on the German and Austrian questions; but the
most propitious moment had passed, the Note lacked any
sense of urgency, and the real answer lay in the wave of arrests
in the Soviet Zone. The Russian government emphasised its
recovery from the shock of the German rising and the fall of
Beria by a demonstrative reception for Grotewohl and a delegation from the Democratic Republic in Moscow. It was now
more heavily committed than ever to upholding the satellite
régime, and the Western Powers and the Federal government
showed equally clearly that the events of June 17th only gave
a greater incentive to West Germany's integration into Western
Europe. All hope of reunification seemed to have gone, and the
two camps to be permanently divided. The hopes that had been
raised by Stalin's death had vanished, and so had Berlin's rôle
in the post-war history of Europe.

Reuter insisted in the following weeks that the rising—this
first expression of the German people's will to freedom since
Hitler—marked the beginning of a new era; that the West had
greater power and greater scope for newer initiatives than at any

time since the war. But he was wrong. The West had been caught in the persistent and fateful dilemma of European history since the end of the war. If it were divided and weak, it could not hope to bring about the liberation of Eastern Europe. If it were united and strong, Russia would be more determined than ever to hold on to its buffer empire. Reuter had hoped that Western unity could bring about a new international order, and for a few weeks in 1953 there was a slender chance that this could come true. But the contradictory tendencies of Western policy had not been resolved; every government had been caught off its guard by the East German rising, and the 17th of June had only reinforced the Pankow régime.

The new voice of Germany was not Reuter's but Adenauer's. Both sides settled down to the *status quo*; and Berlin began to feel its way toward a new form of coexistence with the Soviet Zone, and a return to local government.

Chapter Seven

THE RETURN TO LOCAL GOVERNMENT

THE years between the rising in Berlin and the revolt in Hungary witnessed a more intense debate on the future f Germany than any between Russia and the West since the nd of the war. It was the only period in which the German roblem was seriously discussed between the two sides, and in 'hich there was a genuine, if illusory, search for a solution. rom the Berlin Conference of February 1954 to Khrushchev's ramatic message of November 1956, there was an almost con- nuous round of discussions on 'German reunification', pro- osals of 'disengagement', suggestions for 'European security'. t was also the only period in which Berlin was allowed to recede :om the international horizon, and devote itself to the problems f local government. There is nothing paradoxical in this: as ong as Germany is under consideration, the Soviet Union eels no need to put pressure on Berlin. When, in the end, ecision was once again postponed, Khrushchev began a new ierlin crisis, in order to force the West once more to the egotiating table.

The truth of this position was already demonstrated in 953. After the rising of June 17th, Reuter was determined hat the Western Powers should seize the initiative to begin ew negotiations on the German problem. He was convinced hat the internal weaknesses of the Soviet régime should be xploited to win concessions on German reunification. This was recisely what both sides desired to avoid—because each seemed o be too weak to negotiate. Russia was in no position to offer oncessions over East Germany, which, after the rising, might iave endangered her position throughout Eastern Europe. The United States (and Great Britain) were above all anxious o begin West German rearmament, on which no progress had et been made. They were still bound to the mystique of negotiating from strength', though this meant in effect that hey were not prepared to negotiate at all. The West German government agreed with them. Thus, both sides were for the moment content with the *status quo* in Germany. Berlin was no problem.

Reuter hoped that in this time, as he conceived it, of national emergency, a new 'national government' would be formed in Bonn. He considered it essential that both the SPD and Berlin should be represented in a government dedicated to a new national initiative, and hoped, in case a coalition was formed, to become Foreign Minister.[1] He believed that the Soviet Union had finally lost all chance of conquering Germany; that both sides recognised that peace in Europe could only be achieved through German reunification, and that to achieve this, the West should abandon its intention of integrating the Federal Republic into the Atlantic Alliance beforehand.[2] This seems to indicate that even Reuter would not have been prepared to buy reunification at the price of permanent neutrality. It is hard to judge; he did not formulate his ideas of the future. Perhaps, he still clung to the hope that a United West would be able to achieve international reconciliation.

In the election of September the CDU won a crushing victory. The economic miracle was now really achieving an unprecedented level of prosperity among all classes, and the electorate was in no mood for Reuter's appeals that Germans should give their 'last shirt' for the freedom of the Soviet Zone. There was no question of a coalition with the SPD. The German voters had ratified the international *status quo*. Berlin was pushed into the background.

On September 29 Ernst Reuter died. His heart had long been weak, but the effect of the recent months on his health had not been perceived even by his closest friends. His death was a shock to the whole of Berlin, and throughout the Western sectors candles were placed in every window as a spontaneous gesture of mourning. It was an unique tribute. The city had been uniquely identified with one man, and no one else was able to fill his place. But in fact he could no longer have played the same part himself. He had led Berlin in the hardest struggle of the Cold War, but that era had already passed. Both East and West were resting on the *status quo*, and events in both East and West Germany had only confirmed the situation. Reuter's hopes that the West would be able to mount a new offensive had been destroyed, and could not be translated into purely local action in Berlin. The need there now was not to pursue the Cold War, but to seek a local form of reconciliation. Even if he had attempted this, Reuter, whose name alone held the coalition together, and whose policies now won the support of a bare majority of his own party, would scarcely have been able to succeed.

In Germany the SPD was split after its electoral defeat into 'irreconcilables' and 'reformers'. Reuter had in effect been the protagonist of the latter group, and his disciple Brandt was an open advocate of conscious adaptation to the new age in German politics. But it was the former, the orthodox Marxists, who for a time succeeded. They were still suspicious of coalition; they still adhered to collectivist Socialist principles; they were bitter opponents of German rearmament; and they hoped for reunification through direct negotiation with the Soviet Union. The fact that in the end the party changed to a 'reformist' policy was due to the nature of its position in the capital. But for a time, the situation of Berlin seemed to favour the arguments of the irreconcilables. For the next three years the wider significance of Berlin lay only in the effects it had on the political history of the SPD; while the history of the city itself depended as ever on bargaining between the parties in the coalition.

This was the stage, and these were the two main actions in this history of Berlin during the period. They did not meet until the Hungarian revolt forced the Berliners themselves to reconsider their positions and the SPD to begin a reappraisal of its policies. The final result was that Willy Brandt succeeded to the leadership of Berlin, and ultimately to that of the SPD in Germany. The emergence of this second 'fighting mayor' was not, however, an indication of continuity, but of a painful break with the immediate past.

The attitude of the SPD was, in part, determined from the beginning by the trauma of the foundation of the SED, and the party's subsequent struggle for survival in Berlin. From this period it had drawn two, scarcely compatible, conclusions, both of which were long subscribed to by its members in Berlin. The first was, as Otto Suhr had declared at the all-German conference of the SPD in May 1946, that Berlin's main task was to 'assume a middle rôle between East and West'. The second was expressed by Otto Suhr in December 1956. Berlin's history, he said, showed a small community struggling for freedom and autonomy, yet signified a decisive phase of the Cold War between the two power blocs. Both these views were apparent in Reuter's appreciation of the city's position, and never more clearly than in 1953, when their incompatibility was also most evident. They continued, however, to dominate the attitude of the SPD until Brandt succeeded in imposing a new revisionism after 1956. The change did not come into the open until after the Russian ultimatum of 1958.

Both this immobilism, and the final change, were aided by the position of the SPD in Berlin. Here, in contrast to the national organisation, it was a voters' party with strong public personalities as its chief electoral asset. The CDU in Berlin, like the SPD in Germany, was a members' party dependent for its appeal on an alternative programme. From its base in Berlin the SPD might eventually hope to advance to political victory in the whole country: as long as its foreign policy advocated renewed negotiations with the Soviet Union, it could draw support from the mediatory rôle of Berlin. But when this broke down and the new Russian threat was concentrated against the former capital itself, the new champion of Berlin emerged as the leader of national resistance.

The CDU on the other hand was anxious to maintain the division between the political life of Berlin, where it formed a junior partner in the government, and that of Germany where it was the dominant force. It may be traducing them to suggest that this was a reason for the apparent reluctance of the party leaders in Bonn to encourage closer links between Berlin and the Federal Republic; but it was certainly of a piece with their general attitude that Berlin formed a distinctive and peculiar problem, whose complications should not be allowed to disturb the development of their national policy or the evolution of their diplomacy.

After 1953, in fact, both the main parties were unwilling for reasons of both national and local politics to continue the coalition in Berlin which had been their original response to the crisis of the post-war period. The SPD was always reluctant to subordinate its social policies to the limitations imposed by the Federal government. Though they had no choice if they were

o continue their determined attempts to unite the city with the
ation (and if they were to go on receiving subsidies from
Bonn), they had no desire to assume the permanent respon-
ibility for doing so.* The CDU, which with its allies of the
'DP commanded a narrow majority in the House of Repre-
entatives, was tired of its apparent subservience. Reuter had
eld the coalition together, but only at the price of considerable
dissensions, both between the parties and within his own.
After his death it was an impossible task.

The CDU and FDP now declared against continuing the
oalition, and decided to form a government based on their
wn narrow majority. They were able to retain office for more
han a year in this way. The SPD were less anxious for such a
precipitate break—a vote in a combined session of Represen-
atives and members of the Land Executive only showed a
najority of one against continuing the coalition—but in view
f the configuration of national and international relations at
he time, the majority soon came to favour their oppositional
ôle. Nor would their participation in the government have
nade any great difference: the new administration concen-
rated on a programme of economic reconstruction which it was
nly now possible to undertake on a large scale, and which in
act continued to be directed by Paul Hertz.

Hertz remained a member of the government with the con-
ent of his own party. This was partly on American request, for
he directors of American assistance had unique confidence in
im; partly because he was universally regarded in Berlin as
he man most likely to stimulate American generosity.

In spite of the restiveness which had led to a breakup of the
oalition, there was, thus, no real divergence over economic
policies between government and opposition. Nor was there
ny real disagreement, at the local level of Berlin, over foreign
policy. The meeting of the four Foreign Ministers in Berlin
tself in January and February 1954† only emphasised that the
questions discussed were completely beyond the control of the
enate, or even the German government. No one in Berlin

---

* There were occasional exceptions: Berlin, for example, was permitted to
etain the higher level of pensions which the SPD had introduced there before the
ederal government began a comprehensive scheme.
† See below, Chapter Eight.

disagreed with Adenauer's address to the population: 'I would
like to point out that Soviet policy in Europe at this time i
dominated exclusively by considerations of maintaining th
status quo with regard to the occupation, and with regard to th
political position of all the territories under its control.' I
many members of the SPD did disagree with what followed
'But its plan—and even the most deluded can no longer hav
any doubt about this—is also aimed at making the *status qu*
the basis of a new attack on West Berlin at an opportun
moment',[3] they did not, in any event, dispute the fact that no
thing could be done about the *status quo* for the present.

Thus the demonstrative destruction of Reuter's coalition
was little more than a symbol of underlying disagreements be
tween the parties on a national scale. These disagreements had
been expressed more vehemently when all were partners to a
coalition than they now were between opposite sides of th
House. The only real area of dispute was in fact the adminis
tration, and even here the issues were narrower than they firs
appeared.

The conflict was sharpest during the early months of th
new government. The *Regierender Bürgermeister*, Dr. Walte
Schreiber, had been a minister in the old Prussian government
and was well suited to carrying on the government of Berlin i
this uneventful interim. But he was little interested in day-to
day administration and the problems were serious. The bureau
cracy which had been allowed by Reuter to swell far beyond it
functions* was becoming less efficient as the need for emergency
initiatives gave way to the necessity for implementing long
time programmes. Nor was it only a question of administrative
competence, but of the city's economic efficiency. Berlin stil
lived to a great extent on the pattern of its functions as th
former German capital. Too many people, who would hav
been better employed in the offices of local administratio
proper, occupied positions at the centre which were more suited
to a national capital, and which sometimes impeded efficienc
and increased costs. This was true, for example, in the depart
ments of health and education, where a radical decentralisatio
was needed. Schreiber did not attempt these tasks, and the SPI

* See above, p. 119. There were also political reasons: coalition implied a fai
distribution of jobs among members of different parties.

attacked his short-lived administration both for employing too large a bureaucracy and for failing to decentralise.

Yet when he was succeeded by a Social Democratic coalition after the election of December 1954, matters could hardly be improved. The SPD proportion of the votes in these elections had in fact slightly decreased, but the new distribution of seats enabled it again to head the government. The old President of the Assembly, Dr. Otto Suhr, was now elected *Regierender Bürgermeister*, and his place was taken by Willy Brandt. Suhr and his energetic and authoritarian Senator of the Interior, Lipschitz, were determined now to impose a ceiling on the administration, and to decentralise as far as possible. Their *Stellungplan*, however, came to little: Federal legislation was now demanding the expansion of the administration in many fields, and decentralisation itself imposed an increase in the local forces. Suhr gained credit for ridding the administration of its connotations of a 'spoils system' of coalition government; but his intended reform did not go much further, and Berlin continues to employ a high proportion of its ageing labour force in bureaucratic services.

Suhr's election showed that whatever their differences of outlook, the parties had very little to disagree on in Berlin. His government was devoted to a local reconciliation as well as administrative reform. Success in these comparatively quiet years was limited but noteworthy. His declaration on assuming office already showed that he was determined to come to better terms with the Russian authorities in East Berlin,[4] and the time was propitious. The Berlin question was never more quiescent than in 1955, when the Soviet Union was making more determined efforts than at any time before or since to come to an agreement with the West. It was the only period in which West Berlin was recognised by the Soviet authorities as an autonomous entity: visits were exchanged between the Russian Headquarters and Rathaus Schoeneberg; the radio building in the British sector was handed over by the Russians to the West Berlin government—a gesture which terminated more than a decade of broadcast attacks on the city's leaders from the heart of its territory.

There was naturally never any question of a similar 'normalisation' of relations with the East Berlin régime. It is possible that the Russians hoped that this might follow from their new friendship with the Western government; but, in all shades of Western opinion, the two were mutually exclusive. Better relations with the Soviet Union could only be maintained on the assumption that this was a step towards German reunification: any relations with her protégés in Germany could only hinder this. Such was apparently also Adenauer's view of the situation in 1955, and his relations with Suhr were closer and more cordial than with either the previous or subsequent mayors of Berlin. Thus, it was also in 1955 that the Bundestag began its annual pilgrimage to Berlin to emphasise that this remained the German capital; and relations with Pankow were unremittingly hostile.

But Suhr's administration did succeed in restoring a certain unity to Berlin. The growing financial resources of the city enabled it to institute a scheme for encouraging East Berliners to visit concerts, theatres, cinemas and exhibitions in the West. They paid in East marks at 1 : 1, and the deficit was redeemed by the government. It was more than a gesture: it gave thousands of people the chance to share the cultural life of the city, to see and hear much that they would otherwise never have been able to afford, and retain a sense of participation in the life of the West. In this way West Berlin fulfilled two functions: by the closeness of its relations with the Soviet authorities it modified the rigours of the East German régime; at the same time it continued to give the implicit assurance that this régime would not last. When these relations were broken off after the Hungarian revolt, the Pankow government acquired greater initiative in Berlin affairs.

But though the Rathaus Schoeneberg refused anything more than strictly technical dealing with the Eastern Magistrat or the Pankow government, it did entertain relations with one country that was never recognised in Bonn: Poland. Polish journalists and semi-official representatives of the Polish government frequently visited Berlin for discussions with members of the government on the improvement of German-Polish relations. It was an effort to use Berlin as a springboard for the Federal Republic, and though it was hardly successful, it was the main vehicle for the unofficial negotiations between the two countries which have been pursued intermittently for years. West Berlin also held a strong cultural attraction for Poland. Students were allowed to attend the Free University for some years, and during the International Building Exhibition of 1958, 1,700 Polish architects came to visit the city.

Suhr's policy of 'local reconciliation', thus, achieved a wider success than he had perhaps expected. It also encouraged the SPD to believe in the possibility of a 'solution' through direct negotiations with Russia—though Suhr's own views on foreign policy were probably closer to those of Adenauer than to the official party doctrine. It was during this period that the SPD was most insistent in its demands for negotiations, though it would probably have been embarrassed had it ever been in a position to begin them. There was in reality no basis for negotiations: as long as Russia showed any interest in reunification, she conducted discussions only with those ultimately responsible —the Western Allies. When she dropped this afterwards in favour of perpetuating the division of Germany, the SPD was in no better a position to approach her than the CDU, since neither party would ever consent to the recognition of East Germany or negotiate with the Pankow government. Thus, though the local history of Berlin in this period served to encourage the SPD in its beliefs, its significance remained essentially local. Suhr's success was a function of Russian policy, not the point of a new departure.

For the mass of people in West Berlin, however, the chief significance of these years lay in a programme of economic consolidation and expansion, which was only permitted by the relative stability of international relations, and the local confidence gained by Suhr's policy of *rapprochement*. Since 1953 Berlin has experienced an uninterrupted rise in industrial output and standards of living. This progress was dramatically illustrated by the fall in unemployment and the rise in industrial turnover. But recently new doubts have arisen. Is this economic expansion as safe and certain as it seemed? May the prosperity of Berlin turn out after all to be illusory? The concern which is felt about this is not merely a result of the pressure to which Berlin has been subjected since 1958, though the collapse of earlier hopes in the international sphere has accentuated it: it is a result of the pattern of economic development in this period.

At the end of 1952 there were still over a quarter of a million unemployed in the city. Four years later there were 119,000. In 1959 the figure had sunk to 91,000, and in 1962 it is about as low as can be reached in this artificial situation, some 15,000. Over the same period the production index* rose from 51 in 1952 to 133 in 1959. Industrial orders, when 1952 = 100, rose to 236 in 1959. Industrial turnover rose from 2,902 million marks in 1952 to 7,322 million in 1959.[5]

These are startling statistics of rapid prosperity, which owe much to the careful long-term planning of Senator Hertz and his advisers. But the traditional industrial structure of Berlin on which the new prosperity was built is particularly vulnerable in the circumstances of contemporary Europe, and might need a radical change to survive in the next few years. This problem arises out of the nature of Berlin's industrial structure and financial resources.

After the incorporation of Berlin in the financial system of the Federal Republic, and the Third *Überleitungsgesetz*, the deficits of the city's budget rose. This was natural, since the salaries of public employees, and the level of aid under the Federal *Lastenausgleichsgesetz*† were raised to correspond to those of West Germany. With this increasing deficit, it was impossible to lay a firm basis of industrial expansion without special concessions from the West German government. In 1953 only 52 per cent of Berlin's expenditure could be met from local taxes, and expenditure was still rising sharply. In 1951 it had been 1·2 milliard marks; in 1952 it was 1·6 and in 1953 it was nearly 1·75.[6] If Berlin was not going to become a completely passive dependant of the Federal Republic (and thereby certainly lose much of its population and all hope of ever becoming again the capital of a reunified country) it was essential to expand the city's economic resources as quickly as possible. This was achieved over the next three years by a variety of Federal measures designed to rationalise the industrial structure, and encourage the development of new industry there. As a result a large modernisation programme has been carried out, and a number of new industries have settled in Berlin

---

* 1936 = 100.

† 'Law for the equalisation of burdens,' i.e. a programme of compensation to those who had suffered material losses through the war or under Nazi rule.

because of tax concessions which the national government has offered them. Textile, chemical and printing industries have expanded rapidly, and a wholly new consumer manufacture has begun.* In many respects this programme has been a complete success. Since 1959 there have been many more vacant jobs than unemployed; and in 1961 Berlin began to pay more in Federal taxes to West Germany than it received in direct Federal aid. The standard of living in the city is now practically as high as that in West Germany; and the only form of construction which is still mainly dependent on external assistance is a programme of heavy public works—of intra-city motor-ways and expansion of the Underground network—which is covered by a special allocation of funds,† and public loans at low interest.

Yet in 1962 the economy was still operating on an overall deficit. Berlin's imports exceeded its exports by about 12 million marks a year: and if invisible transactions are included, the total deficit‡ has ranged from 1,620 to 2,160 million marks since 1958.[7] This is still covered by the Federal Republic. It means that in terms of private investment, Berlin is losing money to West Germany. Profits are not invested in Berlin but in the Federal Republic, and many of the more important Berlin firms have established depots there. This movement, which was already important before the crisis of 1961, could well gather momentum if the political pressure of recent years is maintained. Moreover, many of the newer industries in Berlin are no more than small branches of their parent enterprises in the West. They have been placed there to avoid the taxes which have been imposed on the rest of the country to check its breakneck boom—chiefly a turnover tax of 4 per cent. Again, firms in the West which place orders in Berlin are also exempted from turnover tax; and the city's exports to West Germany thus enjoy tax advantages of 8 per cent of their value. Even this has not sufficed to check the overall deficit, and the amount of direct or indirect Federal aid needed to maintain the present economy is some 1,970 million marks a year.

For the biggest industrial city in Germany, which has set

* E.g. shoes and other leatherwork; cigarettes.
† The *Hauptstadt Berlin*—Capital City of Berlin—programme.
‡ I.e. in the *Leistungsbilanz*, the sum of visible and invisible transactions.

itself the task of solvency, this condition is a failure. It arises
from the underlying structure of its industry and population.
In the first place, in spite of the injection of new industry it has
received since 1954, Berlin is fundamentally divided between
two forms of industrial activity. There are the gigantic traditional Berlin firms: Siemens, A.E.G., which are both electrical
(though Siemens has metallurgical components) and the
chemicals firm of Schering. At the other end of the scale there
is a host of minor industries—printing, plastics, woodwork,
breweries, ceramics, which together employ a substantial per-
centage of the working population. Both these sources of employment are extremely vulnerable in present conditions. The
smaller firms because in a period of free European expansion,
they do not have the resources to attract investment or rationalise their own production to the point when it can withstand
competition.[8] The only industry which has succeeded in doing
so hitherto is that of precision tools and optics[9] and that is a
special case. The larger firms are not vulnerable in this sense:
they are continuing to profit from the Common Market. But
the electrical industries are among those in which automation
has made the fastest progress, and where employment is in
consequence severely threatened. In 1959 electrical firms employed some 102,000 people out of a total labour force of less
than 900,000.* The proportion is still much the same, but it
cannot be expected that it will be maintained, and in this case
as in that of the smaller firms, new forms of employment must
soon be provided.

The only way that this can be done, however, is by comprehensive programmes of rationalisation, and attracting private
investment and skilled young labour. The prospects for these
three essentials are not good. Investments can only be maintained at present by public money, such as a special fund of the
European Recovery Programme. This may well be continued,
even internationalised (as an answer to the political problems
of Berlin), but it will clearly depend on the labour available to
implement a programme of rationalisation. This is the crux of
the problem, and the age structure of the population renders it
peculiarly intractable. Every large industrial city suffers a
natural loss of population, which it makes good by fresh im-

* Of which about 315,000 are employed in industry.

migration. In the decade between 1950 and 1960, this was also true of Berlin; the population rose then from 2,150,000 to 2,250,000. But the increase has been replaced by a noticeable exodus, and the proportion of old people is rapidly growing. People of 65 or more accounted for 17 per cent of the population in 1960.* This is expected to rise to 20 per cent by 1965[10] (without taking account of the crisis of confidence provoked in 1961). More, half the present population is over 45, and this proportion too will continue to rise. Even this does not give a true indication of the position: the losses suffered in the war have left the city with a very large majority of women, about 130 to every 100 men. In the age-groups between 35 and 40 the proportions are 171 to 100. This means that in all, out of a population of two and a quarter millions, some quarter of a million are war-widows.

Berlin would therefore have to show a very strong sense of purpose and confidence if it were to attract enough young people to expand productivity and rationalise its industry. The problem has become now more acute than ever before, since it lost natural sources of labour from the East in 1961. 50,000 people lived in the East and worked in the West before the 13th of August, and skilled labour was also recruited from refugees. Both these sources have now dried up; and if Berlin continues to lose population at its present rate (some 21,500 a year before the crisis of 1961) it could soon become a city of ageing pensioners.

This cursory examination is enough to show how vulnerable the present economic and demographic structure of the city and how illustory its prosperity could soon seem. At present, however, the boom which began in the period of local government continues unchecked. The value of exports rose continuously throughout the last decade. In 1950 exports totalled just under 98 million marks. By 1952 they had reached nearly 235 million. By 1954 this had nearly doubled to 461,723,000 marks, and again by 1958, when they stood at 955,031,000. The total for 1959 was 1,135,249,000. Today West Berlin exports 80 per cent of its industrial production, of which over two-thirds go to the Federal Republic and about 10 per cent

* Compared with just over 10 per cent in the rest of Germany. Children under 15 were 13 per cent in Berlin in 1959, compared with 21 per cent in the rest of Germany.

to the rest of the world outside the Communist bloc. More important is that about 75 per cent of electro-technical products go to West Germany, and a still higher proportion of textiles. In fact, Berlin has politically and economically reliable markets for almost all its products. The total exported to East Germany is now something under 1 per cent, and perhaps another 1½ per cent reaches the other East European countries. Of these, Bulgaria is the most important customer: its imports from West Berlin have been rising steadily, while those of the Soviet Union have declined sharply since 1958. The loss of the city's natural economic hinterland has thus so far scarcely affected it; and if it continued to import some food from East Germany until the desperate agricultural crisis of 1961-2, this was chiefly to save transport costs on imports from the West. Berlin has imported the bulk of its fresh food from Western Europe ever since 1950, either directly or via West Germany. The value of these imports has been rising continuously, increasing still further in 1962. The city is as nearly independent as possible from any economic pressure by the East German government, and the only commodity for whose supply it really depends on the Pankow régime, is water. Even this is unnecessary.

The immediate economic security of the city can thus hardly be threatened by any action of the Soviet Union or East Germany. The long-term prospects are, however, much more doubtful, and it is here that political pressure from the Communist bloc may be decisive. If it is maintained, as it has been over the past three years, it may prove impossible either to attract the investment or the skilled young labour force which are needed to maintain present prosperity. If Khrushchev were really anxious to gain control of West Berlin he could then wait for the withered fruit to fall; it could only be saved by an energetic international Western action.

Meanwhile West Berlin has grown from an assembly of inhabited ruins, which it still remained at the time of the blockade, to one of the most interesting and diverse cities in Europe. The housing programme is now practically complete,*

---

* 165,000 new dwellings were completed between 1950 and 1960. The record year was 1959 with over 23,000. Most of these were built under a Social Housing Programme, financed largely from public sources. Rents are low, and gradual purchase easy. See *The Guardian*, 25.5.1960.

and has been carried out on the basis of a comprehensive planning scheme which has avoided the sacrifice of the large forest on the western outskirts, or the Tiegarten in the centre. An 'areas utilisation plan' passed in 1949 outlined the future shape of the city, and a Planning Law of the same period ensured its observance. This Act has been progressively remodelled since: it was replaced by a new measure in 1956, and in 1958 the House of Representatives passed new Building Statutes to ensure the continuity of planning. It is one of the few cities in which the mass of citizens take an active and continuous interest in these principles,—which they combine with a perverse pride in the unhappy brashness of the Kurfürstendamm or the illuminated wilderness of Steglitz.

But many of the results are superb. The new Siemensstadt in Spandau has blocks of flats of differing heights set at sharp angles to one another to provide an interior privacy, an overall unity and a variety of perspective which make much of the LCC's work look like illustrations from Dickens. The masterpiece of the new Berlin is the Hansaviertel in the centre, result of an international architectural competition in which many of the world's leading architects took part. It is a princely quarter and to pass from this to the Stalinallee is to see in monumental form, the difference of outlook between two worlds.

West Berlin still has no geographical centre. The old governmental buildings and main streets are in the East. In the West, the area around the Brandenburg Gate and the Reichstag building has been deliberately left flat, as if to emphasise the expectations of a reunited city. Now it is cut across by the wall of concrete and barbed wire which demonstrate the intentions of the other side. Against it, the Congress Hall in the West looks oddly small and isolated, but incorporates at the same time the legend of the past fifteen years which has created a new city on the outskirts of the old. Some of the public expressions of the legend—the Freedom Bell in Rathaus Schoeneberg, or the John-Foster-Dulles Allee by the Spree— are somewhat affected; but the two universities, the new opera house, the Schiller Theatre, the two leading orchestras and the new Akademie der Künste in the Hansaviertel, all witness the vitality and endurance of the new Berlin. Alongside this, there has been an attempt to revive the 'Isherwood' legend, which has found no lack of supporters among West German and foreign visitors, but which remains self-conscious, constricted —and strictly controlled by the police. There is no break of continuity with the past in the streets of Charlottenburg, or Wedding, but the more recent past is dead. The Berlin which took shape in the period of local government was nevertheless formed by the crisis which preceded it. It is dedicated, wide open to the world, abounding in vitality; and at the same time too aware of its passive dependence on outside support to enjoy its previous extravagance.

The period of local government in Berlin came to an end on October 25th, 1956. It was the day after Russian tanks returned to Budapest to suppress the Hungarian rising. The stability of the previous five years had come to an end, and it was realised immediately in Berlin that new crises would follow. It was also the day on which Willy Brandt established his claim to the succession of Otto Suhr.

Otto Suhr was a sick man for much of his period in office. He became *Regierender Bürgermeister* in January 1955, and fell ill in October. Although he continued his duties, and also became President of the Bundesrat, he never recovered, and died in August 1957. Until the Hungarian revolt it seemed most likely that his successor would be Franz Neumann, the old leader of the SPD in its struggle with the Communists and subsequently Reuter's foremost adversary within the party. Certainly, Neumann represented views more in line with the attitude of the national SPD at the time. But it was also clear that he would have to contend with Willy Brandt, who had already emerged as Reuter's most vigorous defender five years before.*

Brandt was born in Lübeck in 1913. He had been brought up, so to speak, as a Social Democrat, by his grandfather who had apparently been one of the early followers of August Bebel.[11] His first political mentor was Julius Leber, the leading Social Democrat in Lübeck, who was later hanged after the 20th of July 1944. At Hitler's advent, Brandt had escaped to Norway, returning later to Berlin as a Norwegian student, to take charge of the Social Democrat underground there. During the Spanish Civil War, he worked for a time in Spain

* See above, p. 144.

174

as a political journalist, and was again a journalist in Stockholm during the Second World War, though making periodic returns to the occupied country whose nationality he had now adopted. He first returned to Germany to report the Nuremberg Trials as a Norwegian journalist, and at the end of 1946 was sent as a Press Attaché to the Norwegian Military Mission at the Allied Control Council in Berlin. He remained at the time in close touch with the German Social Democrats, attending their conferences at Hanover, and had come to know both Schumacher and Reuter well. It was not at Reuter's suggestion, however, that he abandoned his Norwegian nationality, but at Schumacher's. He became a German citizen again, and took over the Berlin liaison office of the SPD Executive Committee.

Yet Brandt became in essentials a political disciple of Reuter and not of Schumacher. His early radical training and the frustrations of the SPD in exile; the use to which he saw the Communists in Spain put the idealists who hoped for a left-wing alliance; and finally the peculiarities of the Berlin position, all seem to have combined to make him distrust the old radicalism of the SPD, or Schumacher's expectation that Germany could somehow be reunited by eventual agreement with the Russians. In Berlin during the blockade he increasingly identified himself with Reuter, and says himself that 'plotters and schemers' hoped to manœuvre the two into open conflict with the party leaders.[12] Schumacher offered him a safe Socialist seat in Schleswig-Holstein for the 1949 elections, but he chose to remain in Berlin, and became one of the city's representatives in the first Bundestag. He was already advocating a revised national programme for the SPD at that time, and was plainly dissatisfied with its outlook: 'Whoever wants to master the problems of our time ought to leave his collection of quotations at home. A man who always looks back is anything but radical. A party can follow a miserable policy in spite of an excellent programme.'[13]

Brandt refused, however, to enter the Berlin government as 'Reuter's man', though he was offered a position in the Senate in 1949. He established firm roots in the local organisation first, and combined this position in Berlin with that of a non-voting member of the national Central Committee, while in Bonn he made himself the Berlin spokesman on foreign affairs.

It was a shrewd combination, and Brandt was emerging as a prominent pragmatic radical, dedicated more to organisation than ideology, and consciously attempting to adapt his organisation to the straitened circumstances of post-war Europe: a man of the same company as Gaitskell or Kreisky.

At the same time he was a tireless advocate of identifying Berlin more closely with the Federal Republic, demanding the transfer of federal ministeries from Bonn to Berlin, and a general 'March back to Berlin' from which he accused both the German government and the Western Allies of being too ready to retreat.* His public analysis of the position and difficulties of the city is at times somewhat facile, and it is symptomatic that the movement for a return to the capital which he largely launched was stopped short by the Hungarian revolt in 1956.

His position as foreign affairs spokesman, and his European outlook, impelled him to oppose the official SPD policy on German rearmament, and like Reuter or Fritz Erler, the official party spokesman on military matters, he aroused some suspicions among the mass of Social Democrats. This certainly told against him when he ran for the party chairmanship in Berlin against Neumann in 1952, for at the same time as the national movement of identification with Berlin was gathering pace, the Berlin SPD was identifying itself more closely with the national party. Brandt was defeated as a candidate for membership of the Central Committee of the SPD at its Berlin congress in 1954, and again in 1956. It was not until the Stuttgart congress of 1958 that he was officially admitted to the leadership of the party whose candidate for Chancellor he was soon to become. But the essential change occurred in 1956.

At the time of the Hungarian revolt his position in Berlin was already strong. He was President of the Assembly, and vice-chairman of the party. Neumann, however, still seemed the most likely successor to Suhr, and the rivalry of the two men had gained new momentum just before the rising happened.

The day after the Russian tanks returned to Budapest a demonstration of protest was called by all three parties in Berlin. Perhaps 100,000 people assembled in front of the

---

* Brandt even suggests that the crisis of 1958 was launched by the Russians to throw the Allies out of Berlin, as a result of their own hesitation and weakness.

Rathaus Schoeneberg—in a far more embittered mood than the party leaders had realised. Neither Neumann nor Ernst Lemmer, the CDU chairman, were able to make themselves heard above the shouts of the crowd, who soon began to call for a march on the Brandenburg Gate or even the Soviet Embassy.* It was Brandt who diverted them, making his way to the tribune and calling for a demonstration at the memorial to the victims of Fascism at the Steinplatz. Here it was easier to persuade the crowd to disperse, after a measured speech in which Brandt was able to express the feelings of the Berliners without inciting them to rash action. After singing the German 'Song of the Good Comrade', most of the crowd went home.[14] But not all the demonstrators had followed him to the Steinplatz: many thousands had joined the march to the Brandenburg Gate. The majority were stopped on the way† by the West Berlin police, in a number of serious clashes. A few thousands had got to the space before the Gate, and were barely held back from marching into the Soviet sector. On the other side the *Volkspolizei* had drawn up ready to fire, and behind them near the Soviet Embassy were Russian soldiers. Russian tanks were waiting in the side streets by Unter den Linden. The anger of these young demonstrators had been attracted by some British and French cars which they overturned or set on fire as a protest against the diversion of Suez, but they were now concentrating at the Brandenburg Gate, and the situation threatened catastrophe. There is no knowing what would have happened once the *Volkspolizei* opened fire.

It was now that Brandt emerged as the most effective political leader in Berlin. He stopped to disperse the riot on the Strasse des 17 Juni, warning the crowd from a police car that this was playing the Russians' game for them, then drove to the Brandenburg Gate, where the Police President had begun to calm the demonstrators. Brandt was able to speak from the top of a car, and warned them that by their actions they could start a world war. Gradually he formed a procession, which he led to the Soviet war memorial close by, and began the singing of the *Deutschlandlied*. By this symbolic defiance, he averted the real danger.

---

* On Unter den Linden, a few yards behind the Brandenburg Gate.
† In the Strasse des 17 Juni, named after the Berlin rising of 1953.

Brandt's actions on this day ensured that he would become
the next mayor of Berlin. They initially earned him much un
popularity in the SPD organisation in the city, but Neumann's
failure to control the crowd, and Brandt's audacious success
had made his position unshakeable. Otto Suhr died in August
1957. In October Willy Brandt was elected his successor. A
year later a new Berlin crisis began, and Brandt emerged as a
new German international leader. At the elections of December
1958, when 93 per cent of the population voted their defiance
to Khrushchev, he was chosen to lead his party and the city
in its new struggles. His victory was not due to the SPD—he
even induced some of the party leaders to stay away from
Berlin during the election, and concentrated entirely on pre
senting himself as a national figure. Nevertheless he was also
elected to the executive committee of the SPD that year and
began the transformation of the party. The SPD was changed
by the Berlin crisis above all else, into an uncompromising
enemy of Soviet policy in Germany, and Brandt today is far
more determined than Adenauer that the West should make no
concessions which could endanger the position of Berlin.

The international development which led to this new situa
tion had begun during Berlin's period of local government
and the turning point was in 1955.

Chapter Eight

THE TURNING POINT

IT was the Hungarian revolt which ended the era of local government in Berlin; but it became a new centre of international tension as a result of failure at Geneva the year before. In 1955 the leaders of the opposing blocs rounded a cape in European history from which there was no return. After the summit conference of that year, all hopes of German reunification had vanished. The division of Germany was now final, and though the Western Alliance refused to recognise this, it was nevertheless the logical consequence of Western policy. For their part, the Russian leaders abandoned their experiments with the notion of reunification and consciously decided that the two Germanies would remain. For this they found a convenient, if hitherto unavailing, instrument in Berlin.

This question will be discussed in more detail in the next chapter. But its rise can be traced in these earlier years, through the failure of hopes for reunification, and through the sudden and speedy developments of 1955-56. Events now moved with astonishing speed: for three years the two blocs had been preparing—in a dilatory enough fashion—for the long haul towards a German settlement. Now it was abandoned. Instead, both sides were torn by internal crises which they surmounted only to find themselves precipitated into a new and still more complex order, where the demands of thermo-nuclear strategy were tangled with those of new power conflicts to make a European settlement still more urgent and more difficult. These new elements are beyond the scope of this book; but a history of Berlin in this period can be no more than a magnifying glass held over a small section of a world-wide scheme.

This had not always been true before. In the years before the blockade, Berlin had been a distinctive problem which the Four Powers could hope to regulate by separate agreement. In the years of relative stability between 1953 and 1956 it was scarcely even a complicating factor in discussions on Germany. Thereafter, this distinction no longer held good. Although

Khrushchev ensured by his subsequent actions that Berlin would stand at the heart of negotiations on Europe, no agreement could be reached there without reference to a host of other matters. Nothing could be concluded on Berlin without a decision on Germany, and nothing on Germany without agreement on arms control elsewhere. This first became apparent in 1955, and that too is why the negotiations of that year constituted a turning point. Schemes for 'disengagement' were designed to break through this chain, but they were usually out of date before they were mooted. For disengagement which in the early years of the decade was considered as the military counterpart to German reunification was after 1955 conceived as an instrument to bring German reunification about. As such, it was illusory. Any form of disengagement involved a prior political agreement between the two sides, if only because each had to disarm its own Germany, and both had to ensure the permanent neutrality of the country.* Without such an agreement there could be no prospect of a withdrawal from the centre of Europe. And all attempts to define the terms of reunification failed between 1953 and 1955.

Late in 1953 the leaders of the West seem to have been actively considering the possibility of an agreement with the Soviet Union to create, by stages, an all-German government. There has been some discussion of a 'secret Western plan' to this effect, which the SPD revealed in 1959.[1] The details remain obscure, but the West was apparently prepared to tolerate a confederation in which the two German governments would continue to exist until a peace treaty was signed.[2] Until that time the powers of the central German authority were to remain very limited. Whether such a plan were accepted as a programme of action or not,† however, it is very doubtful whether the Soviet Union would have accepted it. As far as can be determined it made no reference to the final neutrality of

---

* Unless, of course, one considers schemes for extending the control of NATO to the whole of Germany. These could form part of a disengagement plan, but would never be accepted by the Soviet Union. Nor does this include such proposals as the Rapacki Plan which have been loosely labelled disengagement but in reality mean arms control.

† It was not discussed among Western governments because the forthcoming Bermuda Conference was delayed by a French ministerial crisis and again by Churchill's illness.

Germany. There is no indication that after a peace treaty the Western leaders would ever have been willing to contemplate a neutral great power in the centre of Europe; and whenever they discussed German reunification they did so on the assumption that the whole country would be under Western control. This attitude never changed, and was expressed repeatedly between 1953 and 1958. As long as they could not achieve reunification on these terms, they preferred to perpetuate the country's division. But they hoped at the same time that in the end they would be successful. In any case they were not prepared to risk an alternative course, and in this Adenauer agreed with them.

This 'secret plan' never came to light because the East German revolt prevented any experiments with the Ulbricht régime to which the Soviet government might have been inclined. After the revolt, and Beria's execution, Russia's primary concern seems to have been to safeguard the security of Eastern Europe. There could not be any immediate question of replacing the régimes she had imposed there. But though both sides had shown little desire to amend the *status quo*, and though they found greater hindrances to any such policy after the events of June each had a powerful incentive to continue the dialogue. And each ultimately hoped to profit from an agreement on reunification.

In the reappraisal of Russian policy that had gone on since Stalin's death there was a new element: fear of war. This seems to have motivated Beria as much as it did Malenkov, and indeed it is probably true that all Stalin's successors were anxious to reduce the risks of war or revolution in Europe which had been raised by his policy. Malenkov was shortly to warn Russia for the first time that she, like the West, would be destroyed in war*. It is possible that Khrushchev later came to power by his very bravado in confronting the risk, and certainly he maintained his position through an alliance with the army. But at the time there were no signs of a split between the politicians and the military on these questions; and the 17th of June, while it inhibited any immediate change, must also have reinforced the underlying desire for new discussions with the West.

* In February 1954. Previous Russian peace campaigns were directed only to external sympathisers.

Stalin's own German policy had, moreover, clearly failed. It seems likely that after 1948 he was determined to oppose any kind of German reunification until American forces had been withdrawn from Europe. This was the sense of his proposal of 1952; but the Soviet position in Europe had ensured not only that American troops would remain, but that they would soon be joined by German contingents. For the next two years Soviet policy was directed towards preventing this, and the Russian government showed great anxiety to find some form of reunification which would do away with the need for German rearmament, induce the withdrawal of NATO and leave Germany open to peaceful penetration. Naturally it failed. Meanwhile, however, this reasoning provided another incentive to renewed negotiations.

In the West, these were also desired. There could be no question of going back on the decision to rearm Germany, and neither Dulles nor Eden believed that neutrality was genuinely possible. But this did not exclude a certain flexibility: a European Security Pact, like that which Churchill had proposed, and Adenauer, with reservations, had supported, might provide the basis for some withdrawal of forces from Germany, open the way to German reunification and serve to limit the extent of German rearmament. These expectations too were disappointed. But there was some hope of fulfilling them eventually, particularly if other obstacles, like the Austrian Peace Treaty, could be overcome first. Thus, though there were no prospects of an immediate change, the West was as willing as the Soviet Union to begin negotiations again.

They were resumed at the Foreign Ministers' Conference in Berlin in 1954. Dulles, Eden, Bidault and Molotov met there in January and February to discuss the prospects of a European agreement. Molotov showed more flexibility on this occasion than at any time since the war: he was apparently anxious to find a basis for settlement, without abandoning the fundamental Soviet position. His approach appears to have been somewhat as follows: East Germany had become a liability to Soviet policy in Europe. It was a source of instability, which, once West Germany rearmed, might extend the dangers of war. And Russian presence in East Germany was the strongest incentive for the West to rearm the Federal Republic. If the West could be persuaded to abandon this in return for the neutralisation of Germany, Russia would be more secure. But it would have to be a genuine neutralisation; a reunified Germany would never be allowed to add her strength to the Western Alliance. The only ultimate guarantee against this was the maintenance either of a pro-Soviet régime in the Eastern half of the country —or, if Germany were to be more than a confederation of two distinct states, the representation of the SED in the government. If this were not assured, the ultimate result of Russian withdrawal would not be that American forces left Europe, but that they advanced from the Elbe to the Oder. This hypothetical reconstruction of Russian ideas at the time may account for Molotov's offer in conversation with Eden to agree to free elections before withdrawal—provided that the Four Powers agreed beforehand on the kind of government that emerged from them.[3] At the time, this was the limit of Russian concessions in all discussion of the modalities of a peace treaty. The Soviet Union may have been anxious to secure a peace treaty on these lines; but it was recognised that such discussions would last a long time. And Molotov also made it clear that if no agreement was reached to this end, he had no interest in clearing minor obstacles like Austria.

The West was not, however, interested in such an agreement. None of the three Foreign Ministers desired to see a neutral Germany. They hoped to secure Russian withdrawal, pure and simple. This lay behind Eden's plan for German Reunification in Freedom, which he presented at the conference, and in which he set forth his demand for free elections as a preliminary to a peace treaty. The West was anxious only that Germany should be neutral in the sense that she was free from Russian interference; and for this reason the Three Powers demanded the right to join in supervising free elections throughout Germany before Russian troops withdrew. Otherwise the SED apparatus would suffice to assure a Communist victory in the Eastern Zone. But neutralisation they regarded as dangerous and utopian.[4] Germany would have to be kept firmly under Western control, and they clearly expected that, after gaining her independence, she would join NATO. Thus, though Molotov insisted that she should be restrained from joining any alliances afterwards, the limit of Western concessions was that she should be free to 'accept or reject' them. They plainly feared that a neutral Germany, in attempting to steer a middle course, would provoke far greater instability than actually existed. She would be open, moreover, to Communist subversion from the Eastern half, or Russian pressure from without. The ultimate result of Western withdrawal would then be the advance of Soviet influence (or even Russian troops) from the Elbe to the Rhine.

In fact, although each side was willing to make apparent concessions to the other—Russia agreeing to the formality of elections, the West to the formality of an independent Germany —there was no basis of agreement between them. The Berlin Conference was from the beginning doomed to failure.

Without agreement on Germany, there was at that time no prospect of settling the other outstanding difficulties which Malenkov had wanted to clear away. Neither the Austrian Peace Treaty, nor the more fundamental discussions on disarmament which were being pursued in the United Nations committee, made any progress. Indeed, the Soviet Union, which had recently shown some willingness to negotiate the German question, had been all the more intransigeant on the question of disarmament. Perhaps the Russian attitude was dictated in both cases by fear of German rearmament.

If this was so, the new turn of events in 1954 must have encouraged the governmental committee in the Kremlin to new concessions, which, they might hope, would impel a new Western approach to the German question. After the fall of Dien Bien Phu, Mendès-France, the new French Prime Minister, announced his intention of ending the war in Indo-China. It was also realised that if the war were pursued to the point of a complete French defeat, American intervention was certain.* Thus, both France and Russia were ready for a compromise peace in Indo-China; and the Russian government may have hoped that if this were achieved Mendès-France's equal determination to settle the problem of EDC might lead to its defeat in the French Assembly. This is exactly what happened.

---

* Bidault had almost succeeded in 'saving' Dien Bien Phu through American intervention. Whether this would have been carried out with atomic weapons (as was believed at the time) or not, it was evident that Dulles was determined at all costs to prevent further Communist advance in Indo-China.

The European Defence Community had collapsed, France was increasingly pre-occupied by the rebellions of her dependencies in Tunisia and Morocco, East and West were for the first time since 1950, everywhere at peace.* More, the strategic reappraisal of the American Chiefs of Staff had resulted in a large reduction of the forces stationed in the Far East; and Congressional disappointment at the failure of EDC was so bitter that the American commitment to Europe itself might be called in question. Not only did German rearmament itself seem to have been defeated, but for the first time there was a prospect that American forces in Europe might be withdrawn.[5] In August 1954, it must have looked to the Russian government as if the alliance between America and Germany, which presented the most serious obstacle to their domination of Europe, was on the point of collapse.

They can hardly have failed to be aware that this success was due to the apparent reasonableness of Russian policy in Europe since 1952. The intimidation of the post-war years had led to the formation of NATO and the promise of EDC. Now the Western Alliance seemed to be crumbling.

In March they had attempted to circumvent the problems of a European Security Pact, and the international control of Germany, by suggesting that the Soviet Union should join NATO.[6] There no longer seemed to be any need for such far-reaching proposals: the position of the West was daily weakening and European obstinacy increasing. But the next three months were marked by startling changes, which brought the Federal Republic into NATO on far freer conditions than those of EDC, and finally granted it full sovereignty. These sudden events forced the Russian government to reconsider its new policy, and to face the final choice that hitherto both Stalin and his heirs had avoided: whether to acknowledge the perpetual division of Germany, or still try to keep the door open for expansion into Western Europe. It is no wonder that all efforts were concentrated for as long as possible on the second alternative. The Soviet leaders attempted more urgently than ever to bring about German reunification. But when they failed, they recognised that the division of Germany was

* Except in Malaya. But it was already clear that the rebels were losing, and that the war would never be more than a local action.

irrevocable, and in consequence they recognised the Federal
Republic. The complications of the period between the London
and Paris Treaties and the Geneva Conference of 1955 can only
be understood in this light, and so only can the sudden but
nevertheless predetermined changes in Russian policy which
followed it.

Between August and October 1954 Eden created a new
European defence community. He had the support of
Adenauer, but faced the initial opposition of both Dulles and
Mendès-France, the first because the new framework was not
'supra-national' enough for American feelings, the second because he had no confidence that a chamber which had just
rejected EDC would ever ratify German rearmament in a still
less controllable form.

But in his determination to preserve the Western Alliance
and for this reason to prevent any possible neutralisation of
Germany, Eden was in reality supported by Dulles and even
by the French Assembly, which, faced with the final alternative
preferred German rearmament to American withdrawal. In
his tour of European capitals in these months, Eden was
finally able to settle the question that had been held up for so
long. In January 1955 the French Assembly ratified the
treaties. These agreements specified that Germany should
commit a national contingent of twelve divisions to NATO
and that she should be recognised as the only German government.* Germany for her part undertook† to renounce in perpetuity the manufacture of chemical, bacteriological and
nuclear weapons, and their means of delivery. The treaties
were finally ratified by the Bundestag in May 1955. The
Federal Republic was now a fully sovereign state.

The Soviet government had made repeated efforts over these
months to prevent the London and Paris agreements from
coming into force. During the final Western negotiations
Molotov made a speech in East Berlin[7] proposing the immediate withdrawal of all occupation forces from Germany, and

---

* Only, as a different clause makes plain, until Germany is reunited. This does
not therefore mean, as is often claimed, that the Western Powers have recognised
the Federal government as having sovereign claim to the whole of Germany. I
does mean that they are bound not to recognise East Germany.

† As also did the Benelux countries.

he reunification of the country—within the framework of a
European security pact. In this event the Soviet government
would be ready to 'discuss' the question of free elections. On
October 29th, the last day of the Paris Conference, Russia
confirmed this offer in a Note to the three Western Powers. If
the decision to incorporate West Germany into NATO and the
WEU were not put into effect, the Soviet government offered
o 'reconsider' the Western plan for free elections throughout
Germany.

This was not much to go on, and it was not to be expected
that the Western governments would scrap the work of years
in return for such a vague proposal. Although the Soviet
Union has normally shown a scrupulous regard for the letter
of any agreement it signs, it has never hesitated to denounce
any verbal arrangements or exploit their ambiguities. This has
not changed since Stalin's time; and in 1962 Khrushchev's
threats to the Berlin air-corridors were made in the same spirit
as that which imposed Communism on Poland, and established
the Oder-Neisse Line before the Potsdam Conference. Nevertheless, it is astonishing that the Soviet offer was so summarily
dismissed. None of the Western Powers was prepared to discuss it, or slow down the time-table of German rearmament
for the sake of new negotiations with Russia. The German
question could only be reopened on the basis of a rearmed West
Germany and Russian evacuation of the East. It is surprising,
not that the NATO powers were committed to such a plan,
but that they hoped to win concessions from Russia in this way.
Yet the next months were to show that they apparently expected to; and Malenkov's and Bulganin's statements revealed
that Russia had not yet abandoned hope of deflecting Western
intentions.

After the failure of the initiatives of October, the Soviet
leaders repeatedly warned the West that the ratification of the
London and Paris agreements would perpetuate the division
of Germany. They affirmed that the Eastern bloc would be
obliged to take counter-measures the moment West Germany
entered NATO. If not, they declared, free elections could be
held throughout Germany in 1955.[8] As ratification drew near,
preparations went on in the East for a counterpart to NATO,
the Warsaw Pact. At the same time the offer of reunification

was repeatedly renewed, only to be ignored in the West. This does not necessarily mean that Russia was now prepared to withdraw from Eastern Europe, or agree unconditionally to setting up a stable and neutralised bloc in the centre of the continent. It might have been possible to bring this about if Western policy had been more flexible, but there was little evidence to substantiate such a hope. It is more likely that, having seen the effects of a display of reasonableness on the fate of EDC, the Soviet Union hoped by similar tactics to prevent the ratification of the subsequent treaties. For Russian policy was itself deliberately ambiguous: the form of free elections which it offered was never specified, nor was the fate of the East German régime in a 'reunified' Germany. But it is true to say that every conceivable concession was tried out, in appearance at least, to test Western reactions. Unhappily there were none.

Instead, the Paris Treaty and the Warsaw Pact were formally ratified and the division of Europe was complete. Yet even now, there was still hope of reaching a limited agreement, which, though it might not offer much opportunity of political expansion, would still secure the essentials of the Russian demand for security. East Germany was not included in the Warsaw Pact, and though it was plain that each side would now retain its own Germany, Russia prepared a new diplomatic campaign to prevent the Federal Republic from participating actively in NATO. Molotov had formally called for a European Security Treaty in December 1954, and the new offensive was designed to meet the new situation. The German settlement that had been established *de facto* would be used as the basis for a security agreement between the Great Powers. West Germany would remain in NATO; East Germany would remain under Russian control. But precisely because neither side need no longer fear the dangers of a neutral reunified Germany, it should be possible for them to reach agreement on the reduction of armaments and tension in Central Europe. If this were achieved, the eventual modalities of reunification could be discussed once more.

This reasoning was not immediately apparent; but it seems to have emerged from the international discussions that took place after May 1955. They were born of the coincidence of negotiations on disarmament, and on European security, which were both being conducted at the same time, and from which the Geneva Summit Conference arose. In June 1955 Molotov still called at San Francisco for a European security pact, which would have involved, in effect, the abolition of NATO, and could have been joined by both Germanies. These would then presumably have been reunified in due course. From this scheme to Bulganin's proposals at Geneva the following month was a short step, but one which involved the reversal of much earlier Russian thinking.

This evolution was matched on the Western side by the preparation, in the conferences of NATO Foreign Ministers, of several alternative schemes, to see which would be the most fruitful at Geneva.[9] They attempted to get round Molotov's sweeping proposals for dismantling NATO to some point of negotiation. One possibility was that Eastern and Western Europe should exchange reciprocal guarantees on the limitation of armaments in Europe, on the model of the voluntary undertakings of the WEU. This originated with Mendès-France, and was later taken up by Eden. Another was that of an agreement between NATO and the Eastern bloc for limiting armaments in certain areas, which would be enforced by inspection. A third envisaged the withdrawal of some American and British troops in return for a thinning-out of Russian forces in Czechoslavakia and Poland.

At the same time the Western Powers were determined to oppose a neutral area or a demilitarised Germany. At best they considered 'accepting' the demilitarisation of East Germany to assure the Russians that they would have no grounds to fear a united Germany in NATO. The limit of any contemplated concessions would be to revise Eden's insistence on the primacy of free elections in favour of Molotov's plan for a transitional provisional government. But in the West this was always linked with the intention of doing away with the East German régime.[10] This was no longer acceptable to Russia, but they hoped to make it so by tying it to a limited disarmament agreement in Europe.

In 1954 the United States had abandoned her previous plans for complete disarmament, enforced by a United Nations body outside the control of the Great Powers. Nor had she any further hope of banning the means of delivery of atomic weapons, or achieving a system of free inspection. She was now concentrating on the possibility of an 'international alarm system', which was also known to be favoured by the Soviet Union—which had already proposed a limited system of (immobile) inspectors, stationed in ports and communications centres. The American intention was that such a scheme should first be applied to Europe, where it would be easier to secure political acceptance than in a universal system. In conjunction with the limitations of the armed forces of all the major powers, on which all had for the moment agreed, this could provide the basis for negoiating a provisional settlement in Europe.

There were, thus, real hopes that the Geneva Conference could lead to fruitful negotiations when it convened in July. But it was soon seen that these hopes depended on the adjustment of tactical positions, rather than a real change of intention by either side. In fact, it met under the shadow of a Russian demand in the United Nations disarmament committee for the dismantling of all 'foreign bases' as part of the first stage of a disarmament programme. This in itself was enough to make nonsense of all attempts to achieve a European settlement as part of a wider scheme. However, the implications of this Russian step had not yet been made explicit, and it was not allowed to dim the atmosphere of the opening proceedings.

The speeches at the beginning of the conference showed how Russian thought had crystallised since Molotov's appearance in San Francisco in June. Bulganin's speech revealed a subtle evolution of the Molotov plan. Federal Germany could, given some kind of a European security pact, remain a member of WEU and NATO. A European security system could now be built around the existing alignments, and Bulganin emphasised that it would be 'absolutely unreal' to think otherwise. But only if agreement were reached to abolish these alliances in the second stage of a security pact. Germany could not be reunified until this stage was reached and both defence systems were dissolved. But this in turn depended on the complete success of the disarmament negotiations then just beginning, and in the meantime Russia was not prepared to consider any system of guarantees. 'Great Powers' Bulganin told Eden cornfully, 'do not need guarantees'. The Soviet government was clearly prepared neither to risk withdrawal from Eastern Europe, nor to risk a reunified Germany until disarmament was complete. Even then, it is doubtful whether Russia would tolerate more than a German confederation in which she would retain control of the Eastern half; perhaps a security pact was designed, as much as anything else, to perpetuate the division of Germany. Certainly, Bulganin declared shortly after the conference that a security pact 'should take into consideration the fact that two German states exist'. This had completely reversed the sense of the Molotov proposals earlier that year, and it was plain that if Russia now proposed to consider the existing alliances as the basis for a security pact, she was not prepared to risk losing control over East Germany.

Both sides had made their maximum concessions before the conference really started—Russia on the continuation of the Federal Republic in NATO, the West on limiting her future armed strength, on joint military inspection to an agreed depth, and on the possibility of a demilitarised zone in Germany. (This was the basis of the 'Eden Plan' put forward at Geneva.) But this last point, it appears, would have embraced essentially East Germany. Fundamentally, the West maintained that security could only be achieved through German reunification; and Russia that reunification could in effect only come about when the Americans left Europe. Neither could meet the other's requirements, and the Geneva conference rapidly declined to the point where Eisenhower's 'Open Skies' offer was all that remained of an international alarm system.

The Western Powers seem to have left Geneva without hopes or expectations from further negotiations with the Soviet Union. At the second Geneva Conference in October, the Foreign Ministers were to take a still more inflexible stand than had their heads of government, on building German reunification and European security side by side. But meanwhile Russian policy had moved with far greater speed. Adenauer was invited to Moscow—and went. By the end of the year Russia, which only a few months before had conceded sovereign status to East Germany, agreed to recognise the Federal Republic. Ambassadors were exchanged between Moscow and Bonn, and the Chancellor's visit, it soon appeared, was

intended merely to consecrate the grave of German unity
Soviet policy has since that date never wavered in its determination to achieve Western recognition of the GDR, and by doing
so, to ensure that any European agreement is based on the
division of Germany.

Why did Adenauer agree? It is hard to believe that the cause
of the German prisoners of war, though of great importance,
was enough to make him change his mind about the wisdom
of diplomatic relations with Russia. Hitherto he had inflexibly
opposed such a step.

In December 1955 the Chancellor declared that after a
decade in which Germany had been only an object for world
politics, the Federal Republic had now gained 'freedom of
manœuvre for the sake of the whole of Germany'. Her recovered sovereignty would enable her 'to pursue the aims for
which she had already been striving: the reunification of
Germany, and the unity of Europe'.[11] Germany's recognition
of the Soviet Union was certainly a function of her sovereignty;
but her recognition by the Soviet Union was nothing but an
obstacle in the path of reunification. The German government
certainly realised this, for in a Note to the NATO powers, it
asked them to reaffirm their undertaking not to recognise the
GDR (with which Russia meanwhile signed a second declaration of the grant of sovereignty).*

Adenauer's motives are still somewhat mysterious. Some
light may be thrown on them by a later confession to his ambassador in Paris, Wilhelm Hausenstein. He had, he told him,
been faced with a 'position of ultimatum' at this time in
Moscow.[12] What can have been Moscow's means of pressure
on him? It seems possible that the proposals which the Western
Foreign Ministers had worked out before Geneva had dismayed
the German Chancellor. The Federal Republic had only acquired full sovereignty a few months before, and the Western
Powers were already contemplating a reduction of their troops
in Germany. These proposals had the support not only of
Britain, but also of the United States, and if they were to be
carried out to a point where German security were threatened,

* It was with this recognition of sovereignty that East Germany also gained
physical control over all civilian traffic to Berlin, a control that after 1958
Khrushchev threatened to extend to military traffic.

the only insurance left was to reach agreement with Russia. Such an agreement certainly ensured that West Germany would acquiesce in Russia's intentions for the future of Europe. Adenauer's discussions in Moscow centred on the clash of priorities which had now emerged in the negotiations between the two sides: the Russians insisting that a security system should precede the reunification of Germany; Adenauer repeating that it could only be the consequence of reunification. But he had, by his action, given way to the Russian order. The existence of two German states was now recognised as the basis for further negotiations. In refusing to acknowledge this, the West was hanging on to an unreal position.

The other Western Powers had, meanwhile, hardened in their insistence that security could only be achieved if the whole of Germany joined NATO. Eden and the British government then and later desired to defer the question of a united Germany's decision until after a system of collective security was arranged. But at the Foreign Ministers' Conference in October, Dulles and Pinay insisted that the last stage of a European security pact—that is, the stage at which the promises of collective defence against aggression could be worked out—could only be achieved if a united Germany joined NATO. Thereafter the policies of the two sides were directly opposed to each other, and were bound at some point to collide.

July 1955 had been the last time when German reunification was possible, even remotely. Thereafter Russia was determined to get the question settled. She did so to her own satisfaction by the end of the year, and has been trying to force acquiescence on the West ever since. This was the turning point which led to the crisis of 1958.

The significance of these developments was hidden for a time by the continuing debate on disarmament, and by new interest in the possibilities of disengagement. Indeed, the plans which the Western foreign ministers presented, for a reduction of troops and an exchange of radar control posts on either side of a demilitarised zone, were the first real official suggestions of disengagement. And the British government moved further and further from the original conception of collective security towards a policy of 'thinned out' zones in the centre of Europe as a first step towards disarmament. This was linked to the reduction of Britain's armed strength, in the belief, which found official expression in 1957, that a nuclear guarantee was of itself enough to preserve the *status quo* in Central Europe. But this belief could not be shared by the Soviet Union until the West recognised East Germany; otherwise there could never be any question of a withdrawal from the centre.

Thus, the concept of disengagement, which began to gain ground in 1957, was already out of date. It was considered valuable precisely because it was clear that Russia would never relax her grip on Eastern Europe in the actual situation. It was hoped that 'disengagement' would provide a break-through— that once troops had been withdrawn, the political question of Germany's alliances would no longer matter. But disengagement had always depended on the political settlement which would define the future of Germany without equivocation. Unless such an agreement were reached beforehand, Russia was completely uninterested in any scheme for disengagement. Bulganin's correspondence in these years repeatedly emphasised this. At best, the Soviet Union was prepared to consider limited plans for the control of armaments in Central Europe— such as those put forward by Adam Rapacki. But there was no chance of withdrawal without a detailed political settlement first.

There had been some grounds for thinking otherwise in November 1956. After the crisis of destalinisation and the Hungarian rising, Khrushchev made a dramatic proposal to the Western Powers for a 'thousand-mile zone' of inspection in Central Europe, and a reduction by one-third of the armed forces stationed in Germany. Ultimately all armed forces were to be withdrawn. But this offer depended likewise on banning atomic armaments and dismantling all foreign bases within two years. This depended on the course of disarmament negotiations and they had already broken down after much progress in 1956. The Western Powers had, under American pressure, suddenly rescinded their proposals for a gradual reduction of armed forces to an agreed ceiling; and though discussions on the fundamentals of atomic disarmament were resumed in 1957, they failed to produce agreement.

Negotiations on every important issue had failed. In 1955 Germany had been linked with a whole range of questions on

which East and West had hoped to reach a limited agreement.
These hopes had gone, and in Russian eyes this was because
the Western Powers refused to come to terms with the realities
of their own policy or the demands of Russian security. When
the opportunity arose, Russia would seek to force this acknowledgement upon them.

Chapter Nine

THE IMPONDERABLE CRISIS

THROUGH the blockade of Berlin the Soviet Union had tried to consolidate its political system in Europe by the direct capture of the city. The second great Berlin crisis, which began in 1958, was no such open assault. Rather, Schumacher's analysis of ten years earlier had come true: it was an attempt to divide Germany, using Berlin as a lever to change Western policy. But Soviet motives appear to have been inconsistent, and Soviet methods were certainly so variable that it was scarcely possible at any one point between the ultimatum of 1958 and the summer of 1961, when the world feared that the crisis had brought it to the brink of war, to work out any settlement which could avert the dangers that had been so rashly evoked. They appeared and receded without any real changes in the position of either side, and it was seldom possible to calculate the consequences of any response to the imponderable threats from Moscow and East Berlin.

The basic confrontation of Soviet and Western policies had remained constant since 1955. Russia had consistently sought to consecrate the European *status quo* into a settlement which would define political spheres of influence and guarantee them by mutual deterrence. This would enable her to withdraw a large part of her forces from Eastern Europe, but would leave her hegemony unchallenged, reduce the risk of war, and leave her free to pursue the peaceful conquest of the rest of the world. The key to such a settlement lay in the definitive division of Germany.

Equally, the Western Powers remained convinced that a European settlement could only be achieved through German reunification. Originally it had been assumed that this could best be secured through the demilitarisation of Central Europe, and the absorption of Germany into a European confederation. But Dulles had been pre-occupied by other considerations, and the absorption of Germany into a European system became confused with the incorporation of Germany into NATO.

Stability was seen almost exclusively in terms of the doctrine of massive retaliation. When, after its brief experiment with the idea in 1955, the Soviet Union abandoned the negotiations for a neutralised Germany, the two approaches were bound to collide at some stage—the more so since Khrushchev was not interested in a permanent settlement in Europe, but only in avoiding the immediate dangers of war.

Since 1956 these fundamentally opposed policies had been fomenting and they came to a head in the crisis of 1958. The moment for Khrushchev's ultimatum was none the less deliberately chosen; but it was the developments of the two preceding years which enabled and encouraged him to act when he did.

The Hungarian revolt had revealed both how unstable the Soviet system in Europe really was, and how illusory was the doctrine of massive retaliation as an instrument of active policy. It was an extension of the principle of deterrence that left no room for any hopes of a neutralised belt in Europe, and inhibited the Great Powers from encroaching on each other's preserves. Hungary's withdrawal from the Warsaw Pact had seemed for a moment to show that the power of deterrence could encourage the development of neutralism, but when, encouraged in part by the Anglo-French diversion in Suez, the Russian forces returned to conquer Budapest, it was revealed that the border-line between 'massive retaliation' and 'self-deterrence' had completely vanished. These lessons followed hard upon the breakdown of disarmament negotiations after a moment of real hope that the West and the Soviet Union could come to terms. In Russian eyes, this failure was entirely the fault of the United States which had insisted on the withdrawal of the Anglo-French proposals after they had been accepted in substance by the Soviet Union. The latter now saw itself confronted by a set of circumstances which dictated a change of method in the pursuit of its policies: the instability of its Eastern European empire, the failure of the West to negotiate on terms which had once seemed acceptable to both sides, and the weakness of a policy of deterrence which offered an admirable chance of exploitation in its most exposed position—Berlin.

Russia's armed strength was not yet, however, sufficiently preponderant to offer immediate possibilities of exploitation.

But it continued to grow throughout 1957. At the very moment when the bankruptcy of pure deterrence had been confirmed, the British government chose to put all its faith in this outworn creed. The Defence White Paper of 1957, following on the heels of the failure at Suez, emphasised the fact that the West not only lacked the conventional strength to match Soviet forces in Europe, but was abandoning the intention of creating it. The Soviet Union, willing as it may have been to reduce the number of its troops, had as yet no intention of going over to a similar doctrine. But that year it created the belief, perhaps ill-founded, that it had secured a decisive advantage in the arms race by launching the first sputnik. And while the relative strength of the Soviet Union appeared to be growing every day, the West showed no sign of contemplating any change in its European policies. In June 1958 Dulles told the Senate Foreign Relations Committee, in answer to a question from the Republican Senator Margaret Aiken, whether a reunified Germany would once again constitute a threat to the peace of Europe: 'I think it is very important, Senator, that a reunified Germany should be integrated into the West by means of her connections with NATO, and through her participation in the Brussels Treaty and West European Union. I believe that a Germany that was left in the condition of neutrality, or, as some people call it, disengagement, would be exposed to the almost irresistible temptation to play off one side against the other, and that this would produce a very dangerous situation—dangerous for the West, dangerous for the Soviet Union and dangerous for the Germans themselves.... I would not consider it wise or prudent to purchase German neutrality at the price of making Germany an independent country. On many occasions I have explained this to the Russians.... I believe that this [Germany's absorption into the West] would be a healthy future for the Germans, for the Russians and for the West.'[1] These remarks were made barely five months before the new crisis began, and while Khrushchev may well have agreed with Dulles' analysis of the problem, he preferred to purchase security at the price of the division of Germany.

Moreover, it now seemed possible to achieve this, since the West had abandoned its tacit guardianship of Europe's future liberation. The refusal to recognise East Germany had always been linked to the assumption that Russian forces would one day be withdrawn from Eastern Europe, and Western presence in the Four-Power city of Berlin had the symbolic function of keeping the light of the future burning behind the Iron Curtain. But while this had contributed to the instability which Khrushchev was now trying to eliminate, the mission had been tacitly abandoned in 1956. Western presence in Berlin was in danger of becoming a 'meaningless anomaly'[2] in the political scheme of Europe, and it offered the ideal target for the exploitation of Western weaknesses. If the bluff of Berlin could be called, the future of Europe could be settled on Russia's terms.

In addition to these underlying reasons there may have been other motives for urgency behind Khrushchev's action in internal political rivalries and the increasing need for manpower in the development of the Russian economy, but they are beyond the scope of this book. If this description has been presented almost wholly in Russian terms, this is only because the Soviet Union had developed an active policy in Europe, while that of the West was limited to whatever responses it could find to the Russian initiative. It is doubtful whether Khrushchev was determined at that time to rid Berlin of its Western garrisons; it is certain that he intended to use them to force a change of attitude in the West, and to make their presence in the city meaningless.

The crisis was slow in developing. Communist threats were concentrated at first on the periphery of the Western system—Quemoy, Turkey and Iran. This probably had a twofold design: both to begin a process of softening up before the real threat was launched, and to exploit Russian and Chinese strength to prevent any bargaining at all until the West was prepared to accede to Soviet desires. But in the early months of 1958 there were unmistakable signs that a real crisis was impending. On March 15th the Deputy Mayor of East Berlin called for a normalisation of the situation in the capital of the German Democratic Republic, and in July this was echoed by Ulbricht in the more important forum of the Fifth Party Congress of the SED. In May, Dulles repeated the Western guarantees for Berlin, and again with greater emphasis in November, shortly after Ulbricht had spoken in the Volkskammer elections of the parallel injustices of Western provocation in Berlin and Quemoy.

On November 10th Khrushchev spoke to a friendship meeting in Moscow of the Polish United Workers' Party, presided over by Gomulka. 'The time has evidently come', he concluded, 'for the powers which signed the Potsdam Agreement to give up the remnants of the occupation régime in Berlin and thus make it possible to create a normal atmosphere in the capital of the German Democratic Republic. The Soviet Union for its part will hand over those functions in Berlin which are still in the hands of Soviet organs to the Sovereign German Democratic Republic.'[3] This announcement marked the real beginning of the crisis. It was followed by a still more emphatic declaration from Gomulka two days later: the Federal German government was the chief prop of the imperialist policy of the reactionary circles of the capitalist world. The threat to the peace and security of all the European governments affected by such a policy could only be overcome through a change in the status of Berlin. Gomulka's was the first shot in a campaign which was taken up by the entire Communist press in Europe, linking the demands for a change in the status of Berlin to the contrast between the peaceful aspirations of the Socialist part of Germany, and the aggressive intentions of the revanchists in Bonn.

The purpose of this campaign was revealed when the Russian ambassadors in Washington, London, Paris and Bonn delivered Notes from the Soviet Government at the end of the month. They contained the famous ultimatum of November 27th, which in 1962 informs the relations between Russia and the West. With this Note, the Soviet government raised the basic questions of the political future of Europe, and ensured that any alterations in the *status quo* would have to begin with a settlement in Berlin.

The Note was remarkable both for its aggressive tone and the number of new concepts it introduced into international negotiations on the future of Berlin. After a long sermon on the tolerance and encouragement shown to Hitler's Germany by the Western Powers before the war, and the unfortunate tendencies developed afterwards through the influence of 'W. Churchill and those who share his views', which had led to epeated violations of the Potsdam Agreement, the Soviet government notified its readers that it regarded as null and void he Agreement on the Administration of Berlin of September 2th, 1944.⁴ It regarded the occupation of Berlin as unlawful, nd accused the Western Powers of abusing their occupation ights to damage the Socialist camp. It added later that 'the Western Powers' insistence on continuing their occupation f West Berlin would lead to the conclusion that the matter is not confined to "indirect aggression" against the GDR and the Soviet Union, and that some other plans are apparently being ept in view for an even more dangerous use of West Berlin'. The dangers of remaining were also specified: '. . . only madmen can go to the length of unleashing another world war over he preservation of privileges of occupiers in West Berlin'.

Alongside these threats the West was offered a series of concessions which would enable West Berlin to retain its distinctive economic and social system, while ending the state of occupation. It would become a Free City, free from intervention in ts internal affairs by 'either German state'. Such an arrangement would represent 'a definite sacrifice' on the part of the GDR for the sake of European peace, but in view of the unrealistic policies of the Western Powers in Berlin, the Soviet government 'would consider it possible to solve the West Berlin question *at the present time*'* in such a manner. In order to give he municipal and national governments in Berlin and Germany time to discuss 'such questions as may arise', the Western governments were being allowed six months to bring the occupation status to an end. If the Russian proposal were inacceptable, the Soviet Union and the Western Powers would have nothing left to negotiate about concerning the Berlin question; and, 'if the above-mentioned period is not utilised to reach an adequate agreement, the Soviet Union will then carry out the planned measures through agreement with the GDR. It is envisaged that the German Democratic Republic, like any other independent state, must fully deal with questions concerning its space, i.e. exercise its sovereignty on land, water and in the air'.

The Note thus contained two distinct ultimatums. In the

* Italics added. The Note also says that this solution would be an important step towards the normalisation of the situation in Berlin.

immediate future the threat of a separate agreement with
East Germany which would leave it free to permit or prevent
at its discretion all Western access to Berlin, without Russian
intervention.* This had not yet hardened into the doctrine of
separate peace treaty which was shortly to be added to the
Russian diplomatic artillery, but the essentials of the threat
were already there. In the long term, the Western Powers
would have to face a third world war if they rejected the Soviet
concessions and insisted on remaining in Berlin.

As an alternative to this fate, they were presented with the
concept of a Free City of West Berlin, which was amplified in a
variety of ways. The Note made mention of a United Nations
association with the future security of the city, of a negotiated
guarantee of 'unhindered communications'—which, however
(though the Note is highly ambiguous on this point†), would
have to be negotiated purely between West Berlin and East
Germany, and even of Russian economic assistance in ensuring
the maintenance of West Berlin's living standards and 'distinctive way of life'. All these have been points of discussion
since, and have only helped to deepen the ambiguity with
which the Soviet demand has been surrounded.

The reasons for this ambiguity are clear: the Soviet government was not prepared to take uncontrollable risks; it preferred
to create an incalculable situation through which the onus of
risk could be placed on the Western Allies. And if they were
not prepared to accept it, the terms of the proffered concessions
were elastic enough to permit continuous extension afterwards.
Thus, West Berlin's freedom from interference in its internal
affairs by either German state contained the implication that, in
accepting the new status, the West would accord practical
recognition to the East German State (without binding it to

* But all the Warsaw Pact Powers would intervene if they judged that the
West had committed any aggression against East Germany.

† 'It is obvious that, considering the specific position of West Berlin, which lies
within the territory of the GDR and is cut off from the outside world, the question
would arise of some kind of arrangement with the German Democratic Republic
concerning guarantees of unhindered communications between the Free City and
the outside world—both to the East and to the West—with the object of free
movement of passengers and freight traffic. In its turn, West Berlin would undertake not to permit on its territory any hostile subversive activity directed against
the GDR or any other state.'

ny agreement on external access to Berlin, since this was to
e in any case within the exclusive competence of the GDR).
There was, at this stage, no mention of Soviet guarantees. Nor
were the offers of Soviet industrial orders for the industry of the
future Free City balanced by any implication that it could con-
inue to trade with the Federal Republic, except in the statement that passengers and freight traffic would have to have
ccess to both East and West.

If the West agreed to the principle of a demilitarised Free
City, it would be faced with an increasing scale of demands.
But the Soviet government had also prepared a way of retreat
or the eventuality—which at that stage it probably considered
emote—that it would encounter open defiance. This was
pparent from the nature of the ultimatum giving the West six
months' grace to arrange its withdrawal from Berlin. The
ime limit is referred to in two different ways in the course of the
Note. In the first place, the Soviet government regarded it as
fully sufficient to *provide a sound foundation* for a solution to
he problems connected with the change'. In the second place,
and much more dangerously, it was said that the six months
hould be used 'for *reaching a relevant agreement*'. There was a
imilar discrepancy between Khrushchev's press conference of
November 27th, and his remarks at a reception in the Albanian
embassy in Moscow the following day. The first was altogether
more challenging. 'You ask', he told a correspondent, 'if the
olicy of the Soviet Union would change in respect to Berlin
f West Germany were to renounce its rearmament programme.
No, it would not change. One must remember that according
o the Potsdam Agreement, Germany should not be armed at
ll. So West Germany's renunciation of a rearmament programme could not be interpreted as a concession which would
bind us to a concession.' Soviet policy on Berlin was immutable,
and the Western Powers had no choice but to agree to it; if
they did not do so within six months, the Soviet Union would
carry out its threat of a separate agreement with the GDR.[5]
But he had retreated from this position the following day: he
was reported, although the Soviet press did not mention it, to
have said that the Soviet government would not take this
action if the Western governments agreed to begin negotiations
within six months.[6]

In fact, there was no hint of the course of action which th
Soviet government had in mind if its demands were refused
It seems to have had none. Nor was there any possibility o
assessing the risks of a separate agreement with the GDR:
would clearly be impossible for East Germany to preven
Western access to Berlin on its own—but it was possible tha
Khrushchev might be impelled to take the gamble of experi
menting with such action by proxy. He desired to give th
Allied governments the choice of risk, and hoped that thei
response would achieve in one form or another his ultimat
objective: that of forcing them to recognise the East Germa
régime, and so ensure the definitive division of Germany, an
Russian hegemony over Eastern Europe.

He was prepared to be flexible while waiting—both in
creasing the scope of his threats, and reducing his terms for a
interim accommodation. But though he had no settled policy
and his reactions to the pressures of his allies or opponents wer
unpredictable and inconsistent, his ultimate aim was clear; an
the West showed little more consistency in its appreciation o
resolve. The Western governments understood that they could
not give way to direct pressure, but they were anxious not t
lay themselves open to renewed pressure whenever Khrushchev
chose. So there was for some time a search for concessions
which was afterwards abandoned. Tactically they were right t
stand firm; but they never worked out a strategy.

The first response of the Western Powers was a simpl
refusal to negotiate under 'ultimatum', which they coupled with
a renewal of their still unanswered proposals of the previous
September for a new discussion of the whole German problem
They refused to treat Berlin as the essential aspect of the
question, and indicated their willingness to discuss the reuni
fication and a peace treaty with the Soviet government. This
must have been to Khrushchev's liking: Berlin was not the
essential aspect of the German problem for him any more than
for the West, and he now had the chance of negotiating on the
peace treaty and European security with the threat behind him
that, if the negotiations failed, he could inflict intolerable loss
on the West in a position where the deterrent could scarcely
hope to work. The Western Powers had taken more than a
month to answer the Soviet Note; he responded within ten

lays with the suggestion of a 'summit conference'. But the erms he proposed in the Note of January 10th, 1959, were precisely those that the West had hoped to avoid by extending the scope of the negotiations: they would embrace not German reunification, but a peace treaty with the two German states.

Coupled with this went a proposal emanating from East Germany that the peace treaty should in fact establish a German confederation—through which the Pankow government would of course be empowered to resist any changes in its régime, whatever the future settlement of Europe. A Note from the GDR to the Soviet government set this forth three days before the Russian summit invitation of January 10th.

The Government of the German Democratic Republic further proceeds from the fact that its agreement to the creation of a demilitarised free city of West Berlin is of great importance to the promotion of an approach between the two German states and to the normalisation of the situation in Berlin. From the establishment of a Free City of West Berlin further important experience would be gained for the creation of a confederation of both the German states. Moreover, such a solution would be favourable for the preparation of a peace treaty with Germany.[7]

In the last paragraph of the Note the East German government declared that it agreed

with the Soviet Government's suggestion of conducting at a suitable time negotiations between governmental delegations of the German Democratic Republic and the USSR concerning the solution of the problems which are connected with the peaceful settlement of the question of West Berlin, and in so doing, proceeds from the standpoint that the time of such negotiations could be settled through diplomatic channels.'

For the first time the prospect of a separate peace treaty had been evoked, and by the East German government.* The history of this Note is obscure: confederation was not a new idea, and it may have been an East German attempt to force Russia's hand by suggesting that either the Western Powers should be squeezed out of Berlin, or that if the scope of negotiations were broadened as they suggested, a confederation

* Speier, *op. cit.*, suggests that the eventuality of a separate peace treaty was first brought forward by Khrushchev in February 1959. But this paragraph is a clear reference to the possibility of a unilateral settlement. It is important not to ignore the part played by the East German government throughout the crisis. It has, within its limited room of manœuvre, shown remarkable ingenuity and tenacity in persuading the Soviet Union to accept its own objectives.

should be established which would ensure their departure any
way. But if neither of these could be assured, the GDR plainl
hoped to influence the course of events by winning a separat
peace treaty, and therewith the control of access to Berlin, a
a compensation from the Soviet Union. It declared in the Not
that it found the situation in Berlin intolerable, and the consis
tent aim of East German policy since that date has been t
bring it to an end. It has attempted bolder *faits accomplis*, bu
this was its first independent intervention in the diplomati
dialogue.

There is no means of judging Khrushchev's immediat
reaction. He was immersed in the Twenty-First Party Congres
during January, which was only indirectly concerned with th
Berlin question in that Malinovsky's boasts of the rocke
strength of the Soviet Union were plainly designed to impres
the West with a fear of resistance. But after this, and perhap
because of the propaganda successes scored at the congress
Khrushchev found it expedient to make use of the threat of
separate treaty. On February 17th he announced that if th
West refused to sign a peace treaty with both German govern
ments before reunification, the Soviet Union would do so wit
the GDR alone.

But though Khrushchev was gradually led to expand hi
threats in this manner, he had also been at pains to present th
West with acceptable alternatives to the *status quo*. While saving
the face of the disputants, they would entail further conse
quences which would bring him nearer his final goal—th
recognition of East Germany and a new form of Europear
stability. He had already made this clear in an interview wit
Philip Noel-Baker and his son Francis in December 1958
Though his demands for the evacuation of Berlin were relent
less, he also insisted that the Soviet Union maintained he
support of the 1956 Anglo-French plan for graduated reduc
tion of forces, and suggested an international control system
The Noel-Bakers concluded: 'The most significant con
clusion . . . was that Mr. Khrushchev and his colleagues wer
glad to seek a comprehensive settlement with the Wester
Powers, if they could be persuaded that the Western Power
would respond'.[8] Similarly Mikoyan, on his good-will tour o
the United States in January, had hinted that the whole crisi

was due to the present occupation of Europe by the troops of the two opposing giants, and had revived suggestions for a common withdrawal from the Elbe. But there was no suggestion that the large demilitarised zone thus created could ever contain a united Germany. To these hints Dulles responded in a press conference which, though it poured scorn on the Soviet proposals for German confederation, conceded a point on which the West had hitherto been adamant (except for a few weeks in 1955): the modalities of reunification. 'There might', he said, be other ways of bringing about German reunification' than those of free elections. The West was approaching the Soviet terms as rapidly as Khrushchev was retreating from his original ultimatum. Both sides were beginning to offer each other the possibilities of negotiations, but neither could be sure of the result if they failed. Russia could not be certain of the success of her ultimatum nor could the West foresee the risks either of compliance or of determination to resist.

In these circumstances Macmillan decided to make a 'reconnaissance' visit to Moscow to try to discover the purposes behind the Soviet threat and the possibilities of negotiation. This episode remains one of the most puzzling of the initial crisis. There is no indication of the conditions proposed by either of the two men, nor how far the conversations of February 1959 affected the subsequent course of events. Their meeting took place after Khrushchev's threat of a separate peace treaty, and though the incidents of the visit highlighted their disagreements, the tone of Khrushchev's speeches at the time was greatly modified. But the communiqué hinted at the areas which they had scheduled for later conferences: 'limitation of forces and weapons, both conventional and nuclear in the agreed area of Europe, coupled with an appropriate system of inspection'.

It appeared that this agreement had in fact changed the Russian stand. The day after its publication, Khrushchev spoke in Leipzig to an international audience including some British visitors, and although he repeated the threat of a separate peace treaty, he emphasised that 'we want to have (the Berlin question) settled not separately but in conjunction with the whole German problem'. But there were two difficulties in the path of even such limited preliminary agreements. Khrushchev

might appear to have dropped the ultimatum on Berlin in favour
of another attempt to solve the German problem in its entirety
but there was no clear connection between a military relaxation
of the sort envisaged by the communiqué and a political agreement. The difficulties of transition from one area to the next
were unaffected. Secondly, the system of inspection on which
a military reduction depended implied an agreement on the
future status of East Germany, or at least a negotiated *modus
vivendi* with the East German régime. There was no chance of
this as long as the Berlin problem remained unsolved, since the
approach of both Germanys to this question was inexorable.
Any working settlement would have involved a concerted
Diktat to the two Germanys by the two leading powers—and
this was impossible unless the military confrontation in Europe
had already been resolved.

Macmillan's visit had not succeeded in even denting this
vicious circle, and none of the hints dropped by the statesmen
of either side had shown any other course to follow. The
subsequent development of the crisis made this clear; and it
continued to swing between attempts to settle the whole
German problem, and immediate efforts at agreement on the
status of Berlin, with a corresponding variation in the intensity
of the threat.

The need to define the scope of negotiation was already
pressing at the time of Macmillan's return. On February
16th the Western Powers had proposed a Foreign Ministers'
conference. Khrushchev had at the time answered that this
would only increase international tension, and suggested instead a summit conference without formal agenda. He was
plainly hoping that this would enable him to win the substance
of his claims. After Macmillan's visit, though it is impossible
to tell to what extent because of it, he had already abandoned
this expectation. At a press conference on March 19th he
agreed to a Foreign Ministers' conference as a preliminary to a
summit meeting, conceded the legality of the Western presence
in Berlin (which all Soviet bloc leaders had firmly denied since
the original Russian Note) and formally withdrew the ultimatum
of November. May 27th, he now indicated, was only an
approximate date, though he clearly desired negotiations to
begin before then and continued to threaten a separate peace if

the West refused to sign a treaty with both German states.

Macmillan was at the same time pursuing his mediatory course through the capitals of the Western world. In this he was entirely unsuccessful. He seemed to envisage proposals for a zone of reduced military tension in the centre of Europe. While it may have been possible to win American support for a working arrangement with East Germany and a progressive relaxation of military tension (as long as this did not imply a formal renunciation of German reunification, or a withdrawal from all bases in Germany),[9] there was no chance of gaining German sympathy for any such move. Both Adenauer and Strauss were at pains to denounce these ideas immediately after Macmillan's visit to Bonn, at the same time as Khrushchev agreed to hold a Foreign Ministers' conference.

Even if it had been agreed to hold negotiations on such lines, it is doubtful whether they could have succeeded; the difficulties of forcing either Germany to concur before a settlement of the Berlin problem were too great. In fact they were dropped before the Geneva Conference of Foreign Ministers began. In the preceding weeks, many of the most influential and respected politicians in the West had produced new plans for disengagement,* but none had overcome the central difficulty of military withdrawal while two hostile states representing the political and military investments of each bloc were left facing each other in the centre of Europe. The Western Powers once again attempted, as they had in 1955, to get round this difficulty by linking their proposals on Germany to a European security system, but this time there was even less connection between the two than before. It was again proved impossible to erect any European system without incorporating East Germany, and they had indicated their absolute refusal to do this at the end of April 1959 by rejecting the Russian proposals for a NATO-Warsaw Pact non-aggression treaty, which would have involved the recognition of East Germany. In these conditions the package deal which they put forward at Geneva was doomed to failure, and it was made clear that they had only succeeded in broadening the scope of the Berlin problem at the price of

* E.g. Senator Mansfield, M. Mendès-France, the leaders of the German SPD (after Ollenhauer, Erler and Carlo Schmid had conferred with Khrushchev). See Hinterhoff, *op. cit.* pp. 263-272.

bringing East German representatives into the negotiations themselves.* The Western plan, and the failure of the Geneva Conference, demonstrated conclusively that there was no chance of a gradual solution of the Berlin problem without the immediate *de facto* recognition of the East German régime. This dilemma has been the burden of East-West relations in Europe ever since.

Briefly, the Western package deal at Geneva presented three days before Khrushchev's original ultimatum was due to expire, proposed a phased procedure for German reunification, coupled with the establishment of a zone of 'controlled armaments' whose boundaries were to be 'mutually determined'. An all-German committee in an East-West ratio of 10 : 25 was to draft an electoral law which would then be approved by a nation-wide plebiscite. City elections in Berlin would be the first step towards national reunification, and after two and a half years elections would take place in the whole of Germany under the supervision of the Four Powers or the United Nations.

This plan was of course rejected, even after considerable amendment to meet Soviet requirements on minor points. It made no attempt to prevent the incorporation of the whole of Germany into NATO after reunification, even though it gave the assurance that Western armies would not, thereafter, advance to the East German frontier. In any case its avowed intention was uncompromisingly opposed to the implicit purpose of the whole Russian campaign—the recognition of East Germany. The negotiations were not to be rescued from this impasse, although they continued off and on until July. The conference did, however, represent some partial victories for each side.

The West had succeeded in reaffirming the legality of its presence in Berlin, and this was not challenged from the Soviet side. It had had the threat of an ultimatum withdrawn, and May 27th passed without incident in Berlin while the Powers were conferring in Geneva. By its suggestion of interim status for the city (which, in fact, meant nothing more than that the

---

* The first days of the conference were spent in wrangling over seating arrangements lest the presence in an advisory capacity of the East German government be held to imply any *de facto* recognition.

present situation would continue unchanged until an all-German solution had been found) it had managed to remove the immediate factors of crisis. The original menace had forced a sortie from the *status quo*, but the West had achieved a victorious retreat.

Soviet successes were more shadowy, but in the long run they boded more danger than appeared at the time. The West had accepted the GDR as a partner in future negotiations on the settlement of Germany. All East German proposals for a mixed commission from the two states had in the past been rejected by the Western governments. They now formed part of their plan and it was even suggested that East Germans could control access to Berlin under the polite fiction that they were agents of the Soviet Union. The status of Berlin was acknowledged to be transitional: although the Western Powers had never claimed that they would exercise their occupation rights in perpetuity, the new formula of an interim status came near to accepting the Soviet imputations that the presence of Western troops in Berlin was 'abnormal'. And this was reinforced by the discussions which were held between the Four Powers on the uses to which West Berlin could or could not be put during the period before a German peace treaty. These did not result in any agreements or undertakings, but the very fact that the representatives of the three Western governments discussed with the Soviet Union the control of espionage in their half of the city gave substance to the original charge of 'indirect aggression' against the Socialist camp in the Note of November.

Although the Geneva Conference thus succeeded in putting off the crisis and gained a breathing-space for the West, it only made it easier for the Soviet Union to renew the threat against Berlin itself whenever it chose. Further time could only be bought by further concessions. This is what happened at Camp David. Fortunately it later proved possible to revoke them—but only at the expense of a renewed crisis, and a sharp and dangerous deterioration of East-West relations, which gave the East German government more room for manœuvre than it had ever enjoyed before and ultimately enabled it to impose its own solution on Khrushchev himself.

During the course of the Geneva Conference Khrushchev

announced that he would shortly visit the United States. This followed a declaration that the Soviet stand at Geneva would not be changed, and that Gromyko would only repeat what he had already said. It is clear that he had given up hope of winning anything useful from a conference of Foreign Ministers, and expected instead to persuade President Eisenhower to concessions which West Germany had hitherto obstructed. In preparation for the visit, the tone of Communist propaganda was immediately softened. At one difficult stage of the Geneva Conference Gromyko had renewed the time limit put forward in November, although he had extended it to one year from the time of the conference. He then extended this by a further six months and emphasised that this was neither threat nor ultimatum. The whole matter was now quietly dropped, and even the phrase 'demilitarised Free City' was amended to Free City *tout court* in the public pronouncements of Communist leaders. The only exception was Ulbricht, who continued to insist on demilitarisation throughout and after Khrushchev's visit to the United States. But this show of an independent line was confined for the moment to verbal divergencies.[10]

It was clear that in any case the demand remained the same, and the change in phraseology was a simple attempt to diminish tension before renewing the attack. In so doing, Khrushchev agreed to reduce pressure while the West prepared for the Summit Meeting at which he hoped to win his final victory. This was the substance of the Camp David talks. They were neither the diplomatic success in achieving a new relationship which a State Department spokesman claimed at the time, nor the defeat which many in Berlin attributed to the communiqué.[11] But they were an important and dangerous development in the process of bargaining. On the one hand Eisenhower agreed that the negotiations on Berlin could not be prolonged indefinitely (and Khrushchev undertook in return to drop the time limit he had imposed at intervals for nearly a year); on the other the Russian claim that the situation in Berlin was 'abnormal' and should speedily be changed was not effectively countered either by the communiqué or by Eisenhower's subsequent press conference. This tacit victory for Khrushchev aroused unjustified alarm in Germany: it was in no sense a step towards a 'sell-out'; but its consequences were none the less serious.

Khrushchev seemed assured that the West was retreating from the firm position it had adopted at Eisenhower's press conference some months before, when he had said that any war over Berlin could certainly not be fought on the ground. He had then opposed the strategic to the tactical threat; now after Dulles' death he had in effect agreed to a new settlement of the Berlin situation and Khrushchev might well have concluded that he had at last succeeded in calling the Western bluff. This impression bought time, but the consequences of his disappointment were revealed when the Summit Conference was finally convened. Secondly, this shadow concession, and the obvious relaxation of international tension that followed, merely stiffened German opposition to any negotiations at all and led to a marked differentiation in the treatment meted out to German and other Western statesmen by Khrushchev.

In their opposition the German leaders in both Berlin and Bonn looked to de Gaulle for support,[12] and the constellation of the Western Powers changed radically in the months before the abortive Paris Conference. The change cannot be attributed directly to Camp David: French and German opposition to Macmillan's initiative was clear immediately after his return from Moscow. But the two axes of the Western Alliance were first delineated at the end of 1959 and have remained virtually unchanged ever since. The possibility of an Anglo-American attempt to impose a settlement on the two leading European powers had been consistently opposed by a Franco-German concert. It is not possible to judge how far this opposition was responsible for changing American policy, but it seems clear that Khrushchev calculated that success lay in winning de Gaulle to the Anglo-American camp. For this reason he visited France in March 1960; but the only result, if any, of his attempts to stir French opinion against the Federal Republic was to convince de Gaulle of the advantages of a divided but armed Germany.[13] France, moreover, needed West Germany as a defence glacis against possible conventional attack, much as Khrushchev seems to have felt the need for an East German buffer state against possible West German designs on Eastern Europe.[14] Because he understood this common need (and in effect agreed to the effective division of Germany) it was hard to see any real threat in Russian pressure, and de Gaulle has never echoed the sense of urgency felt by other Western leaders. Indeed, the Soviet action in precipitating a crisis would make no sense at all unless it were directed towards a final settlement of Europe's outstanding problems; de Gaulle has never believed that these could be dealt with in isolation. Any solution in Europe would require wide agreement in other parts of the world, and a preliminary measure of disarmament. Meanwhile the *status quo* presented less risks because, as an English observer wrote: 'The advantage of the present situation, tense though it be, is that neither side can move without a major war, and therefore will not move unless it deliberately seeks a major war. The engagement of the Great Powers stabilises Central Europe: they protect their weaker allies but also restrain them, since their own forces would be at once involved in any local clash.'[15] These words were written before Khrushchev launched the threat of a separate peace treaty, but they seem to represent a fair summary of de Gaulle's views after that date. The separate peace treaty had been invoked in order to demonstrate to Khrushchev's opponents that Soviet troops would no longer act as a restraining force upon their weaker allies; but it did not succeed in convincing Adenauer or de Gaulle that Russia would thus lightly go to war. Although the suggestion of a time limit was withdrawn after the Camp David meetings, Communist spokesmen continued to threaten a separate peace if the West obstructed a rapid solution to the Berlin problem, notably after a Warsaw Pact meeting in February.[16] But as long as NATO's conventional weakness ensured that any conflict would immediately begin a nuclear exchange, the European leaders did not believe that the danger was real; and Khrushchev cut the ground from under his own feet by his repeated insistence that precisely this was bound to happen. So it came about that Khrushchev attempted to reduce the immediacy of the threat, while emphasising its incalculable consequences, during the course of his visit to France: it would be 'very undesirable', he told a press conference at Rambouillet, for the Soviet Union to sign a separate peace treaty with the GDR. But if there was no other way out, it would be impelled to take this step, and, of course, that would mean the end of all Western rights in Berlin. But such a tactic came very near to asserting that the Soviet Union would deliberately and against its will start a world war, and de Gaulle remained unmoved.

Both France and Germany were far more alarmed at the possibility of a Western surrender to Soviet demands for a change in the status of Berlin. Smirnov, the Soviet ambassador in Bonn, declared repeatedly that an 'interim solution' of the sort proposed in the last days of the Geneva Conference should be the basis of the summit negotiations, and it was noted with anxiety that Gromyko had rejected any such suggestion at Geneva. It had become acceptable after Camp David, and though innocuous if considered in conjunction with a graduated plan for German reunification, it could be highly dangerous if it were regarded as an answer to the isolated question of Berlin. A Western 'summit' meeting at the end of 1959, which declared that the Summit should merely be the first of a series, had not sufficed to allay these fears, and in March Adenauer decided to visit Washington to secure more definitive guarantees.

This visit appeared all the more urgent in view of the attempts of both Russia and East Germany to split the Western Alliance and divide the German public before the Summit Conference. While Khrushchev tried to prise France away from her adherence to Germany, Smirnov made separate approaches to the two German opposition parties with covert suggestions for a compromise on Berlin. What these amounted to is not known, but in February the SPD urged Adenauer to enquire further through diplomatic channels. Such a course would have endangered both the Chancellor's own stand and the Franco-German front, and he firmly refused; but his evident lack of faith in American support made his insistence on the *status quo* seem like a counsel of despair.[17] The fact that Willy Brandt shared this attitude only heightened the impression, particularly in the German SPD, which was still convinced that the only hope of a lasting solution lay in measures of military withdrawal and a European Security Pact.* Berlin appeared to be increasingly threatened throughout these months by a number of insidious actions of the East German régime, which

---

* The *Deutschlandplan* of the SPD, put forward in March 1959. It was only after this plan had been abandoned in favour of supporting Adenauer's foreign policy that the Ruling Mayor of Berlin could become the leader of the SPD and its candidate for the Chancellorship.

at one time displayed its flags on the West Berlin stations of the city railway, at another demanded, in concert with the Soviet Union, that Western aircraft in the air-corridors should observe certain height regulations—which could be extended to involve stringent controls. While refusing to recognise the legality of such limitations, Eisenhower and Herter indicated that American aircraft would not fly above the 10,000-foot ceiling thus imposed. These events were unimportant in themselves, but they increased the misgivings of the Berlin public that the West was unwilling to resist the smallest harassment for fear of provoking a major conflict,* and sharpened the government's pessimism about the outcome of a summit meeting.

Bearing these fears with him, Adenauer flew to Washington in March. He was plainly not encouraged by his conversations with Eisenhower; indeed his next proposal indicated that they had only deepened his dismay, for he now suggested that West Berlin should hold a plebiscite before the Summit meeting to determine the views of the population. This was so unnecessary (and even undesirable, since it weakened the legal case of the Western Powers that their presence in Berlin rested on the right of conquest, and not on their relations with the governments of either Berlin or Bonn) that it can only be regarded as an attempt to forestall any agreements that might be reached in Paris, by demonstrating that they would have to be imposed on an unwilling and helpless population. Behind it lurked the threat that such an open betrayal would shatter Germany's relations with the West and might lead to the destruction of NATO.

Whether it was due to fear of this possibility, to de Gaulle's unswerving opposition, or simply to the impossibility of translating the Anglo-American hopes of a relaxation of tension and an interim solution into any actual terms, it suddenly became clear that the Summit Conference was off. The suddenness of the change was astonishing and is still hard to understand, though one suspects that the American government was acutely conscious of the danger to Western unity that a Franco-German alliance would create. But the lightning reversal probably did

---

* It was at this time that Rakosi's phrase about 'salami tactics' became popular in Berlin; and the Berliners have seen every development since then as another Communist success in nibbling away at the Western position.

as much to anger Khrushchev as the actual failure of his policy. At the beginning of April Herter, who only a few weeks before had assured journalists that Khrushchev's renewed threats of a separate peace treaty did not violate the spirit of Camp David,[18] attacked him for refusing to apply the principle of self-determination to East Germany, declared that a peace treaty should be signed with an all-German government after plebiscites in the whole country, and added that Communist attempts to violate the existing agreements on Berlin would prevent any negotiations on arms control with the Soviet Union. Less than a month before the Summit Conference was due to open, the American Under Secretary of State, Dillon, delivered a still more remarkable attack. Although he repeated that the West was still 'willing to discuss interim arrangements *to reduce tensions in Berlin*',* he made it clear that this 'would not become a first step toward the abandonment of West Berlin' and that 'in the long run the problem . . . could only be solved through German reunification'. A separate treaty, he added, would be 'skating on very thin ice', and remarked that the aim of the Paris Conference would be to minimise the risk of war through miscalculation. If Khrushchev really desired to liquidate the remnants of the Second World War he should withdraw his forces from East Germany and Eastern Europe, and grant self-determination to the Soviet-dominated states there.[19] In other words the West had reverted to the position it had held before the ultimatum of 1958, the efforts that Khrushchev had made ever since to induce a change of mind had been a waste of time, and there could be no discussions of an interim solution unless this were coupled with a Soviet commitment to withdraw from Eastern Europe. The purpose of the forthcoming conference would be to make clear to him that a separate peace treaty would probably lead to war.

These speeches, reported Herter to the Senate Foreign Relations Committee, were made 'in order to keep the record straight'.[20] In fact, they represented a complete reversal of all the developments of the previous year. Those who had feared that Paris would become another Munich were reassured that there would be no change; Khrushchev realised that there was 'nothing to negotiate about'.

* Italics added.

217

'Why did Dillon have to make a statement so obviously out of tune with the tenor of relations between the USSR and the United States since my conversations with President Eisenhower at Camp David?' asked Khrushchev in a speech at Baku, and repeated the threat of a separate peace in stronger terms than ever, adding that if the Western Powers refused 'to sign a peace treaty with the GDR, they . . . will forfeit the right of access to West Berlin by land, water and in the air.'[21] Any attempt to impose these rights would lead to war. But such a threat failed to place the onus of risk on the West. To threaten a separate peace as a consequence of their refusal to negotiate did succeed in placing them in a dilemma; but to threaten before negotiations were due to begin that war would follow unless they joined him in signing a treaty with East Germany was to take too open a risk upon himself. He was in a position from which he could not openly retreat, yet if he persisted the danger of war would become incalculable. It was he who now faced an imponderable crisis, and the only way to circumvent it was to prevent immediate negotiations taking place at all.

It is impossible to say when Khrushchev decided to torpedo the Paris Conference; it is certain that the intercepted flight of an American U2 over Russia presented him with an unhoped for chance of doing so, and that he delayed the announcement of the event long enough to make sure that its international repercussions could not be settled before the conference began.* Had Eisenhower and Herter equally decided that it would be advisable to avoid negotiations at Paris? Or had they calculated that the mutual defiance of the two blocs had reached such a point that it was now essential for the United States to demonstrate its imperturbability in the face of Soviet bluster? In any case they must have known that once the President had admitted responsibility for the U2 flights, the Paris Conference could not go on, even though he gave public orders for them to be discontinued before it started. Khrushchev was now in an easy position: he could demand an open apology as a condition

* Speier, *op. cit.*, suggests that 'the point should not be stretched to mean that Khrushchev was looking for a pretext not to hold the meeting. . . . For many years he had ardently desired to meet the Western heads of state at the Summit'. But though he gives due mention to the speeches of Herter and Dillon, he does not indicate their importance or the sudden change in Western policy that they represented

or negotiations and, when he failed to get this cancel the meet-
ng (and Eisenhower's forthcoming visit to the Soviet Union)
vithout more ado. He did not come face to face with Eisen-
1ower in Paris at any point.

When on his way back, he stopped in Berlin, amid rumours
hat the sector boundary was to be sealed, he could not
completely conceal the failure of his policy. He declared that a
separate peace treaty would be too adventurous for such realists
us the Communist Powers to pursue at this juncture and could
only express the hope that a new summit meeting could be
convened within six or eight months (by which time the United
States would have a new president) and added: 'It will evidently
be necessary to preserve the existing situation until the heads-
of-government meeting that, it is supposed, will take place in
six to eight months'. In other words he admitted defeat.

The separate peace treaty had failed to stir the Western
Powers, and it had failed to materialise. But the defeat which
Khrushchev had suffered was by no means a victory for the
West. The morale of the Berlin population had been greatly
shaken, the irresolution of the Western governments before
the remotest prospect of a nuclear war had been exposed, and
t had been demonstrated that between their commitments to
Berlin and their refusal to treat with the East German government they were unable to devise any alternatives to the *status
quo*. They had shown that they did not consider it feasible to
hold Berlin indefinitely against Soviet pressure, and though
Khrushchev had temporarily retreated, they had also shown
themselves unwilling to resist petty acts of provocation on the
part of the East German régime. Khrushchev could hope to
renew his threat in more favourable circumstances; but if he
did so it was far from sure that he would retain control of a
new crisis. Ulbricht had already given restive signs, and any
further pressure on Berlin was likely to increase his difficulties
inside East Germany. The refusal of either side to force a real
showdown would leave him enough room to manœuvre independently, and the necessity of shoring up his shaky régime
might tempt him into more desperate action than any he had
contemplated hitherto. This was the situation as it developed
between May 1960 and the night of August 13th, 1961.

Chapter Ten

THE TWIN CRISES

At the beginning of 1961, Lord Home gave an interview to a correspondent of the *Deutsche Presse Agentur*, in the course of which he made a remark that attracted great attention in Germany. 'As far as we are concerned,' he said, 'there is no Berlin problem.'[1] At the time, this was an intelligent and realistic reading of the signs, an encouraging indication of the success of Western policy, and an assurance of British firmness in supporting it.* The Berlin crisis had died away, and recent attempts by the East German régime to revive it had proved unsuccessful. Yet within a few months the world seemed to tremble on the brink of war, and the tension in the city seemed about to explode at any moment; both alliances were reinforcing their armies in Central Europe; and the Congress of neutralist states in Belgrade despatched emissaries to the Kremlin and the White House, imploring moderation and restraint.

By 1962 the situation had reverted to a lowering immobility symbolised by the gaunt wall which runs for twenty-five miles through the middle of the city. The American ambassador in Moscow was engaged in exploratory conversation with Gromyko, and Khrushchev was believed to have told Ulbricht that there could be no question of a separate peace treaty that year.[2] But at the same time, Gromyko was unyielding in his insistence on the full Russian demands,[3] including the stationing of Russian troops in West Berlin, and stated[4] that the Western Powers should not 'misunderstand' the postponement of the deadline.†

Dean Rusk had also made it clear that he understood the position. The danger remains, he told a press conference on January 18th: the withdrawal of Russian tanks was no sign of a change in the Soviet attitude.[5] Khrushchev confirmed this

---

* Of which serious (and sometimes frivolous) doubts have been periodically expressed in Germany since Macmillan's visit to Moscow.

† This seems to refer to the postponement beyond 1962.

view by insisting that a separate peace treaty would mean a radical change of the present situation.[6]

Meanwhile Berlin remained ringed with tanks, mines and anti-aircraft guns, and East Germany introduced conscription to place its 220,000-strong[7] armed forces on a regular footing. The temptation of the position was underlined by an unknown aircraft which scattered Albanian tracts over the country, to encourage the population against Khrushchev's 'opportunism' which, they declared, was 'imposed by Russian tanks'.[8]

The crisis had been dropped, but could be resurrected either by the action of the GDR or the Soviet Union whenever they chose. The West was again hoping to buy time, and was still divided about what action it should take when the time ran out. Khrushchev's willingness to co-operate was founded perhaps on the hope that Berlin will eventually 'wither on the vine'.[9] But if, as seems likely, the Western nations engage in an energetic international investment of money and prestige, if the city refuses to wither, they can not hope to avert a third, and possibly final, crisis.

This situation was produced by the pattern of developments after the Paris Conference of May 1960. Before Khrushchev stopped in East Berlin on his way back from Paris, it was still possible to speak of a single 'Berlin crisis', by which was meant a collision of policies of East and West. After he left, there were two distinct crises, not inherently related, but both acting on each other, each rendering the other uncontrollable, until they became so dangerous that a wall was built across Berlin to separate the two. The first was the general upheaval in the political and strategic relationships between the two blocs; the second was the imminent collapse of the East German state.

Khrushchev's speech in East Berlin spelled disaster for the Ulbricht régime. In apparent anticipation of a German peace treaty, the East German government had decided to shore up its crumbling state while it had the time. It imposed the full rigours of the Stalinist economic system before any possible confederation with West Germany could be created. In this way, the social achievements of the Democratic Republic would be safeguarded against subsequent subversion, and the prospects of self-determination ruled out before they could even be adumbrated in Four-Power discussions. The principal, though not the only, means by which this was accomplished was a sudden and massive campaign for the collectivisation of agriculture. Agricultural policies in the GDR had undergone the vicissitudes common to the Eastern bloc since Stalin's death; but the drive for collectivisation had on the whole been relaxed since the flight of the peasants in 1953. Now, in January 1960, a campaign of national persuasion was launched to bring the peasants into the LPG,* by March.

Party agitators were sent into every village and, in some areas, every household to talk the peasants into voluntarily entering the collectives. It was represented as a necessary move for peace; recusants were accused of supporting Adenauer and the revanchists in Bonn. If they were not put on trial, they were allowed no rest. Agitators relieved each other in a constant, and voluble, vigil in their houses, until the exhausted farmers signed. There were widespread suicides. The refugee figures to Berlin mounted sharply; but the East German press continued to report the adherence of each district or each province to the LPGs. By March the whole country had been collectivised.

Other forms of control were also imposed. More and more schools were turned over to the *Alltagsschule* system, whereby the pupils returned home only to sleep, and their extra hours of school were directed to political indoctrination or to working alongside special demonstrators in factories, where they gleaned both technical and political instruction. At the end of 1958 new measures had been passed to prevent 'flight from the Republic', and in particular to prevent inhabitants of the Democratic Republic from coming to East Berlin at all. The number of refugees had dropped after this to about 10,000 a month. Now they rose again to 20,000—the population of a small town. Nor was the country simply losing in numbers: the largest groups of refugees were always young men, and after the flight of industrial workers, there followed a mass exodus of peasants, and a significant proportion of school teachers.

These losses might have been tolerable for a short period. If they had been the preliminary to a German peace treaty,

* *Landesproduktionsgenossenschaft:* the collective farm. There were three types, but the essentials of individual farming were already taken over by the collective at the first stage.

which gave Ulbricht the control of all traffic to and from Berlin, and if he had been able to ensure the continuance of his régime even after a treaty was signed, they would have been worthwhile. But, after abandoning his ultimatum, Khrushchev now came to Berlin and announced that the crisis was off. He would not pursue an adventurist policy; there might be some hope of talking to a new American president in six or eight months' time. The news was disastrous.

Until then, both Russia and East Germany had had common interests and a common strategy in the Berlin crisis. From that moment both interests and strategy conflicted. Ulbricht's crisis was a different one from Khrushchev's, and demanded a more urgent solution. Whenever Khrushchev allowed the question to drop, Ulbricht had to take it up again. If Khrushchev's strategy was one of attrition, Ulbricht was forced into lightning attack. It is now known that Ulbricht had already tried to force a *fait accompli* on both Russia and the West. Twice before this, he had attempted to close the Berlin frontier, but the *Volkspolizei* had been turned back by Russian soldiers as they moved up. He could no longer hope to pull off a similar *coup* in an atmosphere of heightened tension; Soviet vigilance would be still keener. But he had to maintain tension as far as possible, in the hope that a solution would have to be found. In the end he succeeded, but only after a year's efforts which nearly brought about the collapse he feared.

Khrushchev, for his part, had naturally not given up. The reasons which had impelled the original crisis were still as compulsive as ever. But he now hoped to achieve greater success from proceeding more warily. The events of 1959 had shown that both the United States and Britain were prepared to compromise over Berlin because they believed that the ultimate risk of war was real. In Paris, Bonn and Berlin itself the original ultimatum had inspired greater fears of damaging concessions than of actual war, but nevertheless the Soviet tactics had succeeded in creating uncertainty and confusion in the Western Alliance, and the defeat of 1960 was only temporary. If he now concentrated his demands on minor concessions, while still brandishing the threat of nuclear war in the background, Khrushchev could hope to manipulate the crisis more successfully. A more modest ultimatum, coupled with the same risks, would make resistance far more difficult. The West could be forced to define its 'vital interests' more narrowly so that it could clarify to the other side the risks that it would take in trespassing on them; yet by doing so it would already be making important concessions.

This was the essence of Khrushchev's strategy in the coming months. It was not unsuccessful. Kennedy was soon forced to define the vital interests of the West, which he considered unnegotiable. They were: the presence of Western troops in Berlin, Western access to Berlin, and the economic viability of the city. These did not take account of Berlin's relations with West Germany and here lay Khrushchev's opportunity. While he forebore to raise the question of Berlin for a few weeks, he took care to keep the threat of war alive—in contexts where it could do no real harm, notably by threatening the United States with rocket attack in defence of Cuba. And this sabre-rattling served not to renew the demand for Western recognition of East Germany, but to separate West Berlin from the Federal Republic. The immediate occasion for this seems to have been the decision of the SPD at the end of June to support the main lines of the government's foreign policy. Until then, there was always a certain possibility that the SPD could be won over to a scheme for German 'confederation' which seemed to offer a greater chance of German unity. From now on, the SPD was as resigned as the government to eternal opposition to a separate East German state; and the Communist régime immediately began a propaganda offensive against the Federal Republic.

While Khrushchev was proclaiming the virtues of peaceful coexistence in Vienna, the capital of the free and neutral state that was cited so often as an example for the future Free City, Ulbright wrote an open letter to his 'social democratic comrades and dear colleagues' in the German SPD; Berlin was not mentioned, but the mass of workers in West Germany were called on to support the People's Plan for Germany which the SED had been tirelessly propagating for over a year.[10] The reasoning behind this *démarche* was soon revealed. Now that the SPD had abandoned its hopes of reunification through agreement with Russia, the whole of the Bundestag could be accused of revanchism, militarism, of threatening the peace of

Germany and the world; thus justifying any measures Ulbricht himself took to increase tension. The Bundestag was due to meet as usual in Berlin in September.

The opening of parliament had taken place in Berlin every year since 1955. There had been a spate of protests in *Neues Deutschland* each time; but no action against it had been threatened hitherto. But the switch in policy of the SPD, of which the significance was to become more apparent at the end of the year, provided an opportunity to go further than before, while protesting that the only road to peace lay in an agreement between the two German states. While the SED was begging the support of its Socialist brethren, Khrushchev threatened that if the meeting in Berlin were held that year, he would 'perhaps' sign the separate peace treaty after all—so that all the deputies would have to ask Grotewohl for a visa in order to get home.[11] This was hardly adventurous, but it had the desired effect. Adenauer immediately drew back, counseling caution. Both the opposition parties followed Willy Brandt in declaring that firmness was more than ever necessary; the Western governments remained studiously non-committal. Naturally the view of the CDU prevailed, and the session in Berlin was postponed. The first step towards the separation of the city from the Federal Republic had been taken.

It was only a preliminary. Two developments followed, closely linked, in fact, if widely different in appearance. The first was the East German government's experiment in controlling German access to Berlin. The second was Khrushchev's attempt to turn the United Nations Assembly meeting into a preliminary summit.

At the beginning of September a number of West German organisations of the former inhabitants of territories beyond the Oder-Neisse Line were due to meet in Berlin for a 'Homeland Congress'. The speeches made at such gatherings have often been irresponsible and inflammatory. It is one thing for West German politicians not to renounce their public hopes of seeing the lost territories eventually restored; it is another to foment agitation over them, as members of Adenauer's cabinet had frequently done.* Such behaviour has understandably

---

* Not only Seebohm, whose glib demagogy in this respect is notorious, but also Erhard and other members of the Federal Government.

irritated and wearied public opinion among Germany's allies
and the prospects of a celebration in West Berlin gave the
government of the GDR an excellent opportunity to try out
new restrictions. Three days before the Congress was due to
begin, the government prohibited all visits of West Germans to
East Berlin until September 4th. It was only a five-day period,
and the restrictions were, in fact, scarcely enforced: it was an
astute move. But it had serious implications. The Bundestag
had just refrained from meeting in West Berlin because a
symbolic breach of the Four-Power status might at that time
have been embarrassing to the West. Now the East German
government was deliberately flouting these legalities—but in a
manner designed to affect only the West Germans and not the
Occupying Powers. Secondly, the government was asserting its
control over the sector boundary, again in a way that was not
calculated to stir the Western authorities, but which could
have far-reaching effects on the population and the refugees.
Thirdly, in a public warning to the Western Powers 'the
Government of the GDR' drew 'the attention of the governments of the United States, Great Britain and France to the
fact that they alone bore full responsibility for any eventual
consequences of the misuse of the air corridors for the transport of people who attend politically inflammatory meetings
in West Berlin'.[12] This was the most serious implication
of all.

With this measure the East German government was beginning a 'legal blockade' against West Berlin. There was little
or no physical action involved, but every one of the assumptions on which Western presence in Berlin was based was in
practice called into question in the following weeks.[13] It is impossible to say how far Ulbricht was a free agent in this process.
There is no doubt that he had the approval of the Soviet government for his action, but it is also certain that he gained far
greater room for manœuvre in following it through, and in so
doing provoked a crisis in relations between East and West
Germany between September and December 1960. This made
it impossible for the Western Powers (had they ever been
willing) to renew discussion with the Soviet Union over the
whole German question; and just at the time that Khrushchev
succeeded in bringing the world's leading heads of govern-

ment* to the United Nations 'summit', and in cajoling Macmillan into new discussions of the German problem, it became clear that any future agreements would have to be confined to Berlin.

The developments of these weeks were rapid. On September 8th the GDR prohibited West Germans from visiting East Berlin without a special pass, and later declared West Berlin passports (which had hitherto been recognised as identification cards in East Berlin) invalid. The first of these measures was again designed to emphasise that West Germans had no right in Berlin; the second to assert East German sovereignty over the whole of Berlin—a claim which was afterwards made in so many words by a member of the Council of Ministers of the GDR.

There are some indications that the East German government was now going further in this respect than accorded with Soviet policy. Certainly the objective in both cases was the same: to separate the question of Berlin from that of Germany, and from the Western commitment to the Federal Republic. But as Khrushchev prepared to storm the United Nations, Ulbricht was calling (in the East German press)† for direct talks with Brandt on the normalisation of the situation in West Berlin. This can hardly have pleased Khrushchev, who declared to the General Assembly three weeks later that he was 'prepared to wait a while for a solution of the Berlin question although the USSR would *seek agreement*‡ on a German peace treaty at a later summit conference'.[14] At the same time, however, the Soviet Union could not damage its own claims by failing to support East Germany. To the Western Notes of protest at the restrictions imposed in East Berlin, the Soviet reply, therefore, stated on September 26th that this was a matter exclusively within the competence of the Government of the GDR, that the Western Powers should take steps to prevent (West

* With the notable exception of de Gaulle, and naturally of Adenauer.

† Speier, *op. cit.*, quotes this, p. 122, as following up Khrushchev's approach to Brandt via Kreisky during his visit to Vienna. But the two cases are different. Khrushchev's demands were private, and he apparently hoped to persuade Brandt that he had no real support in Bonn or the West. Ulbricht's was public, and couched in terms of the Soviet Note of November 27th, which envisaged direct negotiations between Berlin and the GDR. Khrushchev may have been hoping to isolate Brandt, Ulbricht certainly intended to isolate Berlin.

‡ Italics added.

German) 'revanchist activity' in Berlin, and added that Berlin was on the territory of the GDR and the Western Powers no longer had any legal right there anyway. This Note contained the main elements of Soviet diplomacy throughout this period. The long-term threat remained, but it was made clear that no immediate action was contemplated. It was more urgent to cut the links between Berlin and the Federal Republic—by appealing to the West through an implicit assurance that the threat would not then be renewed for the time being. In the context of Khrushchev's speech and his conversation with Macmillan in New York this may have looked superficially attractive. But at the same time the East German government was doing all it could to maintain the urgency of the situation in Berlin. The contradiction between these two approaches was sharpened in the following months.

Khrushchev was now playing for a summit again, and seems to have received some kind of assurance from Macmillan that in the end he would get one. Certainly, Macmillan remarked after his return from New York that 'negotiations on Germany and Berlin would have to be resumed'. And Khrushchev had agreed that in this case he would take no unilateral action in Berlin. Otherwise 'the countries whose position is that a peace treaty is essential will finally meet and sign a peace treaty. And that will be the end of the occupation status for West Berlin.' The hopes that he attached to a summit were therefore obvious: as a correspondent of *The Guardian* wrote:

. . . He wants the Summit for the very purpose, among others, of compelling the West to make concessions on Berlin. How he would do this is a question of tactics, threats and blackmail which, he may believe, would be more effective if used in the course of Summit negotiations. By bringing other questions into the negotiation, such as the suspension of nuclear tests and disarmament, by threatening and blustering in the full view of a world anxiously watching the Summit proceedings, he might be able—Mr. Khrushchev may believe—to win at least on points.[15]

But this was a strategy extending over many months. It required much preparation, particularly in attempting to separate West Germany from its allies, which was essential if his ultimate aim—the recognition of East Germany—was to be fulfilled. Meanwhile East Germany was upsetting these calculations by the crisis it had provoked in its relations with the

Federal Republic. The result was not only that the two nearly came to a conflict which could have been the beginnings of a new blockade, but that the SPD now fully supported the foreign policy of the West German government, and adopted the Mayor of Berlin as its chief candidate in the election of the following year.

In September West Germany notified the GDR that the trade agreement between the two would expire at the end of the year. The reaction was slow and deliberate. Although such a threat would mean a serious blow to the East German economy (which depended on West Germany for particular metallurgical and chemical imports) and which was already seriously lagging in its export programme,* no arrangement was made to begin negotiations until December. Meanwhile, a series of minor pin-pricks began, to demonstrate how easily the East German government could blockade Federal traffic to West Berlin without affecting the rights of the Western Powers. Tele-printers were confiscated as 'war material'; a lorry was held on the autobahn for several days at the beginning of November. Ulbricht was plainly hoping to treat the threat as bluff and win his point before negotiations began.

These tactics certainly succeeded in dividing the German government, and German opinion even more sharply. When negotiations between the two sides began, the West was under just as much pressure as the East. Not only could the GDR apply a limited blockade to Berlin at any time it chose; but the Soviet Union in a concurrent series of negotiations with Bonn refused to include West Berlin in any new trade agreement. The government visibly hesitated; Brandt insisted that all trade should be broken off unless Berlin was formally included. In the middle of December it seemed that a new Berlin crisis was looming dangerously near, particularly as *Neues Deutschland* announced that the GDR would ask the three Western Com-mandants to negotiate a special agreement for maintaining Allied lines of communication if no new agreement were in force by January 1st.[16] This would have implied *de facto* recognition: if the Western Powers refused, as they certainly would, Khrushchev would have had little choice but to begin

---

* Largely due to shortage of labour—estimated by the East Germans at 500,000. Refugees in September totalled 19,000, in October 22,000.

again the process of announcing a separate peace treaty. Once again East Germany seems to have chosen its most opportune moment to force the pace.

Khrushchev in any case must have decided that this was too dangerous, and would certainly have destroyed all chances of a summit. His ambassador in East Berlin was warned by the American ambassador in Germany of the dangers of such a step. A few days later Smirnov, the Soviet ambassador in Bonn, called on Adenauer, apparently to assure him that the *status quo* would continue. The two German governments quietly renewed the previous trade agreement, and that between the Federal Republic and Russia was likewise continued on the basis of an informal agreement to consider West Berlin a part of West Germany.

It looked, at the beginning of 1961, as if the crisis had again been averted; that in spite of every Communist threat, there was essentially nothing to fear but occasional malicious pinpricks and that there was 'no Berlin problem'. But the form of this latest crisis had shown how precarious the situation was. The GDR's tactics in concentrating its threats on the local issue of Berlin, which were pursued in conjunction with the Russian attempt to separate Germany from its allies, but nevertheless conflicted with it; the crisis in relations between the two German states; the menace of economic warfare and a limited blockade, had all revealed that the Berlin crisis could now hardly be stopped. Each renewal of tension increased the flow of refugees;[17] the desperate shortage of labour in the East German régime's economy increased its determination to stop the gap in Berlin; the tension which this created not only stimulated further flight—it damaged the chances of a successful summit, prevented the two Great Powers from even discussing the German problem as a whole, and ensured that as a result there could be no compromise over Berlin. For the question of Berlin, considered in isolation, can never be settled by compromise. One side will be defeated in any settlement, and the only chance of an alternative arrangement lies in a wider negotiation over Germany. Even so, the chances scarcely exist, but they would be stronger if there were a different régime in East Germany. As it was in 1961, the Ulbricht government was able to prevent any approach to a settlement at all, while its own position grew more desperate every month. The twin crises drew together, and ran in a single thread from the trade negotiations of December to Khrushchev's meeting with Kennedy in June, and finally to the Berlin wall in August.

Khrushchev also had new reasons for urgency, and with them his motives seem to have become increasingly inconsistent. The Sino-Soviet dispute was gathering pace, and he had already suffered a serious setback in his attempt to force a settlement at the Congress of the eighty-one Communist Parties in Moscow in November. A dramatic diplomatic victory over the West was needed to strengthen his own internal position. He was also, it is believed, coming under increasing pressure from his military advisers to resume nuclear testing—if only, as later became obvious, to confirm the spectacular advances that Russian technologists had made in this field since tests were stopped in 1958; but to resume these now would weaken the chances of a successful summit. He had to attempt this first. Moreover, as the Soviet Union attained an increasingly convincing nuclear parity with the United States, the disparity of their conventional forces in Europe gave him added grounds for hope that the deterrent policy by which the United States had hitherto succeeded in protecting Berlin might, after all, turn out to be a bluff.

But there were also signs that the Soviet superiority could not last for ever, and might be threatened far sooner than was expected. Kennedy's victory in the American election, and the appointment of General Maxwell Taylor (a previous commandant in Berlin) to advise him on military affairs, indicated that the United States might soon seriously reconsider its military policy in Europe and begin reinforcing its conventional troops there. This would not of itself greatly affect the Soviet position; but if as a result all the NATO countries fulfilled their military commitments, if the German army were brought up to 12 divisions, and above all if it were armed with tactical nuclear weapons, the possibilities of Khruschev's imposing his own German settlement on the Western Alliance would be destroyed. Indeed, he seemed to be actively afraid of a German army, equipped with nuclear weapons which might drag the Western Alliance into war.* In this case, he had both

* And convinced Walter Lippmann that this was so—probably rightly. See Lippmann's interview with Khrushchev, 10th April, 1961.

to convince the West that in Berlin he held a hostage against such a policy, and at the same time attempt to use Berlin as a lever to achieve a much wider settlement. The two objects were barely compatible, and his behaviour over the coming months was, for these and other conflicting reasons, certainly erratic.*

Neither Kennedy nor Dean Rusk displayed any great enthusiasm for a personal encounter with Khrushchev in the early months of 1961. But Llewellyn Thompson, the American ambassador in Moscow, was certainly engaged in a somewhat vague series of meetings designed to establish better relations between the two powers over a wide range of problems. Khrushchev may have hoped that this was the prelude to more substantial negotiations. Perhaps for this very reason, he again attempted to renew the pressure on Berlin in February—in the form of an *aide-mémoire* to Adenauer, which was handed over by Smirnov. It was Smirnov who had settled the preceding Berlin crisis two months before in conversation with Adenauer. Now he conjured up once more the original threat of a separate peace treaty, in case the Federal Republic opposed a 'peaceful settlement with Germany'. Once again he emphasised that until the treaty was signed a temporary settlement of the Berlin problem was possible—provided a time limit was set. The West had been warned again that the crisis could be renewed at any moment.

Five days later Thompson flew after Khrushchev to Siberia to present a letter from Kennedy. In spite of the chase, it remained unanswered for months. Meanwhile the United States had suffered serious political defeats in Cuba and Laos; the East German régime had already introduced a new labour code,† which was stimulating the flow of refugees still further; and the attempts of the Berlin Senate, in which Brandt had taken a leading part, to renew 'technical contacts' with the government of the GDR had failed—apparently because they excluded the possibility of political discussions.[18] The West

---

* Apart from which, Khrushchev had displayed a violent temperamental instability, both in Paris and New York. It is hard to believe that his behaviour in these places was merely put on.

† Under which it was expected the production norms in the GDR would be raised by as much as 15 per cent in 1961 and wages could be cut by 50 per cent. See *The Guardian*, 1.1.1961.

was in a weak position, and the local problem of Berlin was becoming steadily more menacing. In this situation Kennedy agreed to meet Khrushchev in Vienna in June for a political *tour d'horizon*. Kennedy had, in spite of his cautious statements at the beginning of the year, made no real diplomatic preparations for such a meeting. Khrushchev, for his part, had got the essentials of a summit—a chance to impress the American President face to face. He may have decided that the moment had come to confront him with his apparent determination to achieve a European settlement, in preparation for a real summit later on.

Kennedy said the meeting was sombre. There was every cause for dismay. The Soviet *aide-mémoire* of June 4th was a naked renewal of the 1958 ultimatum. Again the demand for an immediate peace conference was pressed on the Occupying Powers; again the two Germanys were bidden to negotiate their own terms of reunification; and again it was suggested that the Free City of West Berlin might be garrisoned by troops of all four occupying powers, or by contingents of neutrals. In either event, the Western guarantees of Berlin would be at an end. Finally it renewed the ultimatum of 1958: if the two German states had not concluded their negotiations within six months, a peace treaty would be concluded with either both, or one of them.

These points were underlined by Khrushchev in a television interview on June 15th and in subsequent speeches. Yet even now he was more cautious than he had ever been in 1958; he clearly desired and expected that the Western Powers would resign themselves to a *de facto* recognition of the East German state, and as the note expressed it '*de jure* to formulate the immutability of the existing German frontiers'. But he was careful not to insist on a *de jure* recognition of the GDR itself. He hoped that the division of Germany would be acknowledged: not that the United States would exchange ambassadors with East Germany. It is important to an understanding of his objectives that this is borne in mind; and the document of June 4th explicitly assured the American government that the conclusion of a peace treaty need not be linked with the recognition of East Germany. If his sense of the realities of power had led him to take this initiative at a moment favourable to the

Soviet Union, it also prevented him from trying to get more than he could expect. His demands were by his standards modest, and this gave added hope that they would be met. If this lay behind the ruthless bluster of the following weeks, his bluster also concealed a certain sense of responsibility, a sense of proportion—and a fear of war, which was totally lacking in the East German (or Chinese) approach.

It is instructive at this point to consider the evolution of Khrushchev's proposals for disarmament in the preceding period, in connection with his policy towards Germany. He had originally advocated the complete disarmament of all non-nuclear powers before touching ballistic missiles. That is to say, he hoped that Germany would be completely disarmed while the Great Powers retained a deterrent guarantee of European stability. This was subsequently reversed—with the effect that standing forces would be maintained in Germany, while the West was dispossessed of its nuclear capability to threaten any change. The whole programme was then abandoned. Russia adopted the position that each state would need enough forces to keep its régime in power. But in Germany this entailed a very high level of forces in view of the East German (and Russian) arms that would be needed to maintain the government there. Hence, to escape the dilemma, Khrushchev, in 1961, suddenly accepted the need for an international force under United Nations authority* to keep peace in a disarmed world: a proposal which less than a year before 'was reviled by Soviet spokesmen as one of imperialism's most evil devices'.[19]

There is no suggestion that Khrushchev was anxious to assure stability throughout the world by these proposals. Indeed, disarmament was probably always conceived as the prelude to a more intensified stage of 'peaceful coexistence'. But the conjunction of these proposals with the ultimatum of 1961, and with the limitation that Khrushchev himself imposed upon it, does suggest that at the time he was genuinely hoping that his strategy would be successful in securing stability in Europe—as a necessary condition for revolution in those areas where the United States and other Western Powers had just suffered grave defeats.

But the events of the next weeks upset his calculations. The

* Presumably in conjunction with a 'troika'.

first developments were certainly encouraging. The United States reply of July 17th to the *aide-mémoire* of June 4th rejected the Soviet demands, and pointed to the Geneva proposals of 1959 as the best basis for a German settlement. But the Note also remarked that 'the United States is not wedded to any particular arrangement for Berlin'. And a few days later Kennedy announced to the nation that the conventional strength of the United States was to be greatly increased. The Army was to be strengthened by 125,000 men, and this addition was to be used, in part, to reinforce the Seventh Army in Europe. Berlin could not be defended by conventional means, and though these reinforcements formed part of a long-term defence programme, which was the only adequate assurance of a successful deterrent policy, it was probably a mistake to make this move at that time. There can be no doubt that in the summer of 1961 the weakness of the West was its only strength: it could not fight a ground battle in Europe, and it was certain that any war over Berlin would be total. Now the credibility of American deterrence was weakened: Khrushchev responded by reinforcing the Soviet army in Eastern Europe, and appointing Marshal Koniev, the old conqueror of Germany, to its command.* There may have been serious military motives behind this appointment—the necessity of integrating all the forces of the Warsaw Pact into a unified command structure—but its timing also suggests that it was a bit of military bravado to show the West that Russia could always trump any conventional reinforcement. In so doing Khrushchev was playing on the very fears of 'escalation' in Europe which the new American administration had revealed in its demands for greater 'flexibility', and ill-timed reinforcements. Once again, he was able to profit from his adversaries' policies to place the onus of risk on them.

There were also other indications that his policy was succeeding. Brandt, in an effort to deflect the crisis from the

* The real Soviet conventional reinforcements had of course already been announced on July 8th. Russia had, like the United States, already got over the nuclear euphoria which had been contained in Khrushchev's message of January 1960. The new measures seem to have been designed to convince the West that any reinforcements in Central Europe could easily be outmatched at any time by the Soviet Union—leaving the conventional-nuclear imbalance just as it was before.

direction it had now taken—that is, a localised threat to Berlin which by the very fact of its local limitation immediately raised the threat of an all-out nuclear war—had called for a peace conference of all the fifty-two states which had taken part in the war against Germany. In so doing, he had fallen foul of Bonn where the government still hoped for a new postponement—through direct conferences between the Five Powers on the model of the previous December—but feared at the same time that any economic counter-measures, such as those which it had previously threatened, could cause the explosion in East Germany that it desired above all to avoid.[20] These divisions of opinion extended beyond Germany to the Western Alliance as a whole: Chester Bowles, the American Under Secretary of State had told the press on July 23rd that 'much could be negotiated', and that there was a hope of an eventual Central European arms control arrangement. But nothing could be decided until the United States had discussed the matter with its Allies. A Western Foreign Ministers' meeting was due in Paris early in August, but Khrushchev knew as well as everyone else what attitude Adenauer and De Gaulle would adopt towards any attempt to resolve the crisis by a measure of arms control in Central Europe. Macmillan had already failed to persuade them to such a scheme in 1959. These facts, coupled with the State Department's frequent assurances that the Berlin crisis was regarded as one of several crisis sectors and not as an isolated (or universal) problem, could have given Khrushchev grounds for hope that first an 'interim solution' would again be sought, and secondly that this would lead to a recognition, if not of the East German régime, at least of the permanent division of Germany. He could hope after that that a reduction of armaments in Central Europe could take place, but only on this basis. He was plainly uninterested in any other proposals such as those put forward at Geneva in 1959, and again mentioned by Chester Bowles.

Yet this possibility was already vanishing. In spite of his own attempts to prevent it, and the general agreement in the West* to circumvent it, the Berlin crisis *had* become an isolated (and therefore universal) problem. The fact was that the East German state was on the verge of collapse. Its administrative

* Again with the notable exception of De Gaulle.

machinery had been gravely weakened by a purge of the SED*
which Ulbricht had ordered at the beginning of the year,
following hard upon a purge of six months before.[21] Agriculture had almost come to a stop: agitators, who a year before
had coerced the peasants into entering the collectives, were now
pleading desperately with them to work. Whole villages went
on passive, undeclared strikes, ignoring their cattle and their
crops. For the first time since 1953, demands were voiced (and
even published) for free elections and free travel. Refugees
were now crossing into Berlin at the rate of over 1,000 a day.
There were 30,000 in July, 20,000 during the first twelve
days of August.† Women had already comprised some 45 per
cent of the total labour force in January.[22] Now the proportion
was rising every week. Pensioners were forced to return to
work in vital sectors of the economy, on whose maintenance the
rest depended. Industrial production had, in spite of all dis-
advantages, been rising over the previous three years—though
not so fast as the economic plan demanded. Now it was suddenly apparent that if refugees continued to pour out at the
same rate, it would soon collapse. The gap in Berlin had
urgently to be stopped—and knowledge of the fact stimulated
further floods of refugees. The crisis which Khrushchev had
conjured up could no longer be controlled; and if it entailed
a rising in East Germany, or the breakdown of its government, it would threaten the very purposes he intended it to
serve, and even increase the danger of war.

For this reason Khrushchev emphasised the threat of war
with increasing insistence during the days of July, in one
famous incident calling the British ambassador, Sir Frank
Roberts, into his box at the Bolshoi Theatre to tell him how
many bombs were needed to destroy Britain. He similarly
warned Fanfani that Italy was a hostage to the Soviet Union,
adding at the same time that war over Berlin could easily be
avoided. He was plainly hoping to divide and cow the West
into acceding to his demands in time; at least into stimulating

---

* Both these purges coincided with those of the Russian Communist Party.

† It is impossible to guess what proportion these figures represented of the total
who tried to escape. Certainly there were thousands more. The GDR was hardly
in a position to imprison them all but any form of punishment, such as transference
to other locations, dislocated economic planning.

division within the Western Alliance. If he impressed and frightened public opinion to the point where no Western leader could announce that he would 'fight for the Germans' or boast his readiness to be 'blown into atomic dust' for the sake of Berlin,* he might yet force the Western leaders into an agreement that access to Berlin should be negotiated with the GDR before the end of the year.

In this he might have succeeded. The Foreign Ministers' Meeting in Paris was unable to reach any agreement on further action. As the crisis became more acute each day, public opinion at best attempted to ignore it, at worst began to demand the recognition of the GDR. With the possible exception of the United States, none of the Western countries showed any public readiness to contemplate the possible results of refusal. Even in America some leading politicians had made speeches like Senator Fulbright's, suggesting that the GDR, like other sovereign states, had the right to control the movements of its population (by erecting a control net in Berlin?), or like Senator Mansfield's, adumbrating the conversion of the whole of Berlin into a Free City.† Another proposal was being discussed in every country: that of preserving West Berlin by moving the United Nations from Manhattan to Charlottenburg. The chief difficulty with these and other attempts to 'ease tension' was that they stood no chance of being accepted by the Soviet Union. They did not provide a basis for negotiation; but they were indications that Western opinion was alarmed at the implications of the Three Powers' policy towards Berlin. Khrushchev allowed negotiation with McCloy, now the head of the American Disarmament Administration, to continue up to the Paris meeting, but was clearly uninterested in anything but agreement to his demands.[23] He seems to have hoped that the West could not hold out much longer.

But it was already too late. Even while the Foreign Ministers were agreeing in Paris that nothing could be done—because

---

* Perhaps this is why Macmillan declared that it was 'all got up by the Press'. He could hardly announce a retreat. It was impossible in the climate of opinion at the time to remark, as Lord Home did when the crisis had receded, that the country was willing to face nuclear extinction. He had to sidestep these alternatives somehow.

† Mansfield's proposal understandably caused panic in the SED. See Wolfgang Leonhard in *Die Zeit*, 11.8.1961.

concessions might affect the German elections in September, and resistance might provoke an appeal for help from the Soviet Zone[24]—Ulbricht had begun a new campaign in Berlin. It is impossible to tell how far this was an independent initiative, how far agreed beforehand with Khrushchev, but his measures were plainly designed to test Western reaction to an eventual sealing of the frontier. They were directed against the *Grenzgänger*, the Berliners who lived in the East but went to work in the West. This opportunity was the only practical result of the Four-Power status which could still be appreciated by the population; and the new campaign was designed as an open challenge. Economic measures had already been taken against the *Grenzgänger* in July; but now they were openly hauled out of trains at the frontier stations by the *Volkspolizei*. There had already been signs that Ulbricht was again trying to force the pace: after the Vienna meeting he had called a press conference to explain that when West Berlin became a Free City, Tempelhof airport would 'naturally' have to be closed down, along with the refugee camps. The first threat was the more serious; it would have meant that all air traffic had to pass through the control of the East German airport at Schönefeld. Now, in response to the Western protest at the treatment of the *Grenzgänger*, the East German press again renewed their threats, to demonstrate open contempt for the whole principle of the Four-Power status.[25]

The significance of these steps was in doubt for a few days, until it became known that Ulbricht had attended a secret conference of the First Secretaries of the Warsaw Pact countries in Moscow from August 3rd-5th. The communiqué offered no more than a repetition of all the previous Soviet demands for a peace treaty, though in a more than usually insistent form. But it was already suspected that more radical decisions had been taken, and it is most probable that it was now that Ulbricht at last got permission to close the frontier in Berlin. It was high time, for on August 8th 1,700 refugees crossed into the West—apparently impelled by rumours that the frontier was really to be sealed now. On August 10th the total rose to over 1,900.

In these last days, while the West was at last considering a 'summit' proposal, which even a month before would have meant diplomatic victory for Khrushchev,[26] preparations were finally being made to seal the border. Possibly as a deliberate diversion, the Warsaw Pact countries announced on the 12th that new measures would be taken around the perimeter of Berlin to stop the 'kidnapping and human theft' that had been carried out on the territory of the GDR. But no mention was made of the internal frontier of the city. It was possibly also for this reason that Koniev had recently invited the three Western Commandants to his headquarters near Potsdam for private discussions.* At all events no one seems to have suspected what was about to happen.

On August 12th the flood of refugees reached a new level; over 4,000 crossed into West Berlin in little more than twenty-four hours. At half-past two in the morning of Sunday August 13th detachments of East German border police and army guards took up positions along the whole length of the Berlin frontier. Almost immediately squads of workers began to dig up the roads with pneumatic drills and erect barbed wire fences and other obstacles. The city railway was completely stopped, and so were the underground trains, with the exception of one line on which no halts were allowed in East Berlin. At some points, troops were reinforced by tanks and armoured cars.

There has been much speculation ever since on whether it would have been possible to resist. It has been affirmed that Ulbricht, like Hitler when he ordered the march into the Rhineland, was ready to withdraw at the least sign of opposition. Indeed these beliefs have been encouraged whenever possible by both the Russian and East German authorities: nothing could be better calculated to shatter the morale of the inhabitants of West Berlin and destroy their faith in their allies. Even the parallel with Hitler would be of use to Ulbricht. There have also been some signs of confirmation: it is now known that the heavily armed troops who occupied the frontier on the night of the 12th had no ammunition. Yet it is impossible to believe that they would really have withdrawn. Not only did the NCO's and officers carry ammunition: the tanks and armoured cars were loaded with live shells. Heavy concentra-

* There appears to be no truth whatever in the rumours, which still have a certain currency in West Germany if not in Berlin, that the Commandants were told of the impending action.

tions of tanks and armoured troop carriers were waiting at key points behind the frontier. All this indicates that Russia and East Germany were determined to go through with it. The authorities avoided unnecessary risks, which could have arisen if the troops had fired on angry crowds; but they had nothing to fear from local Western action. Once they had decided on the operation, they would not be deterred from carrying it out.

But why had Khrushchev, before announcing that he was travelling to the Black Sea on holiday, made this decision? He seems to have hoped up to the last minute that it would not be necessary: at the Warsaw Pact Conference ten days before, other measures had been worked out, which prevented most East Germans reaching Berlin at all. They demanded enormous numbers of police on perpetual duty over a large network of roads and railways all over East Germany. They could scarcely have been conceived as more than a temporary action —but they had not been tried out when the decision to build the wall was apparently taken. It may be assumed that he agreed to the closing of the frontier if they failed, as they obviously did. And that he agreed because the collapse of East Germany was involving Russia and the West in the danger of war. He had now to separate the two crises at any cost and even though he knew that the West was about to accede to his demands for a summit. For at the same time, the West could not afford to prolong a situation of such tension that it invited the danger both sides were equally anxious to avoid, and imposed the awful moral burden of encouraging refugees. Khrushchev may well have hoped that in consenting to close the frontier he was enabling the West to return to 'his' crisis, that is, the recognition of a divided Germany; but he can hardly have been unconscious of the fact that in so doing, he was destroying the urgency that had been the chief incentive to the West, and making it morally impossible to agree to early negotiation. In the near future he would have to find a means of heightening tension and bringing the adversaries back to the summit without incurring new risks in Berlin.

The West for its part now had to demonstrate its commitment to West Berlin. The barbed wire that was erected on the night of August 12th was a flagrant breach of the Four-Power status, even though thirteen crossing-points were left open at the time to allow Allied circulation throughout the city. For it nevertheless amounted to the final incorporation of East Berlin into the GDR—a situation whose equivalent had never been allowed to develop in the Western half of the city. Nothing had been done about it, because nothing could be. But Kennedy had implied in his speech of July 25th that the United States was prepared for local action in Berlin if necessary.* He had been careful to limit his commitment to West Berlin, but there was some justification for the prevalent feeling in the city that if the West was prepared to put up a fight, now was the time to do it. However, it was a mistaken one. In spite of Kennedy's speech, Khrushchev understood clearly enough that he could not attack West Berlin without the risk of world war, and because of it, he knew that he could take any action he chose in East Berlin.

The fact remained that the inhabitants now demanded 'action'. The Senate met on the morning of the 13th and voiced the desire for energetic counter-action, and in the afternoon the West Berlin police were kept busy holding back crowds of angry demonstrators at the frontiers† while the *Volkspolizei* threw tear-gas shells at groups on the other side. The same day Dean Rusk issued a statement of protest, but observed that 'available information indicates that measures taken thus far are aimed at residents of East Berlin and East Germany and not at the Western position in West Berlin or access thereto'.[27] This clarified the attitude of the United States, but also depressed the West Berliners still further. The Allied protests to Soloviev, the Soviet Commandant, only provoked demonstra-

---

* 'I have heard it said that West Berlin is untenable. So was Bastogne. So in fact was Stalingrad. Any dangerous spot is tenable if men, brave men will make it so. We do not want to fight—but we have fought before.' This was a foolish statement which ignored the whole nature of the crisis: that the West could only maintain its position in Berlin by the threat of thermonuclear war. The only answer to these arguments is, 'So was Dien Bien Phu'. Kennedy's assertion that nothing was dangerous or safe but thinking made it so was belied by the Note that the United States had sent the Soviet Union on July 17th which again attempted to enlarge the Berlin crisis to cover the whole German question. He knew quite well that at this juncture any local action presented intolerable risks—as it also did for Russia, if Western policy hitherto had meant anything at all. If his words had been taken at their face value, Russia could easily have occupied West Berlin. As it was, they constituted an open invitation to seal off the East.

† Though these were smaller and less impetuous than in September 1948 or October 1956.

tions demanding 'deeds, not words', and universal mutterings of 'salami tactics'.* The morale of the West Berliners had been struck a damaging blow by these events, and their import was emphasised in the next week as the number of crossing-points were reduced, the number of refugees who succeeded in finding loopholes diminished day by day, and the wall began to go up. The long concrete scar symbolised the whole history of the city since the war, and the armed guards who looked down at them, the complete helplessness of the population. All they could do was to boycott the city railway. Brave and ingenious men and women still succeeded in crossing through—by swimming the Teltow Canal, which forms a long section of the border, by leaping from windows into West Berlin, or by tunnelling underneath the wall. But the *Volkspolizei* received orders to shoot to kill any who attempted to escape—and did so. On occasion the Western police fired at them, at least once with fatal results. A minor battle began at these border points where refugees were known to cross, and the Western Powers were still helpless to prevent it. Eventually the Wall was extended to enclose the Brandenburg Gate, and the number of transit points was reduced to four.

In the first days it still seemed that something might be done. Adenauer was reported now to favour economic sanctions, but it was soon seen that any action would be purely symbolic. The American Vice-President visited West Berlin and received an enthusiastic welcome. He promised the crowd that the tyranny beyond the wall would not last for ever and distributed ball-point pens. American tanks and soldiers proceeded to Berlin up the Helmstedt autobahn, and Kennedy waited in Washington for news of their safe arrival, though it had been clear for months that there was no danger of a repeated blockade. Some of the tanks were of latest M-60 type, with which the American Seventh Army was slowly being re-equipped. They had an important purpose, though it was not generally

* The concept of 'salami tactics' in the Berlin situation is dangerously misleading. It implies that the main issue for Khrushchev is the possession of West Berlin. He has given repeated evidence that it is not. It implies too that the West can stop further erosion of its position by standing firm. In fact, it is precisely the policy of 'standing firm' that impels Khrushchev to accentuate the crisis further, and of itself erodes the Western position. Only a radical new approach to the whole German question can prevent this.

realised until October. General Clay returned to Berlin, after twelve years, as Kennedy's special ambassador, though his functions were never clearly defined. He is reported to have found the morale of the population unexpectedly low, and to have insisted at intervals thereafter that some demonstrative action was needed—even advocating at one moment that the tanks should be used to punch a few holes in the wall.

During September the situation seemed to have settled down. The wall was reinforced, but the population of West Berlin remained. Alarmist figures of a mass exodus were shown to be completely misleading: the high numbers of emigrants to West Germany were in the main refugees, who could only be evacuated gradually. Meanwhile attention in West Germany was concentrated increasingly on the last few weeks of a some-what sordid election campaign, in which Adenauer seems to have been dominated by the fear that the tragic events of August should prove a political asset to Brandt. In East Germany Ulbricht was restoring his régime after the near collapse it had suffered in the summer. Recalcitrant peasants, earlier *Grenzgänger*, members of the FDJ who had not yet volunteered for military service, were publicly beaten up by picked squads of young factory guards. It was a systematic and extensive operation, which *Neues Deutschland* glorified as 'education by the fists of the workers'. The inhabitants of the border houses in Berlin were evacuated, and so were all those who lived in a 'frontier zone' many kilometres wide along the whole length of the intra-German frontier. This was now mined and fortified so as to be completely impassable, and preparations were announced for combined manœuvres of Russian, German, Polish and Czech armies in the autumn.

The danger of the situation was growing throughout this period. The United States and Great Britain were still anxious to negotiate a settlement of the crisis—apparently on the terms, which had already been explored in 1959 and 1961, of a limited arms control settlement in Central Europe. But Russian policy remained implacably opposed to this reversal of its own priorities: arms control could only follow as a result of a political settlement.[28] The first condition for this was for the West to recognise a divided Germany. At the same time the German government was determined to oppose any settlement which smacked of disengagement. Strauss declared that this was Khrushchev's intention, and the chief danger of the situation; and Khrushchev's conversations in Russia with Spaak and Reynaud confirmed his view.[29] Both before and after the elections, Adenauer's cabinet refused to contemplate any such possibility, and, as always, publicists in Germany (and elsewhere) threatened that if it came to pass, German public opinion would be so demoralised that it would turn 'neutralist' and NATO would be ruined.*

But Khrushchev was unremittingly bent on his summit. The Twenty-Second Party Congress would soon take place, and while it would be pretentious to attempt an explanation of his intentions or tactics before it happened, there can be little doubt that he felt the need of some victory over the West, in view of the increasingly acrimonious dispute with China and the pressure of his own military advisers. But apart from this, his action in sealing the frontier and the inevitable nature of the Western response, had made the Berlin crisis, whether either side wanted it or not, into a crisis of Berlin. Thus, the United States, while making exploratory soundings about future negotiations, had to demonstrate its determination to defend West Berlin; and Khrushchev, while resolved to bring the West into negotiations, had to maintain pressure in Berlin and even increase tension elsewhere. This was certainly not the only reason behind his decision to resume nuclear tests on September 1st, but it may well have informed the timing. Just as the Belgrade Conference was convening, just before the German elections, he announced that the Soviet Union was forced by the aggressive policy of the Western Powers into resuming tests for self-defence. This may also have been an attempt to stop the West negotiating on other terms than his own: by demonstrating his contempt for 'world opinion', he could forestall the announced intention of the United States to appeal to the forum of the United Nations; by openly denouncing the only set of negotiations between the two sides which had

---

* This frequent threat combines two popular and corrupt images, that of the 'furor teutonicus' and that of 'Rapallo'. The first implies that the Germans would be beyond any rational argument, the second that they would turn cynically nationalist *Realpolitiker*. The two are scarcely compatible. Neither are they true. The Germans know very well what their interests are.

hitherto shown some hope of success, he could make the West understand that it could not expect to impose its own timetable for a German settlement. Either these problems could all be settled together (if possible at a summit) or they could not be settled at all.

Meanwhile, in Berlin, the police forces of the two sides continued to fire at each other, and later engaged in tear-gas duels. Soviet helicopters circled the French airport at Tegel in an effort to prevent the Caravelles from landing. Searchlights were directed at pilots coming in at Tempelhof, where it is particularly difficult to come down 'blind'. The checkpoints at which Allied and foreign visitors were allowed to enter East Berlin were reduced to one. Each of these developments carried the risk of lightning escalation if the moment should come when the Western Powers were tempted into responding by a counter-show of force. Russia seemed not only willing to wound, but quite prepared to strike.

In these circumstances Dean Rusk began his private negotiations with Gromyko in New York, with Lord Home as an occasional accessory. France remained aloof. The attitude of the German government was unchanged, and became more inscrutable as the elections approached, and were then succeeded by weeks of wrangling over a new coalition. Willy Brandt pressed the view that any change whatever at this juncture could do nothing but damage to the position of Berlin. Perhaps the American and British Ministers hoped for a relaxation of the crisis, on analogy with the private conversations with Malik in New York that had led to the lifting of the blockade. But the position now was far more complicated: Russia could afford to prolong the situation indefinitely, as she could not in 1949; the West could not confine the negotiations now, as it could in 1949 to the issue of Berlin. Its whole purpose was to enlarge their scope. But it could not resolve the fundamental dilemma. There could be no European settlement without acceptance of the basic Russian premise—the division of Germany. But the American administration had no intention of trying to force this on the West German government. Determined above all to build up NATO to a point where it could achieve greater flexibility of response to new Soviet pressure, the United States needed German collaboration in

Europe more than ever. But if it failed to begin negotiations in Germany, the West would face renewed tension in Berlin, when it was already feared that an explosion could happen at any moment.

Thus, the United States vacillated throughout September and early October. At one point it appears that Rusk approached giving Gromyko an assurance that there was a possibility of new negotiations on 'European security' if the Berlin problem were allowed to die down for the time being[30] without specifying what he had in mind. But the American administration also felt impelled to assure the West German government that there could be no real question of European security without German reunification[31] and publicly emphasised that any disengagement schemes were 'transparent devices intended to weaken and ultimately to destroy the Atlantic Alliance'.[32]

The Soviet Union similarly appeared to offer concessions which likewise depended on conditions it was never prepared to meet. Gromyko gave private assurances that the Soviet Union would not demand a full recognition of the GDR, and also appears to have hinted that free Western access to Berlin would be guaranteed after a separate peace treaty.[33] But this nevertheless implied that the West would come to some arrangement recognising the permanent division of Germany, which the United States was at that very moment denying.

Towards the end of October each side began to express a certain sober optimism, based on the other's concessions. How far it was genuinely felt is impossible to judge: it is hard to believe that either was really convinced. The most notable expression of this mood was in Khrushchev's opening speech to the Twenty-Second Congress, in which, with an air of triumph, he once again withdrew his threat to sign a separate peace before the end of the year, because there was now a chance of a solution acceptable to both sides. He also announced that Russia was about to explode a 50-megaton bomb.

The first, as well as the second of these declarations should have given the West cause for anxiety. It meant that he was going to delay the final showdown once again—but that he could renew it at any time, and that Gromyko's assurances that a separate treaty would do no harm to the Western position had really meant nothing. If an acceptable basis for agreement had been found, he could have signed the treaty immediately— as some Western observers were almost hoping he would. The fact that he chose not to indicated his determination to have the West accede to it in one form or another.

That this, in fact, meant no relaxation of tension was confirmed in the following weeks. The United States and Great Britain had now formulated the hope that the Berlin situation could be saved by a system of technical contacts, which would in effect have recognised the existence of the East German régime: the two Germanys would have discussed with each other the technical problems of trade, and the economic links of West Berlin with the Federal Republic. Since this was no more than a formalisation of what had already been taking place for a number of years, there was some hope, and some indication, that it would have West German support. Further, they hoped that an eventual *modus vivendi* between the Powers could be found on the basis of a separate peace treaty itself: all Russia had to do was sign a guarantee of Western access to Berlin with the three countries concerned (as Gromyko had probably hinted that she might) and then incorporate this into the separate peace with East Germany. The trouble with this scheme was that it ignored Moscow's ultimate and explicit aim, that of securing the signature of the Western Powers to a document affirming the existence of East Germany. But the West could not do this without German consent: it would remain, in whatever form, a violation of the Paris agreements of 1954. And West Germany could scarcely consent merely in order to preserve the *status quo*. If this was the contemplated form of future negotiations, there was some justice in Adenauer's demand that at least the wall in Berlin should be removed before they began. While these feelers were being put out, a new trial of strength began in Berlin.

For Adenauer was reported to be demanding the creation of a 'neutral corridor' through East Germany as the price of any Western concessions over Berlin.[34] It was a point on which no possible negotiations could take place. Instead cautious tests began in Berlin of the possible Western reactions to East German control of Allied traffic in the corridor. There was an opportunity for such experiments at the Friedrichstrasse crossing-point, through which Allied and foreign traffic passed into East Berlin. Allied visitors in uniform, or driven in official cars, were subject to no controls and, as on the autobahn and railways, had no dealings with the East German authorities. Up to this point the East Germans and Russians had scrupulously respected the letter of Allied rights: the wall, it is important to remember, had made no difference to them. Western officials were still able to circulate freely in East Berlin, and frequently did so on principle. But there had been precedents for the new action: in the previous year the American ambassador to the Federal Republic had shown his papers to the *Volkspolizei* when he visited the unrecognised capital of the GDR, and British officials had done so more often to 'avoid incidents'. These were trivial but important concessions: they encouraged a belief that in a trial of strength the West would give way. Ultimately East German control could then be extended to the corridors.

The first of the famous incidents at Checkpoint Charlie occurred on October 23rd, when the United States Minister in Germany was stopped by the *Volkspolizei* on his way to the theatre in East Berlin. They demanded his papers. He called for a Soviet officer. When none appeared, he drove through to the second barrier on the Eastern side, was stopped again, and eventually escorted back by armed American military police. He later drove in again to protest to a Soviet officer, and was afterwards followed by a convoy of American, British and French cars, which came and went without incident. Meanwhile American tanks had taken up positions a few hundred yards behind the checkpoint.

This incident contained all the elements of the silent duel which was fought at the crossing-point later in the month. The American reinforcements in Berlin were now given a new purpose, which they fulfilled with complete success. This was a vital issue, and the American tanks served to demonstrate, as they had done in 1949, that further interference with Allied rights could lead to war. In 1949 tanks had been sent to emphasise that the security of Berlin was, in effect, covered by the new Western Alliance. Now they served in microcosm to fulfil NATO strategy.

In the following days the American authorities in Berlin embarked on a deliberate policy of showing Old Glory in the

Eastern sector. There was every reason to demonstrate in this way, trivial though the individual actions may have appeared. They were strongly supported by the French. There was no attempt to hide the fact that the British were more reluctant. Wrongly, they refused to regard this as a substantive issue: though they made use of their tanks elsewhere and sent an armoured car every day to escort one schoolboy from a British enclave* in the Eastern Zone to school in Spandau, they were far too conciliatory on this vital point. The division of Allied opinion probably encouraged the East Germans to go further. For they began building a concrete barrier which would have made the checkpoint impassable. The Americans threatened to break it down, but work continued cautiously. American tanks then took up permanent positions at the crossing, their crews on day and night watch, their guns loaded; seventy yards away Soviet tanks stood facing them on the other side. It was a dangerous period, when incautious action could have led to shooting at any moment.

The situation was a triumph for the NATO doctrine of the pause. The tanks were withdrawn from their forward positions after a few days; but their presence near the border remained a permanent and valuable source of tension in the coming weeks. Tension in Berlin and in the corridors ran very high. The West Berlin police were rearmed, tear-gas bombs and occasional shots were exchanged with the *Volkspolizei*. The East Germans later closed the civilian railway line from Berlin to Hamburg, and there were signs that they might be preparing a discreet sabotage of other lines.[35] It was in the Western interest to keep tension in Berlin at this moment as high as possible. If the tanks had been prematurely withdrawn, if there had been any indication that the nerves of the local authorities were giving way, there can be little doubt that the incidents at the border and in the corridors would have multiplied. If East German agents had sabotaged the military railway to Berlin, the West could then have found itself in the position it had been trying for so long to avoid: that of firing the first shot. That this did not come about seems to have been due in large part to the

* The Allied enclaves in East German territory were at this time being submitted to a minor blockade. Clay made demonstrative visits to Steinstücken; in fact, they were saved by a helicopter 'airlift'.

tension imposed by the tanks at Checkpoint Charlie. It was a pause in miniature.

There were other reasons for this determination. The quiet negotiations of the preceding months had broken down since the Twenty-Second Party Congress. Khrushchev was now brandishing the threat of a 100-megaton bomb. Concentrating on his battle with Tirana and Peking he was apparently in no mood to discuss eventual concessions over Berlin. The United States was at the same time engaged in a fall-out shelter programme that looked as if it were actively contemplating the possibility of war. And Kennedy was also hindered by his allies in negotiating further. As long as the Franco-German alliance remained, he was in no better a position than Khrushchev to offer concessions or seek a settlement. For this reason he seems to have decided at the end of October that the axis between Paris and Bonn should be broken if possible—for De Gaulle could only obstruct negotiations effectively as long as he was sure of German support. As the champion of German rights De Gaulle was a formidable opponent; shorn of this rôle, he would scarcely be able to hold out alone. It was not France that secured the safety of Berlin.

So Adenauer was invited to Washington, and seemed to be largely won over by Kennedy. After their meeting he was reported to be ready to accede to the American proposals for a wide-ranging East-West discussion of European security[36] within which a new status might be worked out for Berlin. But at the beginning of December it was realised that East Germany was making this impossible. Immediately after Kennedy's first interview with the editor of *Izvestia*, in which he reaffirmed that a solution of European problems could only come about through German reunification, Ulbricht declared that he had failed to appreciate the growing strength of the GDR and that Germany would never be reunited.[37] In this context the foreign policy debate in the Bundestag was bound to reveal that Adenauer had no support for his acquiescence in the American proposals.[38]

In fact, the West had now completed the full circle of its long attempts to sidestep the central issue of the crisis. To avert the danger of a world war over Berlin—which was otherwise indefensible—the United States and Great Britain had consistently

tried to enlarge the scope of the dispute to a discussion of
European security. Naturally this suited Khrushchev's purposes, since his ultimate objective of persuading the West to
recognise the division of Germany could only be achieved by
such negotiations. But to avoid the danger of being forced into
a recognition of East Germany, the West had in the end reverted again and again to insisting on the *status quo*. Each side
had offered apparent concessions in the discussions of the preceding summer, but had once again returned to the same point
—in a more dangerous form than usual. For West Germany
now appeared to be committed to some form of negotiation
while the position of East Germany remained unchanged.
There was no more hope of a compromise over 'technical contacts' in these circumstances, and indeed the only form of
technical bargaining which would have been acceptable to
West Germany would have been a much more thorough-going
guarantee of communications between West Berlin and the
Federal Republic than the GDR was prepared to contemplate.
This left the possibility of negotiating some sort of new status
for West Berlin, which would have strengthened its guarantee
of independence through the Great Powers, but weakened its
links with the Federal Republic. Kennedy was reported to be
considering such a possibility—with the acquiesence of
Adenauer.[39] Brandt rightly recognised that it would mean
political disaster. Berlin could only survive if its connection
with West Germany were continually strengthened. In fact,
Adenauer's policy was leading to a position where to avoid
contacts with East Germany, West Germany would loosen its
contacts with Berlin.[40]

In these circumstances there was no point in negotiating, the
more so as the Soviet Union was again hardening its attitude
to a point where no point of negotiation was left. Menshikov,
the Soviet ambassador in Washington, told the National Press
Club that there would not even be a basis for negotiations if the
purpose of the Western Powers was to get confirmation of their
occupation rights,[41] while, just as the three Foreign Ministers
were discussing the matter in Paris, Khrushchev went out of
his way in a speech in Moscow to announce that there could
be no limited agreement on a new status for Berlin.[42]

It has always been illusory to hope that the West could

maintain its position in Berlin by merely standing firm—it is precisely this policy which permits and encourages 'salami tactics' on the other side. But there is equally no hope for negotiation at a moment when, for reasons of internal politics with the Soviet camp, Khrushchev would clearly prefer no negotiations at all. De Gaulle's inflexibility was not always justified, but his resistance to the whole Western approach throughout this period, and particularly during his discussions with Macmillan at Birch Grove and with Adenauer at Paris, was more prudent and more far-sighted than the attitude of his NATO partners. That they had nothing to fear was revealed in a few days when the Pankow régime again anxious apparently to force the pace, and hoping perhaps to profit from the division within the Socialist camp, announced that Khrushchev had decided to sign a separate peace in 1961 after all.[43] There were seventeen days left. No word of confirmation came from Moscow.

The final position in 1961, achieved at the Paris Conference and at the Macmillan-Kennedy conversations in Bermuda, was that 'soundings with substance' would continue. These went on for some months, but without revealing much of substance. Thompson's conversations with Gromyko in Moscow seemed again to be buying time. The dilemma remained, and time could only be bought as long as Khrushchev was uninterested in more radical negotiations. It was open to him to renew his pressure, and though the tanks were withdrawn by both sides from the Friedrichstrasse crossing-point, he may still in future be able to do so in a manner which does not permit a 'pause' so easily—notably by incidents in the air-corridors.

There has never been any sign that he is willing to risk war over Berlin, but there is no sign that his determination to secure a European settlement—on his terms—has relaxed. And any renewal of pressure on Berlin will continue to divide the Western Alliance with results that may eventually be more damaging than they have been hitherto. Nor is it easy to be confident that in spite of the intentions of both sides, there is no danger of war developing over Berlin. A series of incidents in the air-corridors would be the most likely cause of such an escalation. Action is always relatively easy to limit on the ground. Any hopes for limited war in the air are illusory. The danger may be remote, but it is real. To these political and military dangers is added a third: that West Berlin may indeed 'wither on the vine'. At present emigration from the city has almost ceased, and economic investment is again increasing. But unless its long-term security is assured, these tendencies may be reversed. Such a decay of West Berlin would represent no great loss to the West if it were willing to admit that the Communisation of Germany and Eastern Europe is final. It would be safer and pleasanter to evacuate the population now. But as long as the West refuses to admit that this need be so, it needs West Berlin. For the ultimate significance of Berlin is not political but human. Ever since Stalin failed to conquer it—ever since the resistance of the Berliners themselves impelled the West to defend them—the city has been a symbol that Eastern Europe was not condemned to permanent Soviet domination. If this city were evacuated or abandoned, it would mean not only that Ulbricht had at last won his battle with the Western Allies, but also that the West had given up all hope of changing the history of Europe. And if Berlin were allowed to wither away, if Western presence there became meaningless, the same consequences would follow. It is no bad thing that Khrushchev should have this 'bone in his throat' to remind him that in the end the Soviet Union would be more comfortable without Eastern Europe.

But this end is a long way off, perhaps generations. In the meantime the situation is still dangerous; and the human end must be achieved by political means. There is much that the West cannot do. It can do nothing more than hope that Khrushchev or his successors may disburden themselves of Eastern Europe without risking the collapse of their system inside the Soviet Union. But there are certain conditions which it must meet if Russia is to be assured that withdrawal would not affect her own security. And there are certain conditions that Russia must observe if the West is to acquiesce in arrangements designed for her security. It is only through these that any solution to the Berlin problem can be found, and that this solution can open the way to a wider one.

The first of these has been visible in outline since the end of December 1961. After Khrushchev effectively forbade negotiations at the beginning of the month, there was a startling change in Russian policy. This had earlier been hinted at by the West German ambassador in Moscow, Dr. Kroll, but no confirmation came until Gromyko handed him a new Note on the 27th. Though couched in normal Soviet prose, containing a number of customary allegations about the inner motives of Germany's allies, there can be little doubt that it marked a genuine new departure. Apparently tired of the eternal circle which the threats and negotiations of the previous three years had marked, Khrushchev now seemed determined to by-pass the United States in his search for a solution. He was hoping to secure recognition of the division of Germany from Germany herself.

The most significant passage in the *aide-mémoire* assured the Federal Republic that it was free to remain in NATO, and that there was no question of an exchange of the two Germanys by NATO and the Warsaw Pact in the interests of neutralisation.* At the same time West Germany was urged that it would be in her interests to develop closer relations with the Soviet Union. This was not a temptation to Rapallo. There is no indication that Russia would ever now offer reunification in return for neutrality; but it was a significant step forward from the time (in February 1961) when Germany was told that she had no 'interests' in the Berlin question. Now it acknowledged these directly. Whether it meant that in any future settlement of Berlin, the city's links with the Federal Republic would be genuinely guaranteed was hard to say; but the seriousness of the Note was indicated by two subsequent developments. The first was a television speech by Gerhard Kegel, a member of the East German Central Committee, in which, for the first time 'differences' between the policies of the Soviet Union and the GDR were publicly acknowledged, and, in direct contrast to the Note the 'utter impossibility' of a reconciliation between the two Germanys was rearffimed so long as the Federal Republic remained in NATO. The second was an article in *Pravda* a week later in which the principal 'necessity of the age' was declared to be improved relations with West Germany.

It is unlikely that the Soviet Union will concentrate entirely on wooing the West German government. Soviet policy is highly pragmatic, and the stress of Russian dipomacy will

* While this is the usual starting-point of British speculations and plans for disengagement, it is precisely what is most feared by its German opponents.

doubtless vary between the United States and the Federal
Republic, according to which seems the most promising. But
the significance of the new departure should not be overlooked.
Russia seems prepared to guarantee West Germany's connection with Berlin as long as the Federal Republic abandons its
claims to be the only German state. It is hard to see what
form such a guarantee might take—almost certainly not a
corridor as Adenauer originally desired, but it would probably
involve some arrangement between West and East Germans
under Russian (and perhaps Western) supervision.

This indicates the first condition that must be met if the
Berlin problem is to be solved: Russia will have to admit West
Germany to some share in the future of Berlin, and West
Germany will have to come to terms, on this question at least,
with the GDR.

The second condition that this arrangement implies is that
the West will have to come to terms with an eventual recognition of East Germany. The essential preliminary to an eventual
Soviet withdrawal from Eastern Europe is an initial acknowledgement of the division of Germany. But it would be politically foolish and morally odious to accord recognition to the
present régime in the GDR; after the reign of terror which
Ulbricht has imposed since the wall was built, such a gesture
would be in the worst traditions of appeasement. It would be a
remarkable victory for both Russia and East Germany to win
now the recognition that has been delayed for so long, and it
would demonstrate that the West has neither the moral con-
viction nor the political will to resist a dictatorship that dares
to be ruthless enough. But it would be wrong to equate the
detestable East German régime with the division of Germany.
The first is not inevitable, the second is going to last a long
time. From the Western side the best chance of breaking the
present deadlock would arise from making a distinction between the two questions, and from the Russian side, if Khrushchev is anxious to win recognition of the division of Germany,
the first thing he should do is get rid of Ulbricht. A German
Poland would not inevitably be refused recognition by the West,
and there would be some chance that it could eventually progress to a German Finland. This chance might be slim; but
there is otherwise no chance whatever that the present rigidity

of the West will somehow 'attract' East Germany and reunite the country, or that Khrushchev would take the risk of experimenting in liberalisation if he were assured beforehand of the unvarying hostility of the NATO powers. It would in any case be a risky operation: it could invite revolution. But it could be carried out successfully, as the experience of Poland in equally hazardous circumstances has shown.

The price may be thought too high. It may be thought less dangerous to put up with a succession of crises over Berlin than to risk the alienation of Germany by a recognition of her corrupt rival. But Khrushchev has shown clearly that he is determined to achieve a settlement in Europe before West Germany, as he fears, can dictate her own terms to the West. And if the West seriously fears the prospect of a 'new Rapallo' it is equally in its own interest to secure a settlement before West Germany is in a position to 'do a deal' with Russia independently. There does not, however, seem to be much substance in these fears. They are based largely on the concept of 'Germany' poised uncertainly between the Soviet Union and the Western world, rather than on the political structure and leadership of the Federal Republic. Germany joined the Alliance, not reluctantly, but after a long and persistent effort on her own part, and she did so because she had no choice. By participating in Western rearmament after the outbreak of the Korean War, Adenauer hoped to ensure that Germany would commit the West to the irrevocable protection (and control) of the Federal Republic. Much the same motives seem to lie behind Strauss's campaign for a share in nuclear armament— within the framework of NATO. But there is no evidence that Germany would ever contemplate a 'return to neutralism' or a 'switch of alliances'. Indeed the most active opponents of any schemes of neutralisation in return for reunification have been the German leaders themselves. Far from desiring to play one side off against the other, they greatly fear the condition of friendless neutrality they associate with Rapallo.

However, there could be no question of recognising East Germany without their consent, and there is at present no prospect of obtaining this. But it remains a condition for a settlement of Europe, which has been delayed ever since Yalta, and whose delay is imposing increasing misery on 16 million

Germans. There has not been much evidence that the West German public or its leaders care enough about this to try to consider other ways of relieving their misery than by the long-term and almost fictional insistence on reunification. When the philosopher Karl Jaspers said in an interview in August 1960 that it was the primary duty of the West Germans to help their compatriots to secure a better life rather than insist on unreal hopes, he was greeted with almost universal fury. But this seems the obvious moral duty, not only of the Germans, but of the West, and not only to East Germany, but to all those countries which, as a result of original German action, are now enduring régimes almost as bad as that of Pankow. Perhaps if Khrushchev made a start in Pankow, the West could succeed in inducing Germany to consider a change of policy, of which Adenauer has hitherto managed to thrust the onus on his allies. Perhaps not.

This would not necessarily mean the abandonment of all ultimate hope of reunification, or of the liberation of Eastern Europe. The West must stay in Berlin to demonstrate this—and if its presence could be linked to the formation of a confederation, however vague or tenuous, between the two German states, it would have a real purpose. But genuine reunification could only come about in conditions of general disarmament, which may or may not be possible within the next generation. Meanwhile, it is urgent to achieve greater stability in Europe, and greater liberality in the East, by more limited agreements with the Soviet Union. The first step can only be an acknowledgement of the division of Germany even if this is envisaged as a transitional measure to permit greater progress in the end.

Discussion of armaments raises one last question. If it is true that both sides are now interested in securing a minimum of stability in Europe, the West will have to modify its reliance on a pure deterrent strategy. The ramifications of nuclear strategy are many, and they cannot be discussed here. But as long as the optimistic view prevailed that a threat of nuclear retaliation would suffice to prevent local pressure in Europe, the West was hopelessly exposed to that form of local pressure which the apologists of pure deterrence call 'nuclear blackmail'. In fact the two are inextricably linked; and though the Western Alliance has hitherto succeeded in defending Berlin by this threat, the most astonishing feature of the Berlin crisis has been its persistence. It has been conjured up again and again since 1958, and there is little hope that it has permanently abated now. Each time, both sides have pursued the same diplomatic policy: to place the onus of the risk of escalation on the other. So far this has worked on the whole in favour of the West, but it is doubtful whether the threat can work each time without losing its effect. In the summer of 1961, public opinion in the West was torn by anxiety, and governments were reluctant to commit themselves to the full menace of nuclear war, which alone would have made this position credible. Even while Kennedy was affirming his determination to defend Berlin, he implied that such a defence could be purely local. Such statements, coupled with the conventional reinforcements of the time, might well have encouraged Khrushchev in his intransigeance.

They were signs that the credibility of a straight-forward nuclear deterrent was weakening—yet for this reason, though the timing was probably mistaken, the intention was undoubtedly right. The West must be able to choose between wider alternatives than annihilation or surrender, and it barely succeeded in averting this choice in 1961. If a new Berlin crisis were to arise in the same circumstances as the last, a 'pause' might not be so easy to achieve, and it is even conceivable that if the West again refused to consider the recognition of East Germany, Ulbricht (or even Khrushchev) might well decide that the only course of action was to sever all communication between Berlin and the West. The onus of risk would then lie squarely on the United States and their allies.

The only possibility of transferring it—and of permitting a pause—would then lie in conventional counter-measures. Given the conventional strength, it would this time be safer to break a blockade on the ground than in the air. But America cannot furnish this strength alone, and in view of the present defence policies of Britain and France, the only other source is Germany. For this reason, the German army is being built up at a great pace: but of all European governments, that of Germany is the least enthusiastic for conventional warfare, and the least convinced of the credibility of a pause. Strauss is campaigning tirelessly for tactical nuclear weapons, and has

announced his intention of settling the question in 1962. If
he does, or if he looks like succeeding, it is most probable that
Khrushchev will then be impelled to renew the crisis more
strongly than ever, and even to 'settle the question' of West
Berlin. There is no sign that Kennedy is willing to give way to
Strauss on the issue, or even that he welcomes the preponderant
rôle which Germany is assuming inside NATO. But for the
latter at least he has no choice, and every advance in German
strength is an incentive to Khrushchev to act quickly. The
only alternative to German predominance is a greatly increased
contribution from Britain. At present there seems to be no
prospect of this, but if Macmillan is still anxious to mediate
for reduced tension in Europe, it would seem to be a necessary
preliminary.

This makes no pretence at providing a 'solution' to the intractable problem of Berlin. All that has been done here is to
point to some of the dangers of the present position, and some
conditions for an acceptable alternative. Many difficult negotiations would have to precede even a partial and transitional
settlement. But it does seem that some settlement is becoming
more, not less, necessary as time passes, and that success cannot
be achieved by indefinite postponement. If present developments are allowed to continue unchanged, the situation is
likely in the end to be more dangerous; and Berlin will remain
what it has now become, a city on leave.

NOTES

CHAPTER ONE

(Page references in brackets refer throughout to American editions)

1. Churchill, *The Second World War*, vol. VI, *Triumph and Tragedy*, p. 317 (p. 363)
2. The history of the abortive offer of an American loan is told in J. P. Nettl, *The Eastern Zone and Soviet Policy in Germany*, p. 40
3. Churchill, *ibid.* p. 305 (p. 350)
4. *Ibid.* p. 307 (p. 352)
5. *Ibid.* p. 322 (p. 368)
6. The historian of the conferences between the three leaders, Mr Herbert Feis, has analysed the agreements reached at Yalta and Potsdam in two books: *Churchill, Roosevelt, Stalin* and *Between War and Peace*, both of which give valuable indications of Roosevelt's approach
7. Feis, *Churchill, Roosevelt, Stalin*, p. 540
8. Churchill, *ibid.* p. 446 (p. 467)
9. *Ibid.* pp. 502-503 (p. 523-524)
10. For an account of the concessions for fear of 'premature' unification, see Feis, *Between War and Peace*, p. 243

CHAPTER TWO

Most of the material in Chapters Two and Three is taken from newspaper reports, and *Berlin: Kampf um Freiheit und Selbstverwaltung*, a chronology and collection of documents with an introduction by Professor Hans Herzfeld

1. Leonhard, *Die Revolution entlässt ihre Kinder*, pp. 348-349
2. Clay, *Decision in Germany*, p. 15, gives a different account, but see Feis, *Between War and Peace*, p. 146
3. Clay, *ibid.* pp. 25-26

CHAPTER THREE

1. On the Western attitude to the establishment of the Kommandatura, and to the immediate rôle of Berlin, see also Herzfeld, *op. cit.* pp. 11-12
2. As long as the original Magistrat remained the only organ of city government, the Russians scarcely needed to. See Herzfeld, *ibid.* pp. 22-24
3. At the same time Molotov was resolutely opposing all discussions of a central German administration in the Council of Foreign Ministers. See Boris Meissner, *Russland, die Westmächte und Deutschland*, p. 80 ff.

4. Herzfeld, *ibid.* pp. 21-22
5. Clay, pp. 133-134. See also Howley, *Berlin Command*, pp. 110-112
6. For Soviet arguments on this point, see Davison, *The Berlin Blockade*, pp. 32-36
7. See Herzfeld, *ibid.* pp. 33-36, for Russian attitudes and Western arguments
8. Clay, *ibid.* p. 77
9. Howley, p. 106
10. See Davison, *ibid.* p. 42
11. Herzfeld, *ibid.* p. 19
12. Davison, *ibid.* p. 46
13. Howley, p. 128

CHAPTER FOUR

1. Clay, p. 354
2. Davison, p. 82
3. Brandt and Lowenthal, pp. 332-333
4. E.g., *Telegraf, Tagesspiegel*
5. Hans Herzfeld in *Berlin: Behauptung der Freiheit und Selbstverwaltung*, p. 10
6. Peter Calvocoressi in *Survey of International Affairs 1947-48*, Royal Institute of International Affairs, p. 31
7. Davison, p. 15
8. Calvocoressi, *op. cit.* p. 39. See also Herzfeld, *op. cit.* p. 12
9. Herzfeld, *ibid.* p. 29. Also *Tagesspiegel*, 10.12.1947 and 12.12.1947
10. See above, p. 65
11. Brandt and Lowenthal, pp. 372-374
12. *Ibid.* p. 395
13. Ferdinand Friedensburg, *Berlin: Schicksal und Aufgabe*, p. 61
14. For a summary of the development of the Bi-zone, and the difficulties presented by the currency situation, see Clay, pp. 196-197

CHAPTER FIVE

1. Clay, p. 361
2. Davison, p. 75
3. See, e.g., Clay, p. 367. Sokolovsky's statement in July that technical difficulties would continue until the Western Powers abandoned their plans for a West German government was 'the first admission of the real reason for the blockade'
4. See, e.g., *Stenographische Protokolle der Stadtverordnetenversammlung*, 1948, 64. Sitzung, 65. Sitzung
5. Davison, p. 79. From *Berliner Schicksal*, pp. 47-48

NOTES

6. Davison, p. 84
7. Brandt and Lowenthal, p. 406
8. *Ibid.* p. 407
9. *Ibid.* p. 408
10. *Ibid.* pp. 411-412
11. Davison, pp. 95-98, gives the best account of these events
12. Friedensburg, p. 30. For a more optimistic estimate of that time, see Clay, p. 365
13. Friedensburg, p. 30
14. The report of Bevan's attitude is pure hearsay
15. Clay, p. 366
16. *Ibid.* p. 365
17. Davison, pp. 109, 157
18. For a short analysis of the popular attitudes, *ibid.* pp. 130-144
19. Davison presents the campaign against Füllsack as a deliberate Soviet attempt to split the administration. This is hardy credible. Davison himself implies, p. 175, that it was an attempt to bring the whole city under Soviet administration. See also *Tagesspiegel, Telegraf*, 13.8.1948
20. *Neues Deutschland*, 26.8.1948. *Neues Deutschland* had warned its readers the day before that the Social Democrats were preparing a putsch
21. Brandt and Lowenthal, pp. 450-451
22. Davison, pp. 180-181
23. See, e.g., *Tagesspiegel*, 28.8.1948
24. Clay, pp. 380-383, gives an account of transport needs and conditions
25. Cf. the accounts in *Neues Deutschland* and *Tagesspiegel*, 4.9.1948
26. Davison, pp. 186 and 192, suggests that Kotikov's action may have been designed to provoke the West into sending a military guard to the City Hall. But it was clear by then that the Assembly would no longer meet there
27. *Neues Deutschland*, 9.9.1948. Davison, who also quotes this report, does not attach any great significance to it
28. Davison, p. 188, gives a detailed account of the meeting, and of Allied apprehensions beforehand
29. Plischke and Erdmann, pp. 135-136
30. *Ibid.* p. 136 ff.
31. This reluctance was probably due to the hope that if the Soviet authorities refrained from open violation of the Four-Power agreements, the Western Commandants would permit the Communist mass-organisations to go on functioning in West Berlin. Communist propaganda is still tirelessly active in the West in spite of the hopelessness of the cause. For an expression of the Soviet attitude, see Kotikov's letter to the Magistrat of October 20th, quoted in Davison pp. 220-221
32. See Brandt and Lowenthal, p. 460
33. *Ibid.* pp. 465-465, for a summary of these discussions
34. This summary is taken from *Berliner Wirtschaft in der Blockade*.

Deutsches Institut für Wirtschaftsforschung, Sonderheft, Neue Folgung, Berlin, 1949

35. Davison quotes some interesting remarks of Mr. Hurwitz's on this, pp. 234-435

36. I am indebted to Dr. Georg Kotowski, one of the original founders of the Free University and now a CDU deputy, for the account he gave me of these events

CHAPTER SIX

1. Harry S. Truman, *Years of Trial and Hope*, p. 261
2. *Ibid.* p. 259
3. See Davison, pp. 280-283
4. Brandt and Lowenthal, pp. 482-483
5. *Ibid.* pp. 486-487
6. *Ibid.* p. 501
7. *Ibid.* p. 503
8. A full account of the development of the 1950 constitution is given in Plischke, pp. 75-85
9. *Telegraf*, 31.7.1950; *Tagesspiegel*, 30.8.1950
10. Brandt and Lowenthal, p. 542
11. *Ibid.* p. 545-546
12. The figures quoted here are those for Berlin alone. At that time the West German camps of Giessen and Uelzen received a far higher proportion of the total than they did in the late fifties. The corresponding total for these months is nearly 60,000. From 1953 onwards, more refugees registered in West Berlin than the other centres together. The official figure for the last quarter of 1949 is 16,500, but this takes no account of those who came to live with friends or relatives. It was probably nearer 18,000.

Figures from the monthly list published by the Federal Ministry for Expellees, Refugees and War Victims

13. Quoted in Grosser, p. 280. The best general summary of the party programme, leaders' viewpoints and the workings of the Bundestag at the time is given by Toni Pippin: 'Was jeder von der Bundesregierung wissen muss' (Kerclaer, 1950), where this speech also appears
14. Brandt and Lowenthal, pp. 551-556
15. *Ibid.* p. 645
16. *Telegraf*, 20.8.1950
17. Brandt and Lowenthal, p. 655
18. Sir Anthony Eden, *Memoirs: Full Circle*, p. 31
19. This was in May 1952. Brandt and Lowenthal, p. 657
20. Almost all the newspapers expressed the same belief. See *Der Abend*, *Der Kurier*, *Tagesspiegel*, e.g., 4.12.1950; *Telegraf*, 5.12.1950
21. An account is given of these events in Brandt and Lowenthal, pp. 577-579

22. Dr. Paul Hertz: 'The Economic Recovery of Berlin', paper presented to the International Industrial Development Conference, San Francisco, October 1957
23. Brandt and Lowenthal, pp. 583-584
24. I am indebted to Dr. Zipfel of the Free University of Berlin, who has made a sociological study of the absorption of the refugees, for explaining to me the reasons behind the enormous exodus at the turn of the year, six months before the revolt
25. Eden, *op. cit.* pp. 32, 35
26. Eden's explanation is frank. *Ibid.* p. 45
27. Brandt and Lowenthal, p. 671

Chapter Seven

1. This is denied in Brandt and Lowenthal, p. 697; but I was told of it by a member of the Executive of the Berlin SPD
2. Brandt and Lowenthal, pp. 691-692
3. *Tagesspiegel*, 24.2.1954
4. *Ibid.* 12.1.1955
5. These figures (to the nearest million in the last case) are taken from *Die Industrie Berlins* (*West*)
6. See *Jahresberichte des Senats* for these years
7. See also *The Observer*, 29.10.1961
8. See *Der Mittelstand und die Berliner Wirtschaft*, December 1960
9. *Bewährung der Freien Berliner Wirtschaft*, 1960. Senatsdirektor Otto Busack in 'Mitteilungen des Vereins Berliner Kaufleute und Industrieller', December 1960
10. *Wachsam sein!* Senatsdirektor Otto Busack in *Der Mittelstand und die Berliner Wirtschaft*, January-February 1961
11. Willy Brandt, *My Road to Berlin*, 1960, p. 21. Most of the details of Brandt's career which follow are to be found here
12. *Ibid.* p. 203
13. *Ibid.* p. 205
14. The best account of these events in Berlin is in *Tagesspiegel*, 26.10.1956

Chapter Eight

1. See Hinterhoff, *Disengagement*, pp. 163-164
2. Proposals of this nature had already been made by the East German government and the Soviet Union in 1950. *Ibid.* pp. 149-153
3. Eden, *Memoirs: Full Circle*, p. 66 (p. 75)
4. *Ibid.* pp. 75-76 (p. 84)

5. As Dulles told Eden, *ibid.* p. 163 (p. 183)

6. Note of March 31st to the United States, Britain and France

7. October 6th, 1954. This and subsequent Soviet *démarches*, which went largely unnoticed in the West, are documented in Captain Hinterhoff's book

8. Soviet Government statement, January 15th, 1955

9. See Alastair Buchan in *The Observer*, 3.7.1955

10. See the *Manchester Guardian*, 4.7.1955

11. *Die Internationale Politik 1955*, Deutsche Gesellschaft für Auswärtige Politik, Munich, 1958, p. 353 ff.

12. Wilhelm Hausenstein, *Pariser Erinnerungen*, Munich, 1959, pp. 84-85

Chapter Nine

1. Senate Foreign Relations Committee, June 6th, 1958

2. See Richard Lowenthal's essay 'The Crossroads' in *Encounter*, February 1959

3. *Tagesspiegel*, 11.11.1958

4. All quotations are from the Note to the United States Government

5. *Pravda*, 28.11.1958

6. Speier, *Divided Berlin*, p. 11

7. *Neues Deutschland*, 8.1.1959

8. Hinterhoff, *op. cit.* p. 247-248

9. *Ibid.* p. 281

10. Speier, *op. cit.* pp. 60-61

11. *Ibid.* p. 58-59. For a State Department view of the meeting

12. Interview material

13. De Gaulle is reported to have told Khrushchev that the actual position was in the best interests of each side. It may or may not be true

14. Hinterhoff, pp. 336-340, for military arguments on this point

15. Geoffrey Hudson in *The Observer*, 19.10.1958, quoted in Hinterhoff

16. Speier, *ibid.* pp. 90-92

17. Richard Lowenthal, 'Euphorie des Westens' in *Der Monat*, February 1960

18. Speier, *ibid.* pp. 96-97. He seems to attach no importance to the speeches of Herter and Dillon or regard them as in any way a change of policy

19. Department of State Bulletins of April 25th, 1960 and May 9th, 1960

20. Statement of May 27th: Department of State Bulletin, June 13th, 1960

21. *New York Times*, 26.4.1960

NOTES

CHAPTER TEN

1. Interview with the *Deutsche Presse Agentur*, 17.2.1961
2. See, e.g., *The Times*, 19.1.1962, 20.1.1962
3. *Le Monde*, 17.1.1962, *New York Times*, 16.1.1962
4. *The Times*, 20.1.1962
5. *New York Times*, 19.1.1962
6. *New York Times*, 19.1.1962
7. *Frankfurter Allgemeine Zeitung*, 24.1.1962
8. *Le Monde*, 24.1.1962. The aircraft was said by the West German authorities to be of unknown nationality; the tracts were in the form of a special edition of *Zeri i Populit*
9. *The Times*, 20.1.1962
10. Full text in *Junge Welt*, 16/17.7.1960
11. *Frankfurter Allgemeine Zeitung*, 9.7.1960. Also quoted in Speier, p. 116
12. *Allgemeiner Deutscher Nachrichtendienst*, 30.8.1960. Also quoted in Speier, p. 119
13. See *The Observer*, 25.9.1960
14. *The Guardian*, 4.9.1960
15. Victor Zorza in *The Guardian*, 17.10.1960
16. *Neues Deutschland*, 19.12.1960
17. These factors are discussed, with somewhat different conclusions, in 'Berlin—und was dann?' by Wilhelm Cornides, in *Europa Archiv*, Deutsche Gesellschaft für Auswärtige Politik, Bonn, No. 14, 1961
18. *Frankfurter Allgemeine Zeitung*, 25.2.1961
19. *The Economist*, 22.7.1961. This issue contains the above chronology of disarmament negotiations
20. See *Neue Zürcher Zeitung*, 25.7.1961
21. *Der Kurier*, 21.6.1960
22. *The Guardian*, 2.1.1961
23. *The Times*, 3. 8. 1961
24. *Neue Zürcher Zeitung*, 7.8.1961
25. See *Frankfurter Allgemeine Zeitung*, 4.8.1961
26. See *The Observer*, 13.8.1961
27. *New York Times*, 14.8.1961. Also quoted in Speier, p. 183
28. See above, p. 209
29. See *Die Zeit*, 8.9.1961
30. See Rusk's press conference, 18.10.1961
31. See *Frankfurter Allgemeine Zeitung*, 27.10.1961
32. White House press release, 18.10.1961
33. See, e.g., *Die Zeit*, 27.10.1961
34. *New York Herald Tribune*, 23.10.1961
35. *Frankfurter Allgemeine Zeitung*, 11.12.1961
36. *New York Times*, 2.12.1961

37. *Frankfurter Allgemeine Zeitung*, 4.12.1961
38. *The Times*, 7.12.1961
39. *New York Times*, 2.12.1961
40. See *Die Zeit*, 11.12.1961
41. *The Times*, 12.12.1961
42. See the argument of *Le Monde*, 12.12.1961, on this point
43. *Neue Zürcher Zeitung*, 16.12.1961

NOTES ON SOURCES

Use has been made throughout of the following newspapers: *Der Tagesspiegel*; *Der Kurier*; *Der Telegraf* (all of West Berlin); *Neues Deutschland* and *Die Neue Zeit* (East Berlin). Other constant sources have been the stenographic reports of the proceedings in the City Assembly and the House of Representatives, and the yearly reports of the Magistrat and Senat; the State Department publications on the Foreign Relations of the United States (which for the early years include the Conferences at Malta and Yalta, 1956 and the Conference at Potsdam, 1960); the Surveys of International Affairs published by the Royal Institute of International Affairs, London, and the volumes of the *Internationale Politik* published by the Deutsche Gesellschaft für Auswärtige Politik, Bonn.

For the earlier years books have included:

Winston Churchill, *The Second World War*, vol. VI, *Triumph and Tragedy* (Cassell, London, 1954; Houghton Mifflin, Boston, 1953)

Herbert Feis, *Churchill, Roosevelt, Stalin* (Princeton, 1958)

Herbert Feis, *Between War and Peace* (Princeton, 1960)

Lucius D. Clay, *Decision in Germany* (Doubleday and Company, New York, and Heinemann, London, 1950)

Frank Howley, *Berlin Command* (Putnam, New York, 1950)

Wofgang Leonhard, *Die Revolution entlässt ihre Kinder* (Kiepenheuer und Witsch, Cologne, 1955). (Translated as *Child of the Revolution*, Collins, London, 1957. I have throughout used the German edition)

J. P. Nettl, *The Eastern Zone and Soviet Policy in Germany, 1945-1950* (Oxford, 1951)

Boris Meissner, *Russland, die Westmächte und Deutschland* (H. H. Nölke Verlag, Hamburg, 1953)

Alfred Grosser, *L'Allemagne de l'Occident 1945-1952* (Gallimard, Paris, 1953)

Ferdinand Friedensburg, *Berlin—Schicksal und Aufgabe* (Schulz Verlag, Berlin, 1953)

Hans Herzfeld, *Berlin und das Berlinproblem vom Zusammenbruch bis zu den Stadtverordnetenwahlen des 20. Oktober 1946* in

Berlin: Kampf um Freiheit und Selbstverwaltung, 1945-1946, a chronology and collection of documents published by the Senat (Berlin, 1957)

Berlin: Behauptung von Freiheit und Selbstverwaltung 1946-1948, a subsequent volume published in 1959

Notes on the Blockade of Berlin. From a British Viewpoint in Berlin (British Military Government, 1949)

W. Phillips Davison, *The Berlin Blockade* (Princeton, 1958)

Harry S. Truman, *Memoirs*, vol. II, *Years of Trial and Hope* (Doubleday and Company, New York, 1956 and Hodder & Stoughton, London, 1955)
   For years after the Blockade, sources include:
Otto von der Gablentz, *Dokumente zur Berlinfrage, 1944-1959*. Deutsche Gesellschaft für Auswärtige Politik (Oldenburg, 1959)
Berlin im Blickpunkt der Welt, a collection of documents and commentaries (East Berlin, 1959)
Joachim Rottmann, *Der Viermächtestatus Berlins*. Bundesministerium für Gesamtdeutsche Fragen (Bonn, 1959)
Rudolf Legien, *Die Viermächtevereinbarungen über Berlin. Ersatzlösungen für den Status quo?* (Carl Heymanns Verlag, Berlin, 1960)
Berlin, Brennpunkt deutschen Schicksals. Lectures given at the Otto Suhr Institut of the Free University (Berlin, 1960)
Willy Brandt, *Von Bonn nach Berlin* (Berlin, 1957)
Gregory Klimow, *Berliner Kreml* (Kiepenheuer und Witsch, Cologne, 1952) (Translated as *The Terror Machine*, Faber & Faber, London, 1953)
Albert Worliczek, *Bonn-Moskau. Die Ostpolitik Adenauers* (Isar Verlag, Munich, 1957)
Willy Brandt, *My Road to Berlin* (Peter Davies, London, 1960)
Anthony Eden, *Memoirs: Full Circle* (Cassell, London, 1960, Houghton Mifflin, Boston, 1960)
Hans Speier, *Divided Berlin* (Princeton, 1960)
Eugene Hinterhoff, *Disengagement* (Stevens and Sons, London, 1959)
   Economic sources include:
Berlins Wirtschaft in der Blockade (Deutsches Institut für Wirtschaftsforschung, Berlin, 1949)
Berliner Statistik: Monatsschrift (Statistisches Landesamt Berlin, 1953 ff.)
Statistisches Jahrbuch Berlin (Statistisches Landesamt Berlin, 1952 ff.)
Die Wirtschaft Westberlins 1945-1955 (Industrie-und Handelskammer zu Berlin, 1956)
Mitteilungen des Vereins Berliner Kaufleute und Industrieller (Berlin, November 1953 ff.)
Daten zur Entwicklung der Berliner Wirtschaft (West) (Senator für Wirtschaft und Kredit, 1959)
Die öffentliche Wirtschaft (Die Gesellschaft für öffentliche Wirtschaft, 1951 ff.)
Der Mittelstand und die Berliner Wirtschaft (Berliner Volksbank (West) 1961, monthly)
Die Industrie Berlins (West) 1950-1959 (Senator für Wirtschaft und Kredit, 1959)

INDEX

INDEX